William Shakespeare

Recent Titles in
Historical Facts and Fictions

William Shakespeare

Facts and Fictions

Douglas J. King

Historical Facts and Fictions

An Imprint of ABC-CLIO, LLC
Santa Barbara, California • Denver, Colorado

Library of Congress Cataloging-in-Publication Data

Names: King, Douglas J. (Douglas James), 1958- author.
Title: William Shakespeare : facts and fictions / Douglas J. King.
Description: Santa Barbara, California : ABC-CLIO, [2020] | Series:
   Historical facts and fictions | Includes bibliographical references and
   index.
Identifiers: LCCN 2020008674 (print) | LCCN 2020008675 (ebook) | ISBN
   9781440866746 (hardcover ; acid-free paper) | ISBN 9781440866753 (ebook)
Subjects: LCSH: Shakespeare, William, 1564-1616—Miscellanea.
Classification: LCC PR2900 .K56 2020 (print) | LCC PR2900 (ebook) | DDC
   822.3/3—dc23
LC record available at https://lccn.loc.gov/2020008674
LC ebook record available at https://lccn.loc.gov/2020008675

ISBN: 978-1-4408-6674-6 (print)
       978-1-4408-6675-3 (ebook)

24 23 22 21 20   1 2 3 4 5

This book is also available as an eBook.

ABC-CLIO
An Imprint of ABC-CLIO, LLC

ABC-CLIO, LLC
147 Castilian Drive
Santa Barbara, California 93117
www.abc-clio.com

This book is printed on acid-free paper ∞

Manufactured in the United States of America

Contents

Preface

The life of William Shakespeare has inspired many myths, misconceptions, and fictions. This book explores ten of the most important and common questions regarding Shakespeare and attempts to separate fact from fiction. Along with fact and fiction, a third element often comes into play: subjective opinion. With Shakespeare, the historical evidence often leaves room for much interpretation and conjecture regarding a given biographical issue. In most cases, this book will not present a simple fact-versus-fiction judgment on a given question. Rather, the author has carefully researched the available records on each issue and presents the most salient information for the reader. When a verdict is offered on a particular issue, this book renders judgment based on what seems to be the best and preponderant evidence.

Each chapter deals with one fact/fiction question, and each is structured in three parts: "What People Think Happened," "How the Story Became Popular," and "What Really Happened." The first section makes the case for a narrative that may (or may not) be revealed as false by the third section. In each chapter, one will find historical documents or quotes from the most relevant sources on the question being considered. In most cases, documents and quotes from Shakespeare's time have been gently modernized and notes added to aid in comprehension. All quotes from Shakespeare's works throughout this book are taken from Open-SourceShakespeare (http://opensourceshakespeare.org/).

The ten facts/fictions considered begin with the perennial and fundamental question of who Shakespeare was: "William Shakespeare Was Not the Author of the Works We Know as Shakespeare's." The second chapter moves to the question of Shakespeare's sexuality: "Shakespeare Was Homosexual or Bisexual," and the third deals with his religious outlook: "Shakespeare Was Secretly Roman Catholic." Chapter 4 explores the question of Shakespeare's learning: "Shakespeare Was Poorly Educated," and chapter 5 inquires into his domestic life: "Shakespeare Rejected His Wife and Family." Chapter 6 looks at the sources of Shakespeare's works: "Shakespeare's Plays Were All Recycled and Not Original," and chapter 7 examines the author's creative process and the nature of his inspiration: "Shakespeare Was a Solitary Genius Whose Talents Cannot be Explained." Chapter 8 probes the issue of genre: "Shakespeare, His Colleagues, and His Audiences Saw Tragedies as More Important than Comedies." The ninth chapter considers whether Shakespeare's plays and language are still relevant and accessible to the average reader or viewer: "Shakespeare's Plays are Elite and His Old English is Incomprehensible for Contemporary Readers and Audiences," and the final chapter explores the question of whether and how productions can give modern audiences an authentic Shakespeare experience: "To Give Audiences the Most Authentic Experience Possible, Shakespeare's Plays Should Be Produced with Renaissance Costumes and Staging."

Each chapter ends with a "Further Reading" list, keeping in mind that people have been researching and discussing these aspects of Shakespeare's life for over 400 years and that for most of these issues, the jury is still out—with reasonable and intelligent people continuing to reach different conclusions. Such is the great mystery and appeal of Shakespeare that he and his works continue to elicit such fascination and passionate debate, with no end in sight.

I thank Gannon University for supporting the writing of this book. I greatly appreciate the efforts of the wonderful editorial team at ABC-CLIO, and I dedicate this book to my parents and to Dr. Al Labriola, my mentor from Duquesne University—would that they all had lived long enough to see it.

"When thou dost ask me blessing, I'll kneel down, / And ask of thee forgiveness: so we'll live, / And pray, and sing, and tell old tales, and laugh / At gilded butterflies. . . ." —*King Lear*

Introduction

The name William Shakespeare inspires a range of responses among people: reverence, intimidation, admiration, fear that his writing is difficult and inaccessible, and, most of all, some degree of familiarity; almost everyone has at least heard of Shakespeare. Even among those who've never read, enjoyed, or explored his works, William Shakespeare carries the weighty reputation of "the greatest writer who ever lived." Along with such fascination over the author and his works (comedies such as *Twelfth Night* and *A Midsummer Night's Dream*; tragedies such as *Hamlet* and *Macbeth*; and histories such as *Richard III* and *Henry V*; along with 154 sonnets and five longer poems) naturally comes curiosity about Shakespeare's life. Because Shakespeare lived in an era that, unlike ours, was not known for recording virtually every move of its people, we find huge gaps in his biography; and since his death, scholars and fans have researched, speculated, fomented rumors, and fantasized about various aspects of the life of William Shakespeare from Stratford-upon-Avon, England.

People have discussed and debated Shakespeare more than about any other author, and more has been written about his works than about any literature other than the Bible. The enormous worldwide fascination with this English poet/playwright shows no signs of letting up, over 400 years after his death in 1616. Because Shakespeare elicits so much fascination across the world, readers fervently seek and hope for more information about his life; to the limited facts we have, people have added many fictions—or at least unverifiable theories that often become promulgated and accepted as accurate. This book aims to reach some verdicts regarding ten key debates over Shakespeare; using the best evidence currently available, we attempt to separate the facts from the fictions.

On April 26, 1564, a child was christened at Trinity Church in the medium-sized English town of Stratford-upon-Avon. The church register reads "*Gulielmus, filius Johannes Shakespeare.*" Translating from the Latin, this gives us "William, son of John Shakespeare." Given that document listing April 26 for the christening, but no birth record (they were rare in those days, when babies were not born in hospitals), why then do we celebrate Shakespeare's birthday on April 23? This is a fine example of a good surmise, something in between a fact and a fiction. First, Shakespeare died on April 23, 1616, aged only fifty-two years. Because so much of what we take as factual or accurate about Shakespeare actually stems to some degree from wishful theorizing, there seems a nice symmetry to his having been born and dying on the same day—akin to the poetic justice of American founding fathers and presidents Thomas Jefferson and John Adams dying within hours of each other on July 4, 1826. But more than just wishful thinking causes us to peg Shakespeare's birthday three days back from the date of his baptism; Church of England guidelines from the time would prescribe holding a christening on the Sunday or feast day following a child's birth. But even here we're left with a bit of a mystery, because the Feast of St. Mark fell on April 25; why wasn't infant Will christened then? Some scholars speculate that St. Mark's Day was still viewed as somewhat inauspicious because, traditionally, it was marked in ways rather similar to our contemporary celebrations of All Saints Day/Halloween. Legend had it that on St. Mark's Eve, one could see in the churchyard the spirits of all those who would die in the parish in the coming year. Whatever the reason, Shakespeare was christened instead on the twenty-sixth, the day of England's patron, St. George; and for convenience and symmetry, we celebrate his birthday—matching his death day—as April 23. Thus the circumstances surrounding Shakespeare's entrance onto our planet mirror some of the difficulties we find in separating fact from fiction in many aspects of his life.

Perhaps the first and biggest question—to be considered in depth in chapter 1—is whether Shakespeare really was Shakespeare. The reputation and genius of Shakespeare are so enormous—and his biographical trail so limited—that skeptics have theorized that a son of a small-town, middle-class glove maker, a lad with only a grammar school education (we'll investigate Renaissance English education in chapter 4) could not have produced the works now generally considered the greatest pieces of literature ever written. William Shakespeare of Stratford-upon-Avon as master author is a hoax, goes the theory that comes under the name "the authorship controversy," and which has had its adherents from the nineteenth century through today.

Even among those who grant that Shakespeare was Shakespeare, myriad other theories and mythologies have arisen regarding his life—and some are the subjects of the ten chapters of this book. For most of these issues, we cannot point to irrefutable fact versus fiction. Rather, scholars and laypeople alike can make their cases for one view of a debate regarding Shakespeare; reasonable minds will differ, and barring—for example— discoveries of newly revealed hidden documents, we may never have irrefutable answers. Much of what we think we know about various historical figures is speculative and murky, and even when we have documented facts, the conclusions we draw from them are often debatable. For example, history has preserved a key legal document from the end of Shakespeare's life: his will. In that document, he bequeaths to his wife Anne "the second best bed." This is clear, written fact. However, throughout the ages people have debated the meaning of this ambiguous language, with some reading it as a tongue-in-cheek and even affectionate nod to his spouse (who would by law have been entitled to one-third of William's estate). However, other scholars argue that this phrasing in Will's will is cold and hurtful; that view is bolstered by the fact/fiction that for most of their married life, Shakespeare may have lived in London, far apart from his wife and family. (In chapter 5—"Shakespeare Rejected His Wife and Family"—we will probe the facts and fictions surrounding Shakespeare's family situation.) Thus, even when we have documentation such as the will, the conclusions we draw from the historical record can differ widely.

Because Shakespeare's reputation stands so powerfully, some readers tend to romanticize him, to place him on a pedestal as "The Bard" and "The Swan of Avon," whose genius cannot be accounted for by his upbringing or historical/cultural circumstances (we explore the question of Shakespeare's transcendent and solitary genius in chapter 7). Conversely, since about the 1970s, most Shakespeare scholarship seeks to understand him and his works as very much a product of a particular time and places: between about 1590 and 1613, in Stratford-upon-Avon and London, when and where Shakespeare created the vast bulk of his works. This historical approach may bring us closer to understanding and verifying fact versus fiction in the many mysteries about Shakespeare.

Exploring the historical background of Shakespeare's life takes us into a turbulent and momentous period in English and world history: the Renaissance. However, even the term "Renaissance" brings debate and competition, with several other terms vying for the preferred way to denote the period in which Shakespeare lived. Perhaps the simplest, most fact-based, historical way to refer to an era invokes the rulers of the time/nation. Thus, most people have heard Shakespeare's period called the "Elizabethan" age. However, Queen Elizabeth I died in 1603, quite in the middle of the era and before Shakespeare had written many of his greatest works, including *King Lear*, *Macbeth*, and *The Tempest*. Because King James I succeeded Elizabeth to the throne, we can accurately call Shakespeare's epoch the Elizabethan/Jacobean age ("Jacobus" is Latin for James). Alternatively, taking the two rulers' family names, the period is sometimes called the Tudor/Stuart period (for Elizabeth Tudor and James Stuart). Most scholars and historians of the last fifty or so years have preferred the term "Early Modern Period," which ties the age with—among other developments—the evolution of the English language from Old to Middle to Modern English (we'll explore the language of Shakespeare and his time in chapter 9). That brings us back to the original term used here to denote the period: the Renaissance. This term has fallen into disfavor by scholars who see it as problematic and potentially misleading; however, better than any of the other designations, "Renaissance" points us in the direction of the turbulent and exciting spirit of the era. Literally, renaissance (from the French) means "rebirth." So we should ask: What was being reborn, and how/why?

During the sixteenth and early seventeenth centuries, people in England grew enamored with the art, architecture, literature, and other cultural elements of ancient Greece and Rome. Many works that had not previously been readable were translated from Greek and Latin into English. These works were far more easily disseminated due to the widespread use of the printing press since Gutenberg's invention of movable type around 1450. Classical texts in Latin, such as Ovid's *Metamorphoses* and Plutarch's *Parallel Lives*, became the centerpieces of English grammar-school education, as students learned not just the Classical languages but also the rhetoric, philosophy, history, religion, literature, and more. For aspiring playwrights such as Shakespeare, the newly available English translations of the works of Roman playwrights such as Seneca also served as highly influential models.

As citizens of Renaissance England looked back to the great discoveries and cultural contributions of the Greek and Roman civilizations of past millennia, their lives also exploded forward. The Renaissance was defined by exploration, creativity, and change in virtually all areas of life. The age featured exploratory and trade missions that would—among other discoveries—bring the English to the New World, founding, for example, Jamestown (named for King James) and Virginia (named for Elizabeth, the "Virgin Queen"), as explorers claimed the territories that would eventually become the United States and Canada. Economically, the English Renaissance saw multiplication of new businesses, increased social mobility, and the burgeoning of what would come to be called "the middle class." As a result of economic, political, and cultural opportunities, the London population grew from about 50,000 in 1530 to 225,000 by 1605—a staggering expansion. Among the huge developments of the English Renaissance was the tumultuous journey that forcibly changed the state religion of all English people from Catholicism to the Church of England, back to Catholicism, and finally—under Shakespeare's Queen Elizabeth—back to the Church of England.

In 1527, frustrated by his wife's inability to provide him with a male heir and with his affections pivoted toward Anne Boleyn, Henry petitioned Pope Clement VII for an annulment—a process within the Catholic church whereby a marriage is declared invalid, null, and void. Clement denied Henry's request, and after intensive negotiation and maneuvering that lasted years, in 1533 Henry married Anne; the following year he declared himself the supreme head of the newly formed Church of England, the monumental move known as the English Reformation. Thus in one fell swoop did Henry convert not just himself but all of his subjects (at least in a legal sense) from the Roman Catholic faith to his newly created church. With Henry's move went the country. His subjects had no choice; the Church of England instantly became the state religion, and Roman Catholicism was outlawed. Henry's move only began a roller-coaster ride for English citizens that would last for many decades, throughout Shakespeare's lifetime and beyond.

Thus, the fact or fiction as to whether Shakespeare or his parents practiced Catholicism is no mere curiosity (we explore the question of Shakespeare's religious views in chapter 3: "Shakespeare Was a Secret Catholic"); one's religious practice at the time could be quite literally a matter of life or death. After Henry's death in 1547, the throne passed to his nine-year-old son Edward (VI), who reigned with the aid of a regency council until his untimely death in 1553. Edward maintained the church his father had founded, but upon his death, the throne passed to Henry's oldest surviving heir, Mary Tudor, the daughter from Henry's first marriage. Being the staunchly Catholic child of the Spanish Catherine of Aragon, Mary immediately returned England to Roman Catholicism. Thus, after twenty years of the Church of England as the state religion, with Catholicism a forbidden practice, Mary reversed that equation. Her persecutions of people who held to the Anglican ways—some of whom indeed plotted to overthrow her—earned her the familiar nickname "Bloody Mary." But like young Edward's reign, Mary's was short, and upon her death in 1558, the throne passed to Elizabeth I—daughter of Henry and Anne Boleyn. Elizabeth immediately restored the Church of England as the state religion, again banning adherence to Roman Catholicism. Such was the climate into which William Shakespeare was born in 1564.

Although there was much strife and tumult, the England in which Shakespeare grew and prospered also featured budding opportunities, including new worlds of artistic exploration. Whereas in the Italian city-states, the Renaissance was defined by art and architecture—featuring the masterworks of Botticelli, Leonardo, Michelangelo, and many others—in England, music and literature took precedence. We can loosely think of Shakespeare's literary career as spanning the twenty years between 1590 and 1610; and during that time, playwriting evolved from a little-pursued, nonlucrative, and disreputable avocation to a valid and at least potentially remunerative occupation, with Shakespeare and other playwrights creating and achieving huge financial and artistic success. At the beginning of the English Renaissance, being a respectable writer meant being a poet; by the 1600s, numerous playwrights competed to have their works performed, and playgoing was a wildly popular activity, especially in London.

After Shakespeare's death in 1616, the Renaissance dramatic boom continued; Shakespeare's works remained popular until the cessation of all theater during the English Civil War (1642–51) and through the Commonwealth/Interregnum (1552–60), during which the Puritans, led by Oliver Cromwell, deposed and executed King Charles I (son of James I). The Puritans opposed any form of theater as immoral, and thus during the eighteen-year period from 1642 to 1660, performances were banned, and no plays were produced. With the restoration of the monarchy in 1660, theaters were reopened, and a public hungry for entertainment sought out plays to view. In addition to new playwrights coming forth to mark the new era (known as Restoration Drama), theater companies looked to popular works of the not-too-distant past, with the foremost being the plays of William Shakespeare. In the more than three centuries since then, Shakespeare's plays have enjoyed virtually worldwide popularity, and public fascination with knowing more about the facts and fictions of his life has only increased.

1

William Shakespeare Was Not the Author of the Works We Know as Shakespeare's

What People Think Happened

In 1550, in Essex, just outside London, Edward de Vere was born as the only child of John de Vere, who would die only twelve years later, leaving the boy as the seventeenth Earl of Oxford (he is thus referred to as Oxford, Essex, or Edward de Vere). Because his father had held some lands belonging to the crown, young Edward officially became a ward of Queen Elizabeth and was sent to live with the powerful Sir William Cecil, Secretary of State and closest adviser to the queen. Thus was Edward launched into a life that would feature wealth and wastefulness; great favor, disfavor, and scandal; patronage of the arts; and noted talent as a writer—perhaps even more noteworthy than history has allowed him. For in fact, Edward de Vere was actually the author of the poems and plays of "William Shakespeare."

Sometime in the late 1580s or early 1590s, now a prominent courtier and private writer, Edward de Vere made the acquaintance of a young man named William Shakespeare. Hailing from the small town of Stratford-upon-Avon and new to the London theater scene, William had gotten involved with the theater company known as the Lord Chamberlain's Men as a shareholder (or perhaps de Vere bought Shakespeare his share as part of the arrangement they would make), occasional actor, and perhaps an aspiring writer. Oxford was a patron of the arts, peripherally visible on the burgeoning theater scene and overflowing with experiences, ideas, and talents that he wanted to see come to public fruition. However, playwrighting was not a respectable avocation for an aristocrat; due to his position in life, the earl needed a front man. He contracted with young William such that Shakespeare's name would be attached to the growing canon of great plays and poems Edward was writing. Others in the theater company accepted and perpetuated the conspiracy, which succeeded until and beyond de Vere's death in 1604.

With time, the Oxford/Shakespeare conspiracy succeeded so well that virtually everyone forgot about the real author, and "William Shakespeare" became known worldwide as the greatest author in the history of the English language. At last, in 1920, British teacher J. Thomas Looney published *Shakespeare Identified*, identifying the real author of "Shakespeare's works" as Edward de Vere. Since that time, the majority of anti-Stratfordians (the term used to describe anyone who doesn't believe that Will Shakespeare of Stratford-upon-Avon wrote the works of "Shakespeare") have come to be called the "Oxfordians"—those who recognize the Earl of Oxford as the true author. In addition to biographical evidence, covert references within the plays also link to the earl, and one can find parallels between "Shakespeare's" language and that found in Oxford's letters and poetry. Also, a Bible known to have belonged to the earl contains marked passages that match the biblical references in Shakespearean plays.

Documents from the time mention Edward de Vere as a talented writer of poetry and plays, and the fact that we have no plays in his name suggests that he wrote them but wanted to remain—to use the name of a 2011 film about Oxford/Shakespeare's true identity—*Anonymous*.

How the Story Became Popular

Of the thirty-eight plays commonly attributed to William Shakespeare, only twelve are set primarily in England—most of those being English history plays wherein the author made no real choice as to setting. The other twenty-six plays place readers and viewers in Greece, Turkey, Spain, Denmark, Egypt, Yugoslavia, Scotland, Lebanon, and, most of all, Italy—the setting for ten plays. In addition to geographical diversity, the plays also feature characters ranging from the lowest of peasants to the mightiest of kings and queens, from villains and scoundrels to heroes and great friends and lovers. Thus, scholars and readers face the mystery of how a middle-class son of a small-town glover—a man who never attended university or traveled more than one hundred miles from his hometown—could so wonderfully have produced such a great range of settings, language, and characterizations. Some people speculate that during Shakespeare's "lost years" (~1585–92), he traveled at least to Italy. But we have absolutely no evidence for that, and the mystery provides fuel for the case that someone else—someone well traveled and more cultivated than the grammar school–educated Will Shakespeare—wrote these works.

Whereas some people assert that interest in the "authorship controversy" was in place shortly after Shakespeare's death, it really began centuries later. In 1853, American writer Delia Bacon—partially funded by transcendentalist writer Ralph Waldo Emerson—went to England to research her complex thesis that William Shakespeare was not the writer of the plays commonly attributed to him. The book she subsequently published (*The Philosophy of the Plays of Shakespeare Unfolded*) constitutes one of the first significant written contributions to what has since become famous as the "authorship controversy." Bacon argued that a group of writers—including poet Edmund Spenser, statesman Sir Walter Raleigh, and philosopher Sir Francis Bacon (no relation to Delia)—had written the plays to encode Bacon's occult philosophical ideas, which were too unorthodox to be publicly promulgated. Emerson himself stated of Shakespeare, "He was a jovial actor and manager. I cannot marry this fact to his verse" (Shakespeare Oxford Fellowship 2019). Other prominent nineteenth-century Americans also belonged to the anti-Stratfordian camp; the great poet Walt Whitman posited that "one of the wolfish earls so plenteous in the plays themselves, or some born descendent and knower, might seem to be the true author of those amazing works. . . . I am firm against Shaksper. I mean the Avon man, the actor" (Shakespeare Oxford Fellowship 2019).

But anti-Stratfordians have differed as to who *did* write the works of "Shakespeare." Over the years, candidates have included the Bacon/Spenser/Raleigh cabal; Queen Elizabeth; William Stanley, Earl of Derby; and poet/playwright Christopher Marlowe. The last may be particularly interesting and plausible insofar as Marlowe was a known writer—in fact, the most successful and celebrated playwright in the burgeoning London theater scene of the 1580s and early 1590s. However, that theory has to not only account for a conspiracy to attribute all of Marlowe's later plays to Shakespeare but also fake Marlowe's untimely death, an event that—though shrouded in mystery—is well documented and would certainly seem to have ended his life and playwriting career in 1593. Since the 1920 publication of *Shakespeare Identified*, the chief candidate for the "real author" has been Edward de Vere, 17th Earl of Oxford. Sigmund Freud stated, "I no longer believe that . . . the actor from Stratford was the author of the works that have been ascribed to him. Since reading *Shakespeare Identified* by J. Thomas Looney, I am almost convinced that the assumed name conceals the personality of Edward de Vere, Earl of Oxford. . . . The man of Stratford seems to have nothing at all to justify his claim, whereas Oxford has almost everything" (Shakespeare Oxford Fellowship 2019).

The theory goes that "William Shakespeare" was a figurehead, an untalented actor and aspiring writer loosely connected with the Lord Chamberlain's Men who published the plays as his own, by agreement with the true author—Oxford—who wished anonymity, or that William Shakespeare was a minor actor with a similar name who became erroneously or deliberately credited as the playwright. But what gave rise to the grand, secret conspiracy by which a middle-class country bumpkin was proffered as the author of the greatest plays ever produced, while the real author willfully achieved historical anonymity?

Edward de Vere possessed myriad experiences, connections, and qualities that make him seem better suited as the most famous playwright in history. As a young man, de Vere "dazzled the queen and absorbed the attention of her leisure moments" (Jenkins 1958, 166). Edward was nephew to Henry Howard, the powerful Earl of Surrey, himself a groundbreaking English Renaissance poet; along with Thomas Wyatt, Surrey pioneered what is known as the English or Shakespearean sonnet form. In his translations of parts of Virgil's *Aeneid*, Edward's uncle Surrey innovated blank verse, the unrhymed, iambic pentameter that would be the primary mode of most of the "Shakespearean" plays; he also translated from the Italian the poems of Petrarch, who is known as the father of the sonnet. Another uncle to de Vere was Arthur Golding, famous to history as the English translator of Ovid's *Metamorphoses*, which served as a hallmark of Renaissance English grammar school education—as well as a prominent source and influence on the plays of "Shakespeare." The young Earl of Oxford clearly had tremendous exposure to talented family, literature, and culture in ways the son of a Stratford-upon-Avon glove maker never could.

While living with William Cecil, de Vere received an aristocrat's private tutoring in rhetoric, languages (especially French and Latin), and arts such as painting and dancing. In 1564, Edward received an honorary master of arts degree from Cambridge University (he would later receive one from Oxford as well). Given in his adolescence, these degrees do not indicate prodigal academic achievement but rather the lad's close connection to the queen's inner circle; nonetheless, the breadth of de Vere's education would have easily trumped that of the grammar school–educated boy from Stratford. In 1567 Edward was admitted to law school, though we have no records of him completing his studies or ever practicing law. We do know that in 1575, the queen authorized a license for de Vere to travel abroad; rather than simply traveling as a private individual, as Elizabeth's former ward he received letters of introduction and admittance to the courts of foreign nations. He visited Paris and Strasbourg, France; visited Germany; and then spent several months in Italian states such as Venice and Milan. On Edward's return to Elizabeth's court, he flaunted his immersion in Italian language, manners, and fashions and was apparently dubbed "the Italian Earl."

All these formative experiences establish Oxford as someone more likely than the Stratford swain to compose plays that so often and richly reflect the atmospheres and influences of foreign cultures, languages, nobility, and royalty. One specific connection that would seem to associate de Vere with a "Shakespearean" play came during his return from continental Europe. Pirates from the Netherlands commandeered and plundered his ship; the affair could have turned out worse had not one or more of the corsairs recognized the famous earl. This bizarre episode closely mirrors a strange scene wherein Hamlet reports to his friend Horatio a similar experience of pirates intercepting his voyage to England and then kindly escorting him back to Denmark.

In court, de Vere established a reputation as a poet, with many of his works surviving. We also have references to him as having written plays, though none survive (in his name!); the fact of written allusions to him as a good playwright, plus the lack of any plays surviving attributed to him, may be evidence that his plays *were* published and produced—but under another name. Oxford was also a devoted patron of writing, music, and theater, with at least thirty known books and plays dedicated to him (indicating that he had subsidized the works) by noteworthy playwrights such as John Lyly (who served as de Vere's secretary) and Anthony Munday. Despite rapidly burning through his inheritance, Oxford sponsored various performances and theater companies—both adults' and boys'—and maintained musical and theatrical troupes named after him. Given Oxford's known interests and talents in the arts, why then would he have engineered the huge conspiracy to conceal his true authorship of the masterpieces attributed to "William Shakespeare"?

During the Elizabethan/Jacobean period in which modern drama essentially came to exist and thrive, theater was at first a disreputable and low art form. As theater grew and achieved vast popularity in London between approximately 1590 and 1610 (the main career span of the playwright known as Shakespeare), playwrighting gradually gained acceptance as a valid form of authorship. However, anyone seeking respect as a creative writer wrote poetry, not plays—and even excessive poetry writing was discouraged among courtiers. The theater was generally viewed as a place of sin and degradation, as evidenced by London laws that forbade theaters from being erected within city limits; instead, many were situated on the south banks of the Thames, close to taverns, brothels, and bear-baiting establishments. A courtier as highly stationed as was Edward de Vere simply would not imagine declaring himself a playwright. Oxford also experienced great scandal in his personal life, which would further disincentivize him from seeking the public eye as an author of plays.

In 1571, with the queen in attendance, de Vere had married Anne Cecil, the fifteen-year-old daughter of the powerful Sir William Cecil, Lord Burleigh. During his subsequent visit to Paris, Edward learned that his wife was pregnant, and somehow during his travels, he became convinced (apparently without evidence) that the child was not his. When he returned to court in 1576, he refused to live with Anne and would remain separated from her for five years. Such bouts of powerful and sudden jealousy remind one of events in "Shakespearean" plays such as *Othello* and *The Winter's Tale*. During his separation, Oxford began an affair with Anne Vavasour, one of the queen's ladies-in-waiting, who in 1581 gave birth to Edward's son. The queen was incensed, and de Vere— as well as Anne and the baby—were imprisoned in the Tower of London. Though Oxford's stay in the Tower was short, he was banished from court for two years and never regained his standing as one of Elizabeth's favorite courtiers.

Edward reluctantly reconciled with his wife, who died in 1588. With Anne's passing, de Vere fell even further from the inner circle of power and influence that stemmed from being related to Elizabeth's closest adviser, Sir William. Edward lost custody of the three daughters Anne had borne him, and in 1592 he married again—to another of Elizabeth's ladies-in-waiting. All of this personal tumult and scandal gives ample reason for the Earl of Oxford to have concealed his true literary ambitions and creations. Oxfordians and even many Stratfordians agree that certain characters in the plays are modeled on well-known court figures—mostly highly unflattering portrayals. Most people see the manipulative and controlling character Polonius from *Hamlet* as reflecting William Cecil and the arch-villain Richard III evoking Robert Cecil, Sir William's son. Oxfordians argue that such dangerous, satirical depictions constitute another powerful motive for concealing de Vere's authorship.

It was common for Renaissance noblemen to hide their literary production, even as poets. Now known as one of the great poets of the age, Sir Phillip Sidney only had his collected works published after his 1586 death. Although anonymous publication was the most common way to get around the taboo against noblemen writing poems and plays, the use of *noms de plume* (pen names) or "front men" may have been common. For example, in 1599, historian John Hayward published a history of King Henry IV. Queen Elizabeth found some elements of the book to be treasonous and encouraging rebellion. Hayward was arrested, interrogated, and imprisoned, with the queen accusing him of pretending to be the author in order to "shield some more mischievous person" and threatening him with torture until he revealed the true author.

The 1589 book *The Arte of English Poesie*—which was published anonymously but is now generally attributed to George Puttenham—notes:

> So as I know very many notable Gentlemen in the Court that have written commendably, and suppressed it again, or else suffered it to be published without their own names to it: as if it were a discredit for a Gentleman, to seem learned and to show himself amorous of any good Art. (*Arte of,* Bk. 1, Ch. 8)

Puttenham later names de Vere as first among these nobleman who have hidden their writing talents:

> And in her Majesty's time . . . are sprung up another crew of Courtly makers, Noble men and Gentlemen of her Majesty's own servants, who have written excellently well, as it would appear if their doings could be found out and made public with the rest; of which number is first that noble Gentleman *Edward* Earl of Oxford. (*Arte of,* Bk. 1, Ch. 31)

The 1598 work *Palladis Tamia, or Wit's Treasury* by Rev. Francis Meres discusses and ranks the great authors of the ancient world along with those of the Renaissance; Meres ranks Oxford among "the best for comedy" (unfortunately for Oxfordians, as we'll see in the next section, Meres also mentions Shakespeare in the same paragraph).

Oxfordians point to another sign that "William Shakespeare" was a fraud and a concoction: his signatures. For the lifetime of the man William Shakespeare, history gives us six signatures. Each signature—three from the will of Shakespeare and three from other legal documents—is spelled differently, and none uses our familiar spelling. Instead, we see Willm Shakp; William Shaksper; Wm Shakespe; William Shakspere; Willm Shakspere; and William Shakspeare. Oxfordians argue that none of the signatures looks as though it were written by a man of literature—let alone a highly literary one who spent countless hours writing beautiful words.

The Oxfordian cause is enough entrenched and publicized to have garnered its own organizations—such as the Shakespeare Oxford Fellowship (mostly comprising Americans) and the De Vere Society (based in England). These organizations publish newsletters and hold annual conferences, all based on making the case and spreading the word that Oxford was Shakespeare. Prominent skeptics of Shakespearean authorship throughout the centuries (mostly Oxfordians) have included historian David McCullough; Supreme Court justices Harry Blackmun, John Paul Stevens, and Antonin Scalia; actors John Gielgud, Orson Welles, Derek Jacobi, and Mark Rylance; novelists James Joyce, Daphne du Maurier, and Anne Rice; Helen Keller; Malcolm X; and Robin Williams. Actor-director Charlie Chaplin argued for the author's aristocracy: "In the work of the greatest geniuses, humble beginnings will reveal themselves somewhere but one cannot trace the slightest sign of them in Shakespeare. . . . Whoever wrote [Shakespeare] had an aristocratic attitude" (Shakespeare Oxford Fellowship 2019). With his characteristic colorful cynicism, Mark Twain wrote: "We are The Reasoning Race, and when we find a vague file of chipmunk tracks stringing through the dust of Stratford village, we know by our reasoning powers that Hercules has been along there. I feel that our fetish is safe for three centuries yet" (Shakespeare Oxford Fellowship 2019). Novelist Henry James concurred, saying, "I am . . . haunted by the conviction that the divine William is the biggest and most successful fraud ever practiced on a patient world" (Shakespeare Oxford Fellowship 2019).

The debate over Oxford as Shakespeare probably received its grandest public hearing in September 1987, when art collector, businessman, and philanthropist David Lloyd Kreeger organized a moot-court debate on the Shakespearean authorship question at the American University. The event was broadcast live on C-SPAN and made the next day's front pages in major publications such as the *Washington Post* and *New York Times*. Kreeger managed not only to recruit two prominent DC attorneys to prepare the cases—Peter Jaszi arguing on behalf of "the Plaintiff" (de Vere) and James Boyle on behalf of "the Defendant" (Shakespeare)—but also to enlist three sitting Supreme Court justices (William Brennan, Harry

Blackmun, and John Paul Stevens) to weigh the evidence. The verdict came out resoundingly in favor of Shakespeare; each of the justices found that the case raised interesting questions but that the Oxfordian argument was not proven.

However, some Oxfordians complained that the rules of the proceeding stacked the odds against their man:

> Justice William Brennan announced, in his opening comments, that the three-man Moot Court would follow more traditional legal proceedings, and that in the absence of a lower court ruling on this case (Shaksper vs. Oxford), Brennan ruled that the burden of proof was on the Oxfordians both to dismiss the Stratford man, and to establish Oxford—all in 1 hour! No similar burden was placed on the Stratford side. . . . Brennan stated that since his [Shaksper's] claim went unchallenged for two centuries, it carried with it the presumptive weight of the law and it would take a "preponderance" of the evidence to take the works away from him (not just "reasonable doubts"). . . . With the burden of proof now totally on the Oxfordian side, the outcome of the Trial was a foregone conclusion. (Boyle 2014)

Despite the unanimous verdict in favor of the Stratfordians, each of the justices was affected by the Oxfordian case:

> Justice Brennan confessed that they were all "a little bit at sea," confronting the wealth of evidence the lawyers had assembled. . . . It was, said Blackmun, a matter for historians rather than the courts. The case, that is, is not closed. . . . There remains "a gnawing uncertainty" about the Shakespeare authorship, said Justice Stevens. Stevens had some advice for the Oxford side. . . . [t]hey must address the crucial question of why a man concealed the authorship of the greatest body of literature in the English language. Several people would have had to be involved in the cover-up. That suggests a conspiracy, Stevens said, and the Oxfordians ought not to be timid about using the word. The conspiracy, if such there was, "had to come from a command of the monarch or her prime minister." (Champlin 1987)

Two of the presiding justices later became convinced of the merits of Oxford as Shakespeare. Justice Blackmun later averred that he would now vote the other way (Tombe 1996); in 1992, Justice Stevens wrote a detailed legal article on behalf of the Oxfordian argument. Stevens lays out "five canons of statutory construction" to build the case, including standard Oxfordian points such as the lack of existing manuscripts in "Shakespeare's" hand, the preponderance of characters in the plays of high/noble status, evidence from the plays that their author was highly educated (as was Oxford, not Shakespeare), the lack of any books handed down by the man from Stratford, and the fact that Queen Elizabeth granted de Vere a large annuity for the final eighteen years of his life—suggesting that she was subsidizing his literary ambitions and also partaking of the conspiracy to keep him anonymous (Stevens 1992).

The fact that such sober-minded and highly educated people as Supreme Court justices have embraced the Oxfordian conclusion gives credence to the cause and helps keep kindled the authorship controversy.

What Really Happened

In 1582, eighteen-year-old William Shakespeare married twenty-six-year-old Anne Hathaway somewhere outside of Stratford-upon-Avon (we do not know in which church, but it was not in Stratford's Holy Trinity Church). Six months later their first child (Susanna) was born, which we know from baptismal records. Two years after that, Anne gave birth to their twins, Hamnet and Judith. After the baptismal record of the twins' birth in 1585, we have almost no historical trace of Shakespeare until 1592. The paucity of records pertaining to William for that period between 1585 and 1592 leads some to brand these "the lost years" and gives fuel to the idea that Shakespeare's existence was shrouded in mystery. However, we might keep in mind that extensive historical records exist for very few citizens of Renaissance England; in fact, for an era far less concerned than ours with documenting people's every movement and activity, we actually have a fairly good trail of documentation for Will Shakespeare. Certainly sometime between 1585 and 1592, Shakespeare—for reasons and in ways about which we can only speculate—arrived in London and began a career as playwright, actor, and theater company shareholder. Also purely speculative are any explanations for what the young man did during those "lost years." Because his plays reflect a breadth of knowledge of a wide variety of social classes (from royalty to the lowest commoners) and of other cultures/nations, some suggest that Shakespeare traveled to Italy and elsewhere. Some imagine that he self-directed a deep and broad study of humanity that made up for his lack of a university education and allowed him beautifully to capture in his works the speech, manners, and essences of so many cultures and people.

Nobody can fully explain how the son of a lower-middle-class leather craftsman gained the ability to reflect such depth and breadth of human experience. Audiences throughout the years and across the globe have viewed and read Shakespeare's works and experienced powerful resonance with their own lives, thoughts, and feelings. This level of artistry and erudition seems at odds with Shakespeare's humble, limited background, and this anomaly fuels the authorship controversy. Invariably, when a candidate is proposed as the actual author of Shakespeare's works, that person is of a higher class and/or university educated—as, for example, the Earl of Oxford. While one can reasonably question how a grammar school–educated, middle-class greenhorn became the author of the greatest works in the history of literature, there may also be a touch of snobbishness and classism to anti-Stratfordian theories. The vast majority of people who have studied Shakespeare's life conclude that, indeed, William Shakespeare was William Shakespeare.

But how would young William of Stratford even have conceived the idea of becoming a playwright, actor, and theater company owner? The historical record allows only for tantalizing speculation. In Shakespeare's youth, he very likely was exposed to traveling theater companies that would visit villages such as Stratford-upon-Avon; in *Hamlet* he recreates just such an itinerant company visiting Castle Elsinore and performing in the royal court. Probably his Stratford grammar school education—featuring as it did much recitation and practice of Latin rhetoric—involved Shakespeare in exciting class performances of scenes from, for example, Ovid's *Metamorphoses*. We can deduce that, with such early seeds planted, sometime during those "lost years" from 1585 to 1592, Shakespeare felt the calling to become a man of the theater and headed to London. We cannot be certain as to how often William, Anne, and their children thereafter saw each other (chapter 5, "Shakespeare Rejected His Wife and Family," deals with that question).

To undertake a theater career in Renaissance England was more than daunting, but Shakespeare seems to have made his mark as a playwright quickly enough to ruffle the feathers of established writers on the London scene. A pamphlet published in 1592 alludes to Shakespeare as an "upstart crow, beautified with our feathers . . . supposes he is as well able to bombast out a blanke verse as the best of you" (Greene 1966, 45–46). This attack was published by an evidently jealous writer known for his volatility: Robert Greene, who would die two weeks after that pamphlet was published. Greene's remarks, apparently intended for fellow playwrights, imply that the uneducated newcomer Shakespeare had far overstepped his bounds as an actor by taking on the role of author—and a suddenly successful one at that.

Shakespeare's plays give us our best records of the years between 1592 and 1613, the bulk of his career in the London theater. We also have numerous financial records pertaining to Shakespeare's business and real estate dealings, both in London and in Stratford. After about 1611, Shakespeare seems to have semiretired; in that year, *The Tempest* was published, believed to be his last play written as sole author. After this time, Shakespeare turned over the reins as house playwright for the King's Men—the theatrical company of which he was co-owner—to John Fletcher. Shakespeare's last three plays (*Cardenio* or *Double Falsehood*; *Henry VIII* or *All Is True*; and *The Two Noble Kinsmen*, all dated around 1613) were almost certainly collaborations with Fletcher, and after 1613 he seems to have written no more works.

To make the Oxfordian case, perhaps the biggest stumbling block is Edward de Vere's death in 1604. For over a century, Shakespeare scholars have spent much energy trying to determine the likeliest dates of composition of the plays, and though such dating is imprecise, most scholars believe that about twelve Shakespearean (or at least Shakespeare-collaborative) plays were written after 1604—including masterpieces such as *King Lear*, *Macbeth*, and *The Tempest*. Both Stratfordians and Oxfordians acknowledge that several of the later plays involved collaboration between "Shakespeare" and another author—mostly Fletcher, who succeeded "Shakespeare" as the main playwright for the King's Men. For Stratfordians, textual evidence shows that William cowrote with Fletcher late plays such as *Henry VIII* and *The Two Noble Kinsmen*, both typically dated around 1612–1613. *The Two Noble Kinsmen* lists both Shakespeare and Fletcher as authors on the title page of its original publication. Collaboration between writers was common at the time, and many scholars believe that early Shakespearean plays such as *Titus Andronicus* and *The First Part of Henry VI* also may have featured more than one author. The very fact of collaboration seems illogical for the Oxfordian case. If one imagines this aristocrat creating plays and wanting to avoid being associated with the world of theater, why would he collaborate with common playwrights?

Yet, for Oxfordians to explain away the fact that numerous plays postdate the earl's death, they must also argue that other authors not only collaborated but completed works presumably left unfinished in 1604. For example, *The Tempest* (~1611) not only contains allusions to recent, contemporary events such as a shipwreck and exploration of the New World, but the entire fabric of the play seems influenced by such events, making it hard to imagine Oxford having begun the work in, say, 1602–1603 and someone else grafting on to complete it in 1611.

In addition to the issues of collaborative authorship and the dating of Shakespearean plays well after Edward de Vere's death, the Oxfordian case falls on other rocky ground. Perhaps the simplest one is the fact that so many plays were published and advertised with Shakespeare's name. Oxfordians theorize that this Shakespeare name was a front or pseudonym, which raises the question "Why?" The vast majority of plays published in the era bore no author's name—only those of the publisher and the theater company. It would have been far simpler for Edward de Vere simply to publish "his plays" anonymously, which would have attracted no attention and allowed him to maintain his cover.

In fact, Shakespeare's name was attached to publications—plays and poems—precisely because it had become enormously popular and well known to the public and to his colleagues. The Shakespeare name helped to sell books. Regarding the Oxfordian skepticism over the inconsistency and awkwardness of the "Shakspere signatures," Renaissance English was in fact notorious for flexible and variable spelling of words, including proper names. As to the wobbliness and variability of the handwriting, which Oxfordians point to as signs that the hand that wrote them was not that of a man used to writing, some of this—particularly the three variant signatures on his will—can easily be explained by the fact of Shakespeare's sickness. Quite likely, in 1616, Shakespeare would have been bedridden, in awkward signing position, and ill enough for his shaky penmanship to be the least of his concerns.

We have already noted how William Shakespeare was well known to other writers—whether they invoked his name in resentment, as did Robert Greene (in the "upstart crow" pamphlet), or in deepest admiration and friendship, as did Ben Jonson in eulogizing his friend for the First Folio. As noted in the previous section, the 1598 work *Palladis Tamia, or Wit's Treasury* by Rev. Francis Meres does indeed mention the Earl of Oxford as one of the best comedic writers of the time. But Oxfordians are forced to ignore or explain the fact that in the same paragraph, Meres also lists Shakespeare, indicating that he clearly knew them as separate authors:

> The best Poets for Comedy among the Greeks are these, Menander, Aristophanes . . . and among the Latins, Plautus, Terence . . . so the best for Comedy amongst us be, Edward Earl of Oxford, . . . eloquent and witty John Lyly, Greene, Shakespeare, [and] Thomas Nash. (Meres 1598)

Elsewhere Meres singles out Shakespeare for highest praise:

> As Plautus and Seneca are accounted the best for Comedy and Tragedy among the Latins: so Shakespeare among the English is the most excellent in both kinds for the stage; for Comedy, witness his [Two] Gentlemen

of Verona, his [The Comedy of] Errors, his Love['s] Labors Lost, . . . his Midsummer Night['s] Dream, and his Merchant of Venice: for Tragedy his Richard the 2. Richard the 3. Henry the 4. King John, Titus Andronicus and his Romeo and Juliet. As Epius Stolo said, that the Muses would speak with Plautus's tongue, if they would speak Latin: so I say that the Muses would speak with Shakespeare's fine filed phrase, if they would speak English. (Meres 1598)

The evidence based on dating of the works, on collaborative authorship, and on myriad people knowing William Shakespeare as well as Edward de Vere renders weak the Oxfordian case. In 2007, the *New York Times* surveyed 265 Shakespeare teachers on the "authorship controversy." To the question, "Do you think there is good reason to question whether William Shakespeare of Stratford is the principal author of the plays and poems in the canon?" 6 percent answered "yes," and an additional 11 percent responded "possibly." When asked if they "mention the Shakespeare authorship question in your Shakespeare classes," 72 percent answered "yes." When asked what best described their opinion of the Shakespeare authorship question, 61 percent answered that it was "a theory without convincing evidence" and 32 percent called the issue "a waste of time and classroom distraction" ("Did He" 2007). Thus do the overwhelming majority of teachers and scholars of Shakespeare strongly hold to the Stratfordian view. Ultimately, the debate over Shakespearean authorship will never be resolved so as to satisfy everyone. Likely, Oxford will always have relatively few but fervent believers in his camp, whereas the majority of discerning readers, teachers, scholars, and students will continue to believe that Shakespeare was Shakespeare.

Further Readings

Boyle, William. "Revisiting the 1987 Moot Court Trial." everreader, April 14, 2014. https://everreader.wordpress.com/2014/04/14/revisiting-the-1987-moot-court-trial/

Champlin, Charles. "*SHAKSPERE* SHAKEN BY MOOT COURT." *Los Angeles Times*, September 29, 1987. https://www.latimes.com/archives/la-xpm-1987-09-29-ca-11009-story.html

Craig, Hugh, and Arthur F. Kinney, eds. *Shakespeare, Computers, and the Mystery of Authorship*. Cambridge: Cambridge University Press, 2009.

Crinkley, Richmond. "New Perspectives on the Authorship Question." *Shakespeare Quarterly* 36, 4 (1985): 515–22.

"Did He or Didn't He? That Is the Question." *New York Times*, April 22, 2007. https://www.nytimes.com/2007/04/22/education/edlife/22shakespeare-survey.html

Edmondson, Paul, and Stanley Wells. "Shakespeare Bites Back: Not So Anonymous." The Shakespeare Birthplace Trust, 2011. https://www.shakespeare.org.uk/explore-shakespeare/blogs/shakespeare-bites-back/

Elliott, Ward E. Y., and Robert J. Valenza. "Oxford by the Numbers: What Are the Odds That the Earl of Oxford Could Have Written Shakespeare's Poems and Plays?" *Tennessee Law Review* 72, 1 (2004): 323–452.

Friedman, William F., and Elizabeth S. Friedman. *The Shakespearean Ciphers Examined*. Cambridge: Cambridge University Press, 1957.

Garber, Marjorie. *Shakespeare's Ghost Writers: Literature as Uncanny Causality*. New York: Routledge Classics, 2010.

Gibson, H. N. *The Shakespeare Claimants: A Critical Survey of the Four Principal Theories Concerning the Authorship of the Shakespearean Plays*. New York: Routledge, 2005.

Greene, Robert. *Groats-Worth of Witte, Bought with a Million of Repentance. The Repentance of Robert Greene, 1592*. Edinburgh: Edinburgh University Press, 1966. https://archive.org/details/groatsvvorthofwi00greeuoft/page/n11

Gross, John. "Denying Shakespeare." *Commentary* 129, 3 (March 2010): 38–44.

Halliday, Frank E. *The Cult of Shakespeare*. London: Gerald Duckworth & Co., 1957.

Halliday, Frank E. *The Life of Shakespeare*. New York: Penguin Books, 1961.

Hastings, William T. "Shakspere Was Shakespeare." *American Scholar* 28 (1959): 479–88.

Hoffman, Calvin. *The Murder of the Man Who Was "Shakespeare."* New York: Julian Messner, 1960.

Jenkins, Elizabeth. *Elizabeth the Great*. New York: Coward-McCann, 1958.

Knapp, Alex. "Yes, Shakespeare Really Did Write Shakespeare." *Forbes*, October 19, 2011. https://www.forbes.com/sites/alexknapp/2011/10/19/yes-shakespeare-really-did-write-shakespeare/#61e2a3334011

Looney, J. Thomas. *"Shakespeare" Identified in Edward De Vere, the Seventeenth Earl of Oxford*. New York: Frederick A. Stokes, 1920.

Matus, Irvin L. *Shakespeare, In Fact*. Mineola, NY: Dover Books, 2012.

McCrea, Scott. *The Case for Shakespeare: The End of the Authorship Question*. Santa Barbara, CA: Praeger, 2005.

McMichael, George L., and Edgar M. Glenn. *Shakespeare and His Rivals: A Casebook on the Authorship Controversy*. New York: Odyssey Press, 1962.

Meres, Francis. *A Comparative Discourse of Our English Poets, with the Greeke, Latine, and Italian Poets. Palladis Tamia. Wits Treasury Being the Second Part of Wits Common Wealth*. 1598. http://spenserians.cath.vt .edu/TextRecord.php?action=GET&textsid=32924

Nelson, Alan H. *Monstrous Adversary: The Life of Edward de Vere, 17th Earl of Oxford*. Liverpool: Liverpool University Press, 2003.

Nelson, Alan H. "Stratford Si! Essex No!" *Tennessee Law Review*. 72, 1 (2004): 149–69.

Nicholl, Charles. "Yes, Shakespeare Wrote Shakespeare." *The Times Literary Supplement* 5586 (April 21, 2010): 3–4.

Niederkorn, William S. "Jumping O'er Times: The Importance of Lawyers and Judges in the Controversy over the Identity of Shakespeare, as Reflected in the Pages of the *New York Times*." *Tennessee Law Review* 72, 1 (2004): 67–92.

Niederkorn, William S. "Shakespeare Reaffirmed." *New York Times*, April 22, 2007. https://www.nytimes.com/2007/04/22/education/edlife /shakespeare.html?mtrref=duckduckgo.com&gwh=78E32CA74D B06D9C72F76CB0DCCC4271&gwt=pay&assetType=REGIWALL

Oxfraud. https://oxfraud.com/

PressMartin, Milward W. *Was Shakespeare Shakespeare? A Lawyer Reviews the Evidence*. New York: Cooper Square Press, 1965.

Price, Diana. *Shakespeare's Unorthodox Biography: New Evidence of an Authorship Problem*. Santa Barbara, CA: Praeger, 2000.

Puttenham, George. The Arte of English Poesie. In *Elizabethan Critical Essays*, 1904. Edited by G. Gregory Smith. 1589. https://www.bartleby .com/359/19.html

Saunders, J. W. "The Stigma of Print: A Note on the Social Bases of Tudor Poetry." *Essays in Criticism* 1, 2 (April 1951): 139–64.

The Shakespeare Authorship Page. https://shakespeareauthorship.com/

Shakespeare Oxford Fellowship. "Exploring the Evidence that the Works of Shakespeare Were Written by Edward de Vere, 17th Earl of Oxford." 2019. https://shakespeareoxfordfellowship.org/discover-shakespeare/

Shapiro, James. *Contested Will: Who Wrote Shakespeare?* New York: Simon & Schuster, 2010.

Simonton, Dean Keith. "Thematic Content and Political Context in Shakespeare's Dramatic Output, with Implications for Authorship and Chronology Controversies." *Empirical Studies of the Arts* 22, 2 (2004): 201–13. https://doi.org/10.2190/EQDP-MK0K-DFCK-MA8F

Smith, Emma. "The Shakespeare Authorship Debate Revisited." *Literature Compass* 5 (April 2008): 618–32.

Stevens, John Paul. "The Shakespeare Canon of Statutory Construction." Shakespeare Oxford Fellowship. 1992. https://shakespeareoxfordfellowship.org/canon-statutory-construction/

Syme, Holger. "People Being Stupid about Shakesp . . . or Someone Else." *dispositio*, September 19, 2011. http://www.dispositio.net/archives/449

Taylor, Gary, and Gabriel Egan, eds. *The New Oxford Shakespeare: Authorship Companion*. Oxford: Oxford University Press, 2017.

Tombe, Sheila. "Interview with Charlton Ogburn." Shakespeare Oxford Fellowship. 1996. https://shakespeareoxfordfellowship.org/interview-with-charlton-ogburn/

Vickers, Brian. "The Face of the Bard?" *Times Literary Supplement* 5387 (June 30, 2006): 17.

Vickers, Brian. "Shakespeare and Authorship Studies in the Twenty-First Century." *Shakespeare Quarterly* 62 (2011): 106–42.

Wadsworth, Frank. *The Poacher from Stratford: A Partial Account of the Controversy over the Authorship of Shakespeare's Plays*. Oakland: University of California Press, 1958.

Webster, Archie W. "Was Marlowe the Man?" *National Review* LXXXII (September 1923): 81–86.

Wells, Stanley, and Paul Edmondson, eds. *Shakespeare Beyond Doubt: Evidence, Argument, Controversy*. Cambridge: Cambridge University Press, 2013.

2

Shakespeare Was Homosexual or Bisexual

What People Think Happened

In 2017, Greg Doran, artistic director of England's Royal Shakespeare Company, asserted that Shakespeare may have been gay and that the playwright clearly created characters who can only be understood as homosexual. Several years earlier, leading British Shakespeare scholars had clashed publicly over the issue, with Brian Vickers taking issue with a book reviewer suggesting that Sonnet 116 appeared in a "primarily homosexual context." Debate over the theory that Shakespeare was homosexual or bisexual was hardly new; it had percolated for centuries before these recent eruptions.

As with all theories about the historical Shakespeare, our knowledge of his sexual orientation is limited by sparse data. Biographical records give us the bare facts that at age eighteen, William Shakespeare married Anne Hathaway; that six months later, she gave birth to their daughter Susanna; and that two years after that, she gave birth to the twins Hamnet and Judith. Many people also believe that William lived much of the following three decades apart from his wife—she in Stratford-upon-Avon and he in London. Beyond these few historical documents (marriage and baptismal records) and surmises over a distant marriage, we have virtually nothing to point us toward Shakespeare's sexual proclivities. And so we look to the poems and plays for evidence.

Like other writers of the period (notably Sir Philip Sidney and Edmund Spenser), Shakespeare wrote a sonnet sequence (large batch) at least partly to earn credibility as an author at a time when writing plays promised neither respectability nor remuneration. Shakespeare's sequence consisted of 154 sonnets, and in several of them, we find evidence for same-sex romance.

Initially published in 1609, the sonnets can be broken down according to the figures whom their speaker (presumably Shakespeare) addresses: 126 poems to a young man referred to as the "Fair Youth" and the final 28 to a "Dark Lady." The characters recur and interact with the speaker throughout the sequence. The speaker expresses his affection for the Fair Youth and admiration for his beauty in terms that certainly seem erotic.

The Fair Youth represents a real young man, the same man to whom Shakespeare's sonnet sequence was dedicated: "Mr. W. H., the only begetter of these ensuing sonnets." This mystery-shrouded figure was not only Shakespeare's literary patron but also his lover. Reversing the initials, many have suggested that W. H. represented Henry Wriothesley, Earl of Southampton. Shakespeare's long poems *Venus and Adonis* (1593) and *The Rape of Lucrece* (1594) are dedicated to Southampton, thus marking him as a known patron and acquaintance of the poet. Wriothesley was a powerful and (as evidenced by portraits) good-looking man—though not terribly youthful, as he would have been thirty-six at the time of the publication of the sonnets.

Seven years younger than Southampton, William Herbert, Earl of Pembroke, represents another candidate for the figure of Shakespeare's Fair Youth. Pembroke was also a leading patron of the arts. After Shakespeare's death, the 1623 First Folio (collected works of Shakespeare) was dedicated to Herbert and his brother, suggesting some strong connection with the plays' author. Scholars have for centuries debated the merits of Pembroke versus Southampton as the true "Mr. W. H." Either man could conceivably have been the inspiration for the Fair Youth and also Shakespeare's lover. Some language from the sonnets themselves—as well as from a couple of plays—point us to the idea that Shakespeare was familiar with same-sex relationships and was himself sexually involved with at least one man: the mysterious Mr. W. H. Literary scholar/critic Stephen Greenblatt, in writing about sexuality within Southampton's world, "assumes that something went on—'whether they only stared longingly at one another or embraced, kissed passionately, went to bed together.'"

How the Story Became Popular

In 1640, the second edition of Shakespeare's sonnets was published. Evidently, the publishers noted the controversial issue of the male figure to whom the majority of the sonnets seem to be addressed, for they altered most of the pronouns from masculine to feminine. That modified version became the best-known edition of the sonnets until 1780, when famous Shakespearean scholar Edmund Malone republished the works with their original language; this edition kindled the debate that rages through this day regarding Shakespeare's sexual preferences.

In 1780, critic George Steevens, upon reading Shakespeare's reference to a young man as the "master-mistress of my passion," opined that "it is impossible to read this fulsome panegyric, addressed to a male object, without an equal mixture of disgust and indignation" (Rollins 1944, 233). The most renowned poets of the nineteenth century took up the debate, with William Wordsworth writing that "with this key [the Sonnets] Shakespeare unlocked his heart" (Schiffer 1999, 28)—implying homo-erotic tendencies—and Wordsworth's cofounder of the Romantic poetry movement, Samuel Taylor Coleridge, arguing that the sonnets expressed only a pure, nonsexual male love. Moving into the twentieth century, a 1944 edition (Rollins) of the sonnets included an appendix with short essays by dozens of critics weighing in on both sides of the issue, and the debate continues today, with no end in sight. We see that the theory of Shakespeare's homosexuality or bisexuality stems primarily from the son-nets. However, some scholars and critics argue that some plays also pro-vide significant evidence of Shakespeare's interest in same-sex romance.

To better understand the sexual and theatrical world of Shakespeare's London, we must imagine a scene where, for starters, women were for-bidden to perform. Little is known about whether women would have been active backstage in theatrical companies—for instance, as costume mistresses—but with few, clandestine exceptions, they did not appear onstage. Thus we are immediately presented with an interesting dynamic regarding sexuality in plays: All female roles—including the many parts Shakespeare created for scenes calling for wooing, kissing, and other romantic activity—were played by young men/adolescent boys. Some scholars speculate that these boy players were subjected to homosexual predation by members of the companies, but we lack solid evidence of this—from a time and place that featured strict laws against homosexual conduct. In any event, we are left to envision the stage dynamics of boys playing women's parts.

Imagine oneself as a playgoer, perhaps of the lower class, watching love scenes between, say, Romeo—perhaps acted by a man you knew—and Juliet—perhaps acted by the son of a neighbor. Throughout the thou-sands of performances of Shakespeare's plays during his lifetime, this spec-tacle (two males very publicly kissing, caressing, and so on) took place over and over. In many cases, the dynamic was further complicated by the notion of cross-dressing within the play's narrative. That is, at least eight of Shakespeare's plays (*Twelfth Night, As You Like It, The Taming of the Shrew, The Merry Wives of Windsor, Cymbeline, The Merchant of Venice, A Midsummer Night's Dream*, and *Two Gentlemen of Verona*) feature female characters who dress as men for portions of the play. These plots sometimes play on the notion of a male actor/character being attracted to a young man (the actor) who dresses as a woman (the original character) who then dresses as a man (his/her alter ego within the plot). Given all this gender bending, the suggestion of homosexual attraction was inevitable. It may be significant that all these plays are comedies (and generally, the most meaty and intricate of Shakespeare's female roles come in comedies). Shakespeare and other English Renaissance dramatists knew full well that such gender confusion would be conducive to comedy, implying that any homosexual implications would be laughable. However, comedy could not have been Shakespeare's intent with myriad other romantic and sexualized scenes that he knew would be staged between male actors, including great and tragic romantic relationships such as those found in *Romeo and Juliet* and *Othello*.

Of course, romantic scenes, and all others, would eventually (beginning with the Restoration) come to be played by actors matching the gender of the characters, and the complexity surrounding the depiction of heterosexual romance by male-only casts would diminish. In fact, it is less than completely accurate to assert that women never performed during the English Renaissance. During Shakespeare's time, women did appear on certain, more private stages—in courtly masques. In addition to the well-known and popular plays performed in outdoor theaters such as the Globe and indoor theaters such as the Blackfriars, a more elite form of entertainment was played throughout the Renaissance, and at least one queen herself enjoyed and performed in masques: Queen Anne of Denmark, wife of King James. Masques were single-performance, high-budget affairs featuring elaborate spectacles and special effects. On the court stage, Anne and some of her ladies played parts—although their roles seem mostly to have been silent, focusing on displaying the physical beauty of these women.

Decades after Shakespeare's death, the Restoration theater scene featured women on the public English stages. During some years of the Commonwealth and Protectorate (1649–60), King James's grandson, the exiled Charles II, took refuge in the French court of his cousin King Louis XIV, himself a great patron of the arts. There, Charles and his courtiers likely enjoyed theatrical entertainments that featured female performers. When the monarchy was restored and Charles crowned, he not only allowed but enthusiastically supported plays that featured women. The first recorded professional production with female cast members was Shakespeare's *Othello* in 1660. From records and artworks of the Restoration theater, we know that not only were women allowed to act on stage, they were also featured as objects of sexual desire, with costumes expressly designed to highlight their bodies—some of which became known as "breeches parts," after the tight-fitting pants they wore, sometimes with slits to further show off the legs. However, even as women began to command attention through their roles, the phenomenon of boy actors playing female roles continued in the Restoration. And about a century later, famed London actress Sarah Siddons would flip the equation by herself playing the title role in *Hamlet*, some nine different times in her life. It would seem that whatever Shakespeare's personal sexual preferences may have been, the plays he created allow producers, performers, critics, and audiences to project their own desires and visions in whatever direction they wish.

What Really Happened

In addition to our clear knowledge that William Shakespeare married and fathered three children, the only possible evidence we have of his sexual biography comes from one anecdote that suggests that while staying in London, he was not faithful to his marriage vows. From the 1602 journal of lawyer John Manningham, we get the picture of Shakespeare enjoying the perks of his theatrical fame:

> Upon a time when [Shakespeare's company partner and lead actor Richard] Burbage played Richard the Third there was a citizen grew so far in liking with him, that before she went from the play she appointed him to come that night unto her by the name of Richard the Third. Shakespeare, overhearing their conclusion, went before, was entertained and at his game ere Burbage came. Then, message being brought that Richard the Third was at the door, Shakespeare caused return to be made that William the Conqueror was before Richard the Third. (Schoenbaum 1975, 152)

However, a source closer to Shakespeare suggests that he was actually more of a recluse while in London. William Beeston, son of Christopher Beeston, a comic actor in Shakespeare's company, reported to the seventeenth-century biographer John Aubrey regarding Shakespeare: "The more to be admired, he was not a company keeper. [H]e . . . wouldn't be debauched, and if invited to, writ [wrote] that he was in pain" (Schoenbaum 1975, 205). Because the older Beeston was verifiably a colleague and likely friend of Shakespeare, the provenance of this account would seem to carry more weight than does the unsourced and legendary anecdote from Manningham's diary.

Beyond the clear facts of Shakespeare's marriage and children, plus Manningham's amusing but hardly reliable tale, everything said or written about Shakespeare's sexuality is entirely speculative—and wholly based (as we have seen above) on interpretations of his plays and especially his poems. Whereas many critics see the sonnets directed to the Fair Youth as expressing sexual love, others counter that these passages could refer to intense, deep, nonsexual friendship. People of Shakespeare's age had a quite different view—and even different vocabulary—to express the bonds of male friendship, drawing on traditions going back to Greek and Roman times.

In the Renaissance, male friendship was expressed in terms of deep affection and love, and we should resist projecting contemporary assumptions that such language implied anything sexual. The friendship between two men was commonly expressed as "love"; that form of love was widely believed to surpass the bond between male-female lovers and to be unbreakable. During the Renaissance, sodomy (defined then as including sex between two men) was punishable by death. Whether Protestant, secret Catholic, or even agnostic, the vast majority of people feared for the fate of their souls enough to avoid homosexuality even if they felt attracted in that direction.

Whatever speculations or conclusions we are tempted to draw from the sonnets—for example, that homoerotic feelings are described therein—it is also far from certain that we should assume the speaker/narrator of the poems to be Shakespeare. The writer was, after all, rather adept at creating characters through his plays and poems. Prudently, scholars rarely argue that any of those characters speaks directly for Shakespeare, yet in eagerly projecting the case for Shakespeare's homo- or bisexuality, some critics make exactly that assumption. Also, not all scholars accept the theory that so many of the poems are indeed addressed to a young man rather than to a woman. And even the ones clearly addressed to the Fair Youth exhort him to marry—a clear call to heterosexual union with a woman, and subsequent procreation.

In *Looking for Sex in Shakespeare*, Stanley Wells longs for a middle ground between the deniers of any possible homoerotic expression in the sonnets and critics who have "swung too far in the opposite direction" and allowed their own sensibilities to influence their understanding. One element that complicates the question of Shakespeare's sexuality is that same-sex friendships in the Renaissance were often characterized by shows of affection (e.g., bed-sharing, professions of love) that contemporary readers associate with modern-day sexual relationships.

Even the speculation regarding the elusive "Mr. W. H."—the alleged real figure represented by the Fair Youth of Shakespeare's sonnets and, in the dreams of some critics, Shakespeare's lover—comes up against newer insights. In 2015, American researcher Geoffrey Caveney proposed that rather than the wealthy and powerful earl of Southampton or of Pembroke, the likeliest candidate for W. H. is William Holme, a humble apprentice at the shop that printed *Shakespeare's Sonnets* in 1609 (Alberge 2015). The dedication—where we find the titillating reference to "Mr. W. H."—ends with "T. T.," presumably the initials of the publisher, Thomas Thorpe. Caveney recently discovered that William Holme died in 1607, two years before the publication, and argues that the dedication serves not to honor Shakespeare's wealthy patron/putative lover (Southampton or Pembroke) but to memorialize Holme. Many prominent Shakespeare scholars have become persuaded by Caveney's assertion that the book's dedication page was set so as to invoke a Roman funeral tablet—featuring, for instance, oddly placed periods throughout the inscription, which would have resembled such a Roman memorial rather than a typical book dedication. If Caveney's hypothesis is correct, it puts a significant dent in the idea of either of the dashing possible dedicatees—Southhampton or Pembroke—and further weakens the theory of Shakespeare's homoerotic proclivities.

But long prior to Caveney's proposal of William Holme as "W. H.," scholars had faced a significant obstacle in identifying the sonnet dedicatee as Southampton or Pembroke. Not only is the "W. H." a mystery, but the "Mr." provides even more of a challenge. That is, an aristocrat of such high standing as those two earls would not be addressed as "Mr."; in fact, such an address would be insulting, as that title could be used for any common man. An earl would be addressed as "His Lordship" or "Lord."

The mysteries of the identity of the "Fair Youth" and of the sonnets' dedicatee remain with us, and those mysteries constitute the closest anyone has gotten to demonstrating that Shakespeare experienced same-sex attraction. Ultimately the argument for Shakespeare's homosexual orientation is entirely speculative and often seems to involve projecting contemporary sensibilities back onto a man who lived 400 years ago. In the absence of any evidence of Shakespeare ever engaging in homosexual relations, and given plentiful evidence of his being married and fathering children, it seems wisest to conclude that William Shakespeare was a heterosexual man—perhaps even a faithfully married one.

PRIMARY SOURCE DOCUMENTS

MARCUS TULLIUS CICERO, "DE AMICITIA" ("ON FRIENDSHIP") (44 BCE)

One could not name a more influential Classical figure for the people of the English Renaissance than Marcus Tullius Cicero, known simply as Cicero (106–43 BCE). More of Cicero's writings survive than of any other Roman writer, and through the writings of others about him, we know that Cicero was foremost known as a great orator—a skill he put to great use as a lawyer and as a consul (only two people at a time served as consuls, the highest elected office during the Roman Republic). Cicero's works formed a cornerstone of the grammar school education of Renaissance English children, including Shakespeare, who would insert Cicero in one scene of his Julius Caesar *(ironically, the historically loquacious Cicero utters only short speeches almost as a straight man to Casca, one of the conspirators soon to assassinate Caesar).*

Cicero's "On Friendship" takes the form of a dialogue between real historical figures, and uses as a backdrop the death of Scipio Africanus, known to history as Scipio the Younger. Cicero places in dialogue Laelius—the great friend of Scipio—and Laelius's two sons-in-law, Fannius and Scaevola. Cicero actually knew Scaevola, who related to him the discussions with Laelius (on the subject of Scipio) that form the basis for Cicero's treatise on friendship. The beginning of the essay contains questions and prompts from Fannius and Scaevola, but the bulk of it—including the excerpts below—consists of Laelius expounding on the subject of friendship, both in general and sometimes specifically regarding his deep bond with Scipio. The terms used describe a deep love, and this conception of profound male friendship—nonsexual but deeply intimate—permeated the thinking of Renaissance writers such as Shakespeare.

"On Friendship" is dedicated to Cicero's friend Titus Pomponius Atticus.

Friendship is nothing else than entire fellow-feeling as to all things, human and divine, with mutual good-will and affection; and I doubt whether anything better than this, wisdom alone excepted, has been given to man by the immortal gods. Some prefer riches to it; some, sound health;

some, power; some, posts of honor; many, even sensual gratification. . . . Those, indeed, who regard virtue as the supreme good are entirely in the right; but it is virtue itself that produces and sustains friendship, nor without virtue can friendship by any possibility exist. . . . Among such good men as there really are, friendship has more advantages than I can easily name.

[. . .] How could you have full enjoyment of prosperity, unless with one whose pleasure in it was equal to your own? Nor would it be easy to bear adversity, unless with the sympathy of one on whom it rested more heavily than on your own soul. Then, too, other objects of desire are, in general, adapted, each to some specific purpose—wealth, that you may use it; power, that you may receive the homage of those around you; posts of honor, that you may obtain reputation; sensual gratification, that you may live in pleasure; health, that you may be free from pain, and may have full exercise of your bodily powers and faculties. But friendship combines the largest number of utilities. Wherever you turn, it is at hand. No place shuts it out. It is never unseasonable, never annoying. Thus, as the proverb says, "You cannot put water or fire to more uses than friendship serves." I am not now speaking of the common and moderate type of friendship, which yet yields both pleasure and profit, but of true and perfect friendship, like that which existed in the few instances that are held in special remembrance. Such friendship at once enhances the lustre of prosperity, and by dividing and sharing adversity lessens its burden.

Moreover . . . friendship . . . lights up a good hope for the time to come. . . . For he, indeed, who looks into the face of a friend beholds, as it were, a copy of himself. Thus the absent are present, and the poor are rich, and the weak are strong, and—what seems stranger still—the dead are alive, such is the honor, the enduring remembrance, the longing love, with which the dying are followed by the living. . . . If it is not perfectly understood what virtue there is in friendship and concord, it may be learned from dissension and discord. For what house is so stable, what state so firm, that it cannot be utterly overturned by hatred and strife? Hence it may be ascertained how much good there is in friendship. . . . [A] certain philosopher . . . sang in Greek verse that it is friendship that draws together and discord that parts all things which subsist in harmony, and which have their various movements in nature and in the whole universe.

[. . . O]n friendship, the foremost question . . . is, whether friendship is craved on account of conscious infirmity and need, so that in bestowing and receiving the kind offices that belong to it each may have that done for him by the other which he is least able to do for himself, . . . or whether, though this relation of mutual benefit is the property of friendship, it has yet another cause, more sacred and more noble, and derived more genuinely from the very nature of man. Love, which in our language gives name to friendship, bears a chief part in unions of mutual benefit. . . . But in friendship there is nothing feigned, nothing pretended, and whatever there is in it is both genuine and spontaneous. Friendship, therefore, springs from nature rather than from need,—from an inclination of the mind with a certain consciousness of love rather than from calculation of the benefit to be derived from it.

[. . .] Love is, indeed, strengthened by favors received, by witnessing assiduity in one's service, and by habitual intercourse; and when these are added to the first impulse of the mind toward love, there flames forth a marvellously rich glow of affectionate feeling. If there are any who think that this proceeds from conscious weakness and the desire to have some person through whom one can obtain what he lacks, they assign, indeed, to friendship a mean and utterly ignoble origin, born, as they would have it, of poverty and neediness. If this were true, then the less of resource one was conscious of having in himself, the better fitted would he be for friendship. The contrary is the case; for the more confidence a man has in himself, and the more thoroughly he is fortified by virtue and wisdom, so that he is in need of no one, and regards all that concerns him as in his own keeping, the more noteworthy is he for the friendships which he seeks and cherishes. What? Did Africanus need me? Not in the least, by Hercules. As little did I need him. But I was drawn to him by admiration of his virtue, while he, in turn, loved me, perhaps, from some favorable estimate of my character; and intimacy increased our mutual affection.

[. . .] It is like taking the sun out of the world, to bereave human life of friendship, than which the immortal gods have given man nothing better, nothing more gladdening. . . . Therefore the pain which must often be incurred on a friend's account is not of sufficient moment to banish friendship from human life, any more than the occasional care and trouble which the virtues bring should be a reason for renouncing them.

[. . .] Since virtue attracts friendship, as I have said, if there shines forth any manifestation of virtue with which a mind similarly disposed can come into contact and union, from such intercourse love must of necessity spring. For what is so absurd as to be charmed with many things that have no substantial worth, as with office, fame, architecture, dress, and genteel appearance, but not to be in any wise charmed by a mind endowed with virtue, and capable of either loving, or—if I may use the word—re-loving?

[. . .] But it is those in whose very selves there is reason why they should be loved, that are worthy of friendship. A rare class of men! Indeed, super-latively excellent objects of every sort are rare, nor is anything more diffi-cult than to discover that which is in all respects perfect in its kind. But most persons . . . most love those friends, as they do those cattle, that will yield them the greatest gain. Thus they lack that most beautiful and most natural friendship, which is to be sought in itself and for its own sake; nor can they know from experience what and how great is the power of such friendship. One loves himself, not in order to exact from himself any wages for such love, but because he is in himself dear to himself. Now, unless this same property be transferred to friendship, a true friend will never be found; for such a friend is, as it were, another self. But if it is seen in beasts, birds, fishes, animals tame and wild, that they first love themselves . . . and that they then require and seek those of their kind to whom they may attach themselves, and do so with desire and with a certain semblance of human love, how much more is this natural in man, who both loves himself, and craves another whose soul he may so blend with his own as almost to make one out of two!

[. . .] I had these things to say to you about friendship; and I exhort you that you so give the foremost place to virtue without which friendship cannot be, that with the sole exception of virtue, you may think nothing to be preferred to friendship.

Source: Marcus Tullius Cicero. *Cicero De Amicitia (On Friendship) and Scipio's Dream.* Translated with an Introduction and Notes by Andrew P. Peabody (Boston: Little, Brown, and Co., 1887).

MICHEL DE MONTAIGNE, "OF FRIENDSHIP" (1580)

Montaigne's most enduring legacy is his Essays, *a ten-volume work he composed throughout and beyond a ten-year period of reclusive and voluminous reading and writing in the library of his family castle. Montaigne is in fact credited with pioneering the essay as a form of writing, and his magnum opus includes influential pieces on subjects including psychology, education, prayer, sleep, solitude, vanity, monstrous children, cannibals, and—of course—friendship.*

Unlike Aristotle, who believed friendship to constitute one soul in two bodies, and Cicero, who viewed the bond as "almost" making one soul out of two, Montaigne clearly saw the two souls as separate beings; nonetheless, his experience and expression of friendship strikingly brings home the common Renaissance humanist view that the bond between two men was superior to that between male and female lovers. So profound and rare was this relationship that a man could have only one such friend at a time—and perhaps only one in a lifetime. Montaigne speaks on the subject based on his personal experience with his dear friend, Etienne de La Boétie, whom he only knew for four years—until the great bond was broken by La Boétie's untimely death in 1563. Being a quintessential humanist, Montaigne also injects his essay with quotes from classical sources, including Cicero. We don't know if—or with whom—Shakespeare experienced such a deep bond of friendship, but Montaigne's essay—which Shakespeare likely read, just as he had read Cicero's— gives us context for the deep expression of male, nonsexual love such as we find in some of the plays and sonnets.

We are not here to bring the love we bear to women, though it be an act of our own choice, into comparison, nor rank it with the others. The fire of this, I confess . . . is more active, more eager, and more sharp: but withal, 'tis more precipitant, fickle, moving, and inconstant; a fever subject to intermissions and paroxysms, that has seized but on one part of us. Whereas in friendship, 'tis a general and universal fire, but temperate and equal, a constant established heat, all gentle and smooth, without poignancy or roughness. Moreover, in love, 'tis no other than frantic desire for that which flies from us: so soon as it enters unto the terms of friendship, that is to say, into a concurrence of desires, it vanishes and is gone, fruition destroys it, as having only a fleshly end, and such a one as is subject to satiety.

Friendship, on the contrary, is enjoyed proportionably as it is desired; and only grows up, is nourished and improved by enjoyment, as being of itself spiritual, and the soul growing still more refined by practice. Under this perfect friendship, the other fleeting affections have in my younger years found some place in me . . . so that I had both these passions, but always so, that I could myself well enough distinguish them, and never in any degree of comparison with one another; the first maintaining its flight in so lofty and so brave a place, as with disdain to look down, and see the other flying at a far humbler pitch below.

[. . .] And therefore it is that they called it sacred and divine, and conceive that nothing but the violence of tyrants and the baseness of the common people are inimical to it. . . . I return to my own more just and true description: "Omnino amicitiae, corroboratis jam confirmatisque, et ingeniis, et aetatibus, judicandae sunt." *["Those are only to be reputed friendships that are fortified and confirmed by judgement and the length of time."—Cicero, De Amicitia., c. 20.]*

[. . .] For the rest, what we commonly call friends and friendships, are nothing but acquaintance and familiarities, either occasionally contracted, or upon some design, by means of which there happens some little intercourse betwixt our souls. But in the friendship I speak of, they mix and work themselves into one piece, with so universal a mixture, that there is no more sign of the seam by which they were first conjoined. If a man should importune me to give a reason why I loved him, I find it could no otherwise be expressed, than by making answer: because it was he, because it was I. There is, beyond all that I am able to say, I know not what inexplicable and fated power that brought on this union. We sought one another long before we met, and by the characters we heard of one another, which wrought upon our affections more than, in reason, mere reports should do; I think 'twas by some secret appointment of heaven. We embraced in our names; and at our first meeting . . . we found ourselves so mutually taken with one another, so acquainted, and so endeared betwixt ourselves, that from thenceforward nothing was so near to us as one another. . . .

Our souls had drawn so unanimously together, they had considered each other with so ardent an affection, and with the like affection laid open the very bottom of our hearts to one another's view, that I not only knew his as well as my own; but should certainly in any concern of mine have trusted my interest much more willingly with him, than with myself.

[. . .] "Nil ego contulerim jucundo sanus amico." *["While I have sense left to me, there will never be anything more acceptable to me than an agreeable friend."—Horace, Sat., i. 5, 44.]*

The ancient Menander declared him to be happy that had had the good fortune to meet with but the shadow of a friend: . . . for . . . if I compare all the rest of my life, though, thanks be to God, I have passed my time pleasantly enough . . . free from any grievous affliction, and in great tranquillity of mind . . . if I should compare it all . . . with the four years I had the happiness to enjoy the sweet society of this excellent man, 'tis nothing but smoke, an obscure and tedious night. From the day that I lost him:

"Quern semper acerbum, Semper honoratum (sic, di, voluistis) habebo." *["A day for me ever sad, for ever sacred, so have you willed ye gods."—Aeneid, v. 49.]*

I have only led a languishing life; and the very pleasures that present themselves to me, instead of administering anything of consolation, double my affliction for his loss. We were halves throughout, and to that degree, that methinks, by outliving him, I defraud him of his part.

[. . .] I was so grown and accustomed to be always his double in all places and in all things, that methinks I am no more than half of myself:

"Illam meae si partem anima tulit Maturior vis, quid moror altera? Nec carus aeque, nec superstes Integer? Ille dies utramque Duxit ruinam." ["If a superior force has taken that part of my soul, why do I, the remaining one, linger behind? What is left is not so dear, nor an entire thing: this day has wrought the destruction of both."—Horace, Ode, ii. 17, 5.]

There is no action or imagination of mine wherein I do not miss him; as I know that he would have missed me: for as he surpassed me by infinite degrees in virtue and all other accomplishments, so he also did in the duties of friendship:

"Quis desiderio sit pudor, aut modus Tam cari capitis?"
["What shame can there be, or measure, in lamenting so dear a friend?"
—Horace, Ode, i. 24, I.]

Source: Michel de Montaigne. *Essays of Montaigne, Vol. 2.* Translated by Charles Cotton, revised by William Carew Hazlett (New York: Edwin C. Hill, 1910).

A SELECTION OF SONNETS (1609)

Shakespeare's sonnets (published in 1609) are all untitled, and are commonly referred to by number or first line. More than any other lines by Shakespeare, those in Sonnets 20 and 63 fuel the fire of those who would make the case for Shakespeare's homosexuality or bisexuality. Both poems are clearly addressed to a man—the mysterious figure most critics call the Fair Youth, and both include language that is at least ambiguously erotic. For example, Sonnet 20 begins by noting that the young man resembles a woman, then calls him the "master mistress of my passion." As with so many of the facts and fictions surrounding Shakespeare, these words provoke controversy. To most contemporary readers and some critics, the word "passion" denotes sexual desire; however, other critics note that more commonly in Shakespeare's time—and in Shakespeare's other usages—it suggested suffering, as in the evocation of the passion of Christ on the cross. Sonnet 63 evokes language of deep love ("My sweet love's beauty")—which was commonly used in the Renaissance to express male friendship—and laments the aging and death that will inevitably come. As in another of Shakespeare's best known poems—Sonnet 18 ("Shall I compare thee to a summer's day," which uses no gendered pronouns)—the poet declares that decay and death can only be defeated by his poems, which will last forever and preserve the subject's memory and beauty: "His beauty shall in these black lines be seen, / And they shall live, and he in them still green."

Sonnet XX

A woman's face with nature's own hand painted,
Hast thou, the master mistress of my passion;
A woman's gentle heart, but not acquainted
With shifting change, as is false women's fashion:
An eye more bright than theirs, less false in rolling,
Gilding the object whereupon it gazeth;
A man in hue all hues in his controlling,
Which steals men's eyes and women's souls amazeth.
And for a woman wert thou first created;
Till Nature, as she wrought thee, fell a-doting,
And by addition me of thee defeated,
By adding one thing to my purpose nothing.
But since she prick'd thee out for women's pleasure,
Mine be thy love and thy love's use their treasure.

Sonnet LXIII

Against my love shall be as I am now,
With Time's injurious hand crushed and o'erworn;
When hours have drained his blood and filled his brow
With lines and wrinkles; when his youthful morn
Hath travelled on to age's steepy night;
And all those beauties whereof now he's king
Are vanishing, or vanished out of sight,
Stealing away the treasure of his spring;
For such a time do I now fortify
Against confounding age's cruel knife,
That he shall never cut from memory
My sweet love's beauty, though my lover's life:
His beauty shall in these black lines be seen,
And they shall live, and he in them still green.

Source: *Shakespeare's Sonnets.* Available online at https://archive.org/stream/shakes pearessonn01041gut/wssnt10.txt

DEDICATION PAGE, *SHAKE-SPEARES SONNETS* (1609)

Two little letters ("W. H.") from this dedication have fueled hundreds of books and articles, with many writers attempting to link those mysterious initials to the Fair Youth of Shakespeare's sonnets—and by extension to establish a connection with a male object of Shakespeare's affections. Throughout the twentieth century and beyond, the two most discussed candidates for "Mr. W. H." have been Henry Wriothesley, earl of Southampton (which immediately presents the issue of the inversion of the "W" and the "H") and William Herbert, earl of Pembroke. As we have seen, more recently, William Holme has been proposed as the "only begetter." Holme was not only an associate of publisher Thomas Thorpe but had his own London bookshop and was connected with the literary and theatrical scenes—including, likely, with Shakespeare. In their zeal to associate Shakespeare with W. H., many overlook the fact that Thorpe—not Shakespeare—actually wrote the dedication, as indicated by the T. T. at the bottom. Shakespeare may or may not have had any input, and the "only begetter" could have been Thorpe's way of crediting his deceased friend Holme with having provided him with the manuscript of the sonnets. Note, too, that the page layout resembles a funeral memorial, as does some of the language, such as "eternity" and "setting forth."

TO THE ONLY BEGETTER OF
THESE ENSUING SONNETS
MR. W. H. ALL HAPPINESS
AND THAT ETERNITY
PROMISED
BY
OUR EVER-LIVING POET
WISHETH
THE WELL-WISHING ADVENTURER IN
SETTING
FORTH
T. T.

Source: *Shake-Speares Sonnets.* 1609. Available online at http://www.shakespeares -sonnets.com/sonnet/ded2comm.htm

EXCERPTS FROM *THE MERCHANT OF VENICE*

The character Antonio begins the play in a state of melancholy, for which he says he has no explanation. Throughout the play, he displays powerful devotion

to his friend Bassanio, to the point of lending him huge sums of money so his friend can woo his beloved Portia. Later in the play, after he forfeits his bond to the moneylender Shylock, he expresses his willingness to die for his friend. Whereas some contemporary critics read Antonio as being in homoerotic love with Bassanio, others argue that Antonio represents ideal male friendship, culminating in the apex of Christian love—on the model of Jesus, he is willing to lay down his life for another.

Antonio. I pray you, good Bassanio, let me know it;
And if it stand, as you yourself still do,
Within the eye of honour, be assured,
My purse, my person, my extremest means,
Lie all unlock'd to your occasions. *I.i.142–46*

Antonio. Give me your hand, Bassanio: fare you well!
Grieve not that I am fallen to this for you;
For herein Fortune shows herself more kind
Than is her custom: it is still her use
To let the wretched man outlive his wealth,
To view with hollow eye and wrinkled brow
An age of poverty; from which lingering penance
Of such misery doth she cut me off.
Commend me to your honourable wife:
Tell her the process of Antonio's end;
Say how I loved you, speak me fair in death;
And, when the tale is told, bid her be judge
Whether Bassanio had not once a love.
Repent but you that you shall lose your friend,
And he repents not that he pays your debt;
For if the Jew do cut but deep enough,
I'll pay it presently with all my heart. *IV.i.2210–26*

EXCERPT FROM *TWELFTH NIGHT*

The sailor character—also named Antonio—expresses his unswerving loyalty to his friend Sebastian. Contemporary critics and productions of the play often play up the relationship of the two as homoerotic, though the Antonio role is miniscule, and Sebastian ends up marrying the Countess Olivia.

One, sir, that for his love dares yet do more
Than you have heard him brag to you he will. *III.iv.1864–65*

Further Readings

Alberge, Dalya. "Has the Mystery of Shakespeare's Sonnets Finally Been Solved?" *Guardian* online, January 31, 2015. https://www.theguardian.com/culture/2015/jan/31/shakespeare-sonnets-mr-wh-dedication-mystery

Alexander, Catherine, and Stanley Wells, eds. *Shakespeare and Sexuality.* Cambridge: Cambridge University Press, 2001.

Bray, Alan, and Laurie Shannon. *Sovereign Amity: Figures of Friendship in Shakespearean Contexts.* Chicago: University of Chicago Press, 2002.

Bromley, James M. *Intimacy and Sexuality in the Age of Shakespeare.* Cambridge: Cambridge University Press, 2012.

de Grazia, Margreta. "The Scandal of Shakespeare's Sonnets." *Shakespeare Survey* 46 (1994): 35–49.

Hammond, Paul. *Figuring Sex Between Men from Shakespeare to Rochester.* Oxford: Oxford University Press, 2002.

Hubler, Edward, Northrop Frye, Leslie A. Fiedler, Stephen Spender, and R. P. Blackmur. *The Riddle of Shakespeare's Sonnets: The Text of the Sonnets with Interpretive Essays.* London: Routledge, 1962.

Innes, Paul. *Shakespeare and the English Renaissance Sonnet: Verses of Feigning Love.* Basingstoke: Macmillan, 1999.

Keevak, Michael. *Sexual Shakespeare: Forgery, Authorship, Portraiture.* Detroit: Wayne State University Press, 2001.

Pearce, Joseph. *Shakespeare on Love.* San Francisco: Ignatius Press, 2013.

Pequigney, Joseph. *Such Is My Love: A Study of Shakespeare's Sonnets.* Chicago: University of Chicago Press, 1985.

Rollins, Hyder Edward, et al., eds. *A New Variorum Edition of Shakespeare: The Sonnets.* Philadelphia: J. B. Lippincott & Company, 1944.

Roy, Pinaki. "Who's the Man?: A Very Brief Study of Ambiguous Gender-roles in *Twelfth Night.*" *Yearly Shakespeare* (April 12, 2014): 46–55.

Schiffer, J. *Shakespeare's Sonnets: Critical Essays.* Abingdon-on-Thames: Routledge, 1999.

Schoenbaum, Samuel. *William Shakespeare: A Documentary Life.* New York: Oxford University Press, 1975.

Sedgwick, Eve Kosofsky. *Between Men: English Literature and Male Homosocial Desire.* New York: Columbia University Press, 1985.

Shakespeare, William. *The Sonnets.* Project Gutenberg. https://archive.org/stream/shakespearessonn01041gut/wssnt10.txt

Smith, Bruce R. *Homosexual Desire in Shakespeare's England: A Cultural Poetics.* Chicago: University of Chicago Press, 1994.

Smith, Bruce R. *Shakespeare and Masculinity*. New York: Oxford University Press, 2000.

Tilney, Edmund. *The Flower of Friendship, 1568*. Ed. Valerie Wayne. Ithaca: Cornell University Press, 1992.

Vendler, Helen. *The Art of Shakespeare's Sonnets*. Cambridge: Harvard University Press, 1997.

Wilson, Ian. *Shakespeare: The Evidence*. New York: St. Martin's Griffin, 1999.

3

Shakespeare Was Secretly Roman Catholic

What People Think Happened

The England in which Shakespeare lived was religiously charged. Throughout the reigns of the Protestant rulers Queen Elizabeth and King James, secret networks of Catholics—both laypeople and clergymen—kept up their practice of the old religion, with some of them also plotting to overthrow the monarch. William Shakespeare was immersed in this climate throughout his upbringing and maintained his Catholic allegiance throughout his adult life and professional career.

Shakespeare's parents wed in 1557, during the reign of "Bloody Mary," when the couple could freely practice their Catholic faith. Such freedom was short-lived, as Mary died without an heir the next year, bringing in the decidedly Protestant Queen Elizabeth and the prohibition of practicing "the old religion." Catholic families such as the Shakespeares had little choice but to conform to the state-mandated Church of England, at least outwardly. Nonetheless, the Shakespeare family's Catholic roots were strong, and young William went out into the world knowing that he must carefully conceal his true faith. Beyond his immediate family, he would have other close contacts with the forbidden religion throughout his young life.

William almost certainly attended King's New School in Stratford-upon-Avon, where his headmasters would have included several men clearly identified as Catholics, such as Simon Hunt, who later became a prominent Jesuit priest, and Thomas Jenkins, who studied with the famous Jesuit Edmund Campion, who would be executed for treason in 1581. We lack records of Shakespeare's precise years at King's New School or his specific teachers, but almost certainly he studied with one or more of these Catholic men.

It is reasonably and commonly assumed that William left school at age fourteen, and the next record we have is his 1582 marriage at age eighteen to the pregnant, twenty-six-year-old Anne Hathaway. The unusual circumstances of his wedding may provide more evidence of Shakespeare's Catholic sympathies. The couple's marriage license was issued not in Stratford but in the smaller town of Temple Grafton, some five miles west. At the time, the vicar of the Temple Grafton church was John Frith, who, a few years later, would be cited by the authorities as a priest "unsound in religion"— likely meaning that though he outwardly operated as a loyal priest of the Church of England, he secretly performed Catholic ceremonies.

During the "lost years"—the period between the births of his children (1583 for Susanna and 1585 for the twins, Hamnet and Judith) in Stratford and the beginning of his London theatrical career around 1592— Shakespeare inhabited a shadowy and dangerous underground world with other recusants (clandestine practitioners of "the old religion") in the English countryside.

Shakespeare may also have secretly attended Oxford University, certain colleges of which were known to be friendly to Catholics, who would audit classes but not officially matriculate. After Shakespeare launched his playwrighting career and had residences in London for two decades, he never registered with his local Anglican church as required by law, and in fact, he was listed among those who failed to attend services. By law unable openly to practice Catholicism, instead he embedded within numerous of his plays and poems references to the plight of persecuted English Catholics.

How the Story Became Popular

Archdeacon Richard Davies, a seventeenth-century Anglican cleric, wrote of Shakespeare: "He dyed a Papyst" (Schoenbaum 1975, 79). As a Protestant clergyman, Davies might be expected to argue against Shakespeare's Catholicism, but instead he adds fire to the theory. The earliest biographical notation we have of Shakespeare comes from a 1679 paragraph in which John Aubrey reports that Shakespeare "understood Latin pretty well: for he had been in his younger years a schoolmaster in the country" (see the full Primary Source Document at the end of this chapter). "The country" may refer to Lancashire County, where young William may well have worked for Alexander Hoghton, a wealthy Catholic. Hoghton Tower (Alexander's huge estate) was a main station for recusants, including Edmund Campion and other Jesuits of the "English Mission" to infiltrate Catholic priests into England and to support the recusants. Hoghton also facilitated and patronized the arts, maintaining a private theater in his home, complete with musical instruments and expensive costumes. Quite possibly in this Catholic safe house, William not only practiced the forbidden religion but also cultivated his passion for theater craft. Hoghton's 1581 will bequeaths to his brother all those instruments and "play clothes," stating that if his brother does not want them, they will go to his (Catholic) brother-in-law Thomas Hesketh, owner of a large nearby estate. Hoghton adds that he hopes Hesketh will take in to his service "William Shakshafte," currently living with Hoghton. Shakespeare's name often appears in records with different forms and spellings, including puns on "spear" versus "shaft"; and documents as far back as Shakespeare's grandfather sometimes used Shakeshafte as the spelling for the family name. Thus it seems likely that Hoghton's will indeed refers to Shakespeare, which gives the best evidence of Shakespeare's presence in this Lancashire hotbed of Catholicism.

Some scholars believe that the marginal notes in the Hoghton family copy of Edward Hall's *Chronicles*—an important source for Shakespeare's early history plays—can be identified with Shakespeare. The intrigue deepens when we consider that records exist for young William seemingly seeking licenses to wed two different young women—Anne Hathaway (whom we know he did marry) plus Anne Whateley, who disappeared from history but who came from a Temple Grafton family with Catholic sympathies. Some speculate that this record was merely a clerical error, but others suggest that Shakespeare was betrothed to the Catholic Whateley but was forced to marry Hathaway because of her pregnancy.

The names "Arthurus Stratfordus Wigomniensis" (King Arthur's compatriot from Stratford) and "Gulielmus Clerkue Stratfordiensis" (William, clerk from Stratford) are found in registers dating from 1585–89 at the Venerable English College, a seminary in Rome that had long trained Catholic clergy serving in Britain. Scholars have speculated that these names might refer to Shakespeare, which would also show him as having traveled to Italy—as many have speculated.

Other tantalizing evidence of the Shakespeare family's continued Catholicism came later. In 1757, a man working on the roof of a house on Henley Street in Stratford—Shakespeare's home of birth and childhood—found a "Spiritual Testament" signed by John Shakespeare. This tract closely modeled one circulated by the Jesuit priest Edmund Campion, who infiltrated areas of England in the 1580s before being captured and eventually executed. This document would certainly stand as proof of John's continued Catholicism; unfortunately, we don't have the document but only reports that it existed. Thus, it serves mostly to amplify the debate over the Shakespeare family's putative Catholicism, as some scholars argue that whatever tract existed was a forgery, and others embrace it as authentic and highly significant (see the full Primary Source Document at the end of this chapter).

Another document sometimes cited as evidence of John Shakespeare's secret Catholicism is the 1592 "Recusancy Return." The wardens of the Church of the Holy Trinity in Stratford-upon-Avon (where William Shakespeare is buried) listed William's father as a nonattender at church services. The local commissioners later added that they "suspected" that some of those on the list absented themselves not because they shunned the Church of England but because they were in debt, and appearing in public might subject them to being served with legal papers or even arrested. Thus once again we find a document that divides scholars, with some arguing that the commissioners' notes discredit the interpretation that Mr. Shakespeare's absence from church stemmed from his recusancy but others insisting that John (and others on the list) could actually have cited their debts to excuse the real reason for their absence: their Catholic beliefs. In 1606, Will Shakespeare's daughter Susanna was similarly listed among those who had failed to appear in church; some scholars believe that Susanna was Catholic, but others argue that Susanna's religious beliefs tended to the other end of the Catholic/Protestant spectrum: Puritanism. As we have noted, Shakespeare himself was cited for missing services at his London parish church—certainly not because of any debt problems, as he seems always to have managed his considerable income very well. One must wonder why a prominent public figure such as Shakespeare would take such a chance with the religious laws as to fail to keep up appearances of conformity; his appearance on the "Recusancy Return" gives more fuel to the idea that he held Catholic beliefs.

What Really Happened

For citizens of Renaissance England, religion was no mere question of differences in beliefs—it was a decision that determined the eternal fate of one's soul. The nation had gone through a rollercoaster ride that began when Henry VIII—formerly honored by Pope Leo as "Defender of the Faith" for his vigorous rebuttal of Martin Luther's nascent Protestant Reformation—himself split from the Roman Catholic church, declaring himself Supreme Head of the Church of England in 1534. England had been Catholic since its founding sometime in the fifth century CE, and families who had never known any other way of worship were suddenly told they had to turn away from Rome or face dire consequences. Such was the situation into which Shakespeare's parents were born (1531 for his father and 1537 for his mother). John and Mary Shakespeare would marry in Stratford in 1557, during the reign of Queen "Bloody" Mary, who had returned England to Catholicism upon her accession in 1553. However, by the next year, as the couple began having children (eventually eight, though three died under age ten), Queen Elizabeth ascended to the throne, Catholicism was again outlawed, and adherence to the Church of England was mandatory.

Typically, in the English Renaissance as now, religion began in the home, and although William was not himself alive for those roller-coaster flips that took England from Catholic to Protestant to Catholic and finally back to the Church of England under Queen Elizabeth, his parents were. Whereas nobody knows for certain if William ever held Catholic beliefs or sympathies, we know that both his parents did. The question is, at what periods, and how avidly, did Mary Arden Shakespeare or John Shakespeare hold to "the old religion"? Shakespeare's mother came from the noble Catholic Arden family that had been granted land by William the Conqueror and had been prominent in Warwickshire (the county encompassing Stratford-upon-Avon and environs) since long before that.

A mostly overlooked but intriguing piece of evidence for Shakespeare's Catholicism is his 1613 purchase of Blackfriars Gatehouse, a location long known for covert Catholic activity, including the hiding of refugee priests. At the very least, the transaction raises the question of why Shakespeare, having rented various London residences for over twenty years, would buy a London house just as he retired to Stratford-upon-Avon to live in New Place, the huge house he had purchased in 1597 (chapter 5, "Shakespeare Rejected His Wife and Family," explores the question of whether Shakespeare retired to Stratford or had mainly lived there all along). Some theorize that Will's purchase of Blackfriars Gatehouse (which was originally a Dominican monastery) was simply a financial investment. Such speculation leaves open questions such as: Why buy an investment property in London just as one is closing up one's affairs there?

Why not buy another house in Stratford? Adding to the intrigue, we know that Shakespeare immediately leased the Gatehouse to John Robinson, a young man from a well-known Catholic family that included John's brother, a priest. Robinson was also no mere tenant from whom William could derive rental income; he was a good friend who would soon serve as one of the witnesses to Shakespeare's will. Ultimately, though we can't be sure of what Shakespeare believed in his heart and soul, we do have a great deal of circumstantial evidence that he was deeply and repeatedly involved with Catholic people (including parents, teachers, friends, and tenants) at a time when such involvement was tremendously dangerous.

We also find evidence of Catholicism from Shakespeare's works. Scholars such as Peter Milward, Claire Asquith, and Joseph Pearce have identified coded Catholic messages within many plays and poems, and some of these claims seem irrefutable. Even without diving that deeply into hidden textual clues, we can find clear evidence that Shakespeare—uniquely among playwrights of his time—embedded Catholic references and created sympathetic Catholic characters. Given the state-sanctioned religious climate of Elizabethan and Jacobean England, Catholic clerical characters in plays by other writers invariably were depicted as sinful, comically incompetent, and/or downright evil. For example, John Webster's *The Duchess of Malfi* (1613) features a Catholic cardinal who viciously controls his sister (the title character), assigns a nefarious spy to watch over her, and orders her execution when he learns she has married and borne children without his consent. The cardinal reveals his wicked deeds to his mistress and then murders her by getting her to kiss a poisoned Bible— the perfect metaphor for how most Protestants viewed the corruptions of Catholic clergy.

Such caricatured depictions of evil Catholic figures dominated the Renaissance stage, with the notable exception of two characters written by one playwright: William Shakespeare, who created Friar Francis for the comedy *Much Ado about Nothing* and Friar Laurence for the tragedy *Romeo and Juliet*. These friars (religious brothers) still incline toward the scheming and plotting stereotypical of Catholic characters, but they at least bear good intentions. In *Romeo and Juliet*, Friar Laurence devises the plan to have Juliet take a potion that would simulate her death so that she might be whisked away and reunited with her husband Romeo; the plot goes awry through no fault of his—though at the play's tragic end, he does seem most concerned with saving his own reputation rather than with the death all around him. In *Much Ado about Nothing*, Friar Francis's similar plan to simulate the death of the female character named Hero actually succeeds in bringing together the lovers and facilitating the play's happy ending.

Not only does Shakespeare create sympathetic Catholic clerical characters in bold defiance of sociocultural expectations; he also explores Catholic doctrine, notably with his clear depiction of purgatory in *Hamlet*. The concept of purgatory stands as one of the clear dividing points between Protestantism (such as the Church of England of Shakespeare's time) and Catholicism. Protestants generally believe that after earthly life, the human soul is bound either for heaven or hell. By contrast, Roman Catholics teach that the soul may ascend to heaven or descend to hell, but they add a third possibility: purgatory. In purgatory, the soul that is not yet ready to merit direct entry to heaven may purge away the remnants of earthly sins and, after a period, will then enter heaven. In Act I of *Hamlet*, Prince Hamlet meets the ghost of his father, who describes how he has returned from the grave to converse with his son:

> I am thy father's spirit,
> Doom'd for a certain term to walk the night,
> And for the day confined to fast in fires,
> Till the foul crimes done in my days of nature
> Are burnt and purged away. (I.v.745–49)

Hamlet Senior very clearly describes his current dwelling place as purgatory, leaving us with the question of how and why Shakespeare would include such a clearly Catholic reference in a play meant for public consumption (and which indeed became hugely popular). This scene begs the questions: If Shakespeare were not a Catholic or someone bearing strong Catholic sympathies, why would he include such provocative language? If he were indeed a recusant, why would he take the risk of creating such a scene and calling attention to its unambiguously Catholic content?

We lack definitive proof that Shakespeare believed in and/or practiced Roman Catholicism. Of course, even if he was indeed Catholic, his life would largely have revolved around concealing that fact. Most scholars ignore the issue, preferring to believe that Shakespeare was a humanist who professed no strong religious belief. However, there exists such ample historical, biographical, and textual evidence that an open and inquiring mind should not ignore the strong possibility that Shakespeare indeed was involved with the forbidden religion and may even have practiced Catholicism throughout his life.

PRIMARY SOURCE DOCUMENTS

JOHN AUBREY, BRIEF LIVES, 1679

Aubrey was an historian, philosopher, and archaeologist who discovered and recorded some features of Stonehenge still known as the "Aubrey Holes." He is best known for his biographical sketches of historical figures, including writers such as Ben Jonson, Francis Bacon, John Milton, and, of course, Shakespeare. This entry features the tantalizing assertion that Shakespeare "had been in his younger years a Schoolmaster in the Country," which fuels speculation that Shakespeare lived among recusant Catholics during his "lost years."

He [Shakespeare] was wont to go to his native Country once a year:

I think I have been told that he left 2 or 300 per annum there and thereabout: to a sister. I have heard Sir William Davenant and Mr. Thomas Shadwell (who is counted the best Comedian we have now) say that he had a most prodigious wit, and did admire his natural parts beyond all other dramatical writers. He was wont to say that he never blotted out a line in his life; said Benjamin Jonson, "I wish he had blotted out a thousand." His Comedies will be witty as long as the English tongue is understood: . . . our present writers reflect too much on particular persons, & coxcombeities, that 20 years hence, they will not be understood.

Though, as Ben Jonson says of him. that he had little Latin and less Greek; He understood Latin pretty well: for he had been in his younger yeares a Schoolmaster in the Country.

Source: John Aubrey. *Brief Lives.* Bodleian Library, MS. Aubrey 6, folio 109 recot. Available online at https://shakespearedocumented.folger.edu/exhibition/document/brief-lives-john-aubrey-including-mr-william-shakespeare

ARCHDEACON RICHARD DAVIES, BIOGRAPHIES, 1688

Davies wrote a series of short biographies of figures from earlier in the seventeenth century, including this brief entry on Shakespeare. The archdeacon was a senior member of the Anglican Church, which leads those arguing for Shakespeare's Catholicism to give credence to Davies's stark assertion that "he died a papist." That is, why would he so definitively proclaim Shakespeare's Catholicism rather than trying to claim the playwright as one of his own?

William Shakespeare was born at Stratford upon the Avon in Worcestershire about 1563–4. From an actor of plays he became a composer. He died Apr. 23, 1616, aged 53, probably at Stratford, for there he is buried, and hath a monument. Much given to all unluckiness in stealing venison and rabbits, particularly from Sir Lucy, who had him often whipped and sometimes imprisoned, and at last made him fly his native country to his great advancement; but his rising was so great that he is his Justice Clodpate; and calls him a great man; and that in allusion to his name bore three horses rampant for his arms. He died a papist.

Source: George B. Allen. "The Question about Shakespeare's Religion." *Records of the American Catholic Historical Society of Philadelphia*, Volume 33. Published by the Society, 1922, p. 269.

SPIRITUAL TESTAMENT OF FATHER CHARLES BORROMEO, ALLEGEDLY FOUND IN THE NAME OF JOHN SHAKESPEARE

In 1757, Thomas Hart, descendant of William Shakespeare's sister Joan and owner of the Shakespeare family home on Henley Street, hired workers to retile the roof. One of them found a small book in the rafters, which consisted of a profession of the Catholic faith. As years went on, the document changed hands, and the great Shakespeare scholar Edmond Malone eventually acquired it. Malone initially declared the "spiritual testament," which bore the name of Shakespeare's father, John, to be genuine, and published a portion of it in his 1790 edition of Shakespeare's works. Later, Malone began to doubt the authenticity of the document, which was subsequently lost, leaving it as a central mystery in the debate over the Shakespeare family's putative Catholicism.

The "Last Will of the Soul, made in health for the Christian to secure himself from the temptations of the Devil at the hour of death" was created by Milanese Cardinal Carlo Borromeo, who died in 1585. In 1580, he had been visited by English Jesuit missionaries Edmund Campion and Robert Parsons on their way from Rome to England. The priests may have received and made thousands of copies of the document, to be distributed to Catholic recusants in England with the goal of saving the souls of people who could not outwardly practice their faith. The danger involved in possessing such a document would explain why it was hidden in the Shakespeare house rafters. The Last Will of the Soul contained fourteen chapters, and it has been abridged and its language modernized here.

I.

In the name of God, the Father, Son, and Holy Ghost, the most holy and blessed Virgin Mary, mother of God, the holy host of archangels, angels, patriarchs, prophets, evangelists, apostles, saints, martyrs, and all the celestial court and company of heaven, I, John Shakspear, an unworthy member of the holy Catholic religion, being at this my present writing in perfect health of body, and sound mind, memory, and understanding, but calling to mind the uncertainty of life and certainty of death, and that I may be possibly cut off in the blossom of my sins, and called to render an account of all my transgressions externally and internally, and that I may be unprepared for the dreadful trial either by sacrament, penance, fasting, or prayer, or any other purgation whatever, do in the holy presence above specified, of my own free and voluntary accord, make and ordain this my last spiritual will, testament, confession, protestation, and confession of faith, hoping hereby to receive pardon for all my sins and offences, and thereby to be made partaker of life everlasting, through the only merits of Jesus Christ my Saviour and Redeemer, who took upon Himself the likeness of man, suffered death, and was crucified upon the cross, for the redemption of sinners.

II.

Item, I, John Shakspear, do by this present protest, acknowledge, and confess, that in my past life I have been a most abominable and grievous sinner, and therefore unworthy to be forgiven without a true and sincere repentance for the same. But trusting in the manifold mercies of my blessed Saviour and Redeemer, I am encouraged by relying on His sacred word, to hope for salvation and be made partaker of His heavenly kingdom, as a member of the celestial company of angels, saints and martyrs, there to reside forever and ever in the court of my God.

III.

Item, I, John Shakspear, do by this present protest and declare, that as I am certain I must pass out of this transitory life into another that will last to eternity, I do hereby most humbly implore and intreat my good and guardian angel to instruct me in this my solemn preparation, protestation, and confession of faith, at least spiritually, in will adoring and most humbly beseeching my Saviour, that He will be pleased to assist me in so dangerous a voyage, to defend me from the snares and deceits of my infernal enemies, and to conduct me to the secure haven of His eternal bliss.

IV.

Item, I, John Shakspear, do protest that I will also pass out of this life, armed with the last sacrament of extreme unction: the which if through any let or hindrance I should not then be able to have, I do now also for that time demand and crave the same; beseeching His divine majesty that

He will be pleased to anoint my senses both internal and external with the sacred oil of His infinite mercy, and to pardon me all my sins committed by seeing, speaking, feeling, smelling, hearing, touching, or by any other way whatsoever.

IX.

Item, I, John Shakspear, do here protest that I do render infinite thanks to His divine majesty for all the benefits that I have received as well secret as manifest, and in particular, for the benefit of my creation, redemption, sanctification, conservation, and vocation to the holy knowledge of Him and His true Catholic faith: but above all, for His so great expectation of me to penance, when He might most justly have taken me out of this life, when I least thought of it, yea even then, when I was plunged in the dirty puddle of my sins. Blessed be therefore and praised, forever and ever, His infinite patience and charity.

XII.

Item, I, John Shakspear, do in like manner pray and beseech all my dear friends, parents, and kinsfolks, by the bowels of our Saviour Jesus Christ, that since it is uncertain what lot will befall me, for fear notwithstanding lest by reason of my sins I be to pass and stay a long while in Purgatory, they will vouchsafe to assist and succour me with their holy prayers and satisfactory works, especially with the holy sacrifice of the mass, as being the most effectual means to deliver souls from their torments and pains; from the which, If I shall by God's gracious goodness and by their virtuous works be delivered, I do promise that I will not be ungrateful unto them, for so great a benefit.

XIV.

Item, lastly I, John Shakspear, do protest, that I will willingly accept of death in what manner soever it may befall me, conforming my will unto the will of God; accepting of the same in satisfaction for my sins, and giving thanks unto His divine majesty for the life He has bestowed upon me. And if it please Him to prolong or shorten the same, blessed be He also a thousand thousand times; into whose most holy hands I commend my soul and body, my life and death: and I beseech Him above all things, that He never permit any change to be made by me, John Shakspear, of this my aforesaid will and testament. Amen.

I, John Shakspear, have made this present writing of protestation, confession, and charter, in presence of the blessed Virgin Mary, my angel guardian, and all the celestial court, as witnesses hereunto: the which my meaning is, that it be of full value now presently and forever, with the force and virtue of testament, codicil, and donation in cause of death; confirming it anew, being in perfect health of soul and body, and signed with mine own hand; carrying also the same about me; and for the better declaration hereof, my will and intention is that it be finally buried with me after my death.

Pater noster, Ave Maria, credo.
Jesu, son of David, have mercy on me.
Amen

> **Source:** "John Shakespeare's Spiritual Last Will and Testament." Available online at http://op54rosary.ning.com/profiles/blogs/john-shakespeares-spiritual

WILLIAM ALLEN, *DEFENSE OF ENGLISH CATHOLICS* (1584)

In the following excerpt, Cardinal William Allen points out what he saw as the illogic of England's outlawing and maltreating the very faith that had been England's universal religion as recently as the reign of Queen Mary I (1553–58) and for over a millennium before Henry VIII's break from Rome in 1534.

And specially for that we would christianly give warning to all princes and provinces that yet happily enjoy the Catholic religion, and the only true liberty of conscience in the same, to take heed by our miseries, how they let this pernicious sect put foot into their states, which by promise of liberty and sweetness at the beginning, entereth deceitfully, but when she is once in, and getteth the mastery, (as she often doth where she is not in season constantly resisted), she bringeth all to most cruel and barbarous thraldom, procuring her followers to hate and persecute the Church, their own only true and old Mother, far more deadly than the heathens themselves do, and turneth all the laws made by godly Popes and princes for punishment of heretics and malefactors, to the spoil and destruction of innocent men and Catholics, for whose defence they were made. Into which misery our country, to us most dear, being fallen and having no other human helps to recover it and our Prince and peers (excepting this case of heresy, of excellent good nature and clemency) with millions of souls that there do perish; we will not fear nor fail to pray and ask it of God with tears and blood, as we have begone: *Donee miser aalur nostri*: till he be merciful both to us and to our persecutors. Our days of affliction cannot be long, their felicity will have an end, both sides shall shortly have their doom [judgment], where the dealings of us all shall be truly discussed, and the just shall stand with great constancy against them that vexed them. Interim in the testimony of a guiltless conscience in all things whereof we be accused by our adversaries, and in joyful expectation of that day, we will continue still this work of God to our own and our country's salvation: *Per infamiam et bonam famam* ["Through ill repute and good repute"], as the Apostle willeth us; and through other miseries whatsoever man's mortality is subject unto.

[. . .]

That we now have great cause to complain of unjust persecution, intolerable severity and cruelty towards Catholics in England; and their Protestants no reason to do the like for the justice done to them in Queen Mary's and other Princes' days, and the cause of the difference.

THE libeller, by sophistical reasons and popular persuasion, going about to make men think the English persecution to be nothing so violent as is divulged, nor anything comparable to the justice exercised towards the Protestants in the reign of the late Queen Mary, telleth of hundreds of our scores, as also of the qualities of them that then suffered, of their innocency in all matters of State, and treason, and such like.

To which we say briefly, clearly, and to the purpose: that we measure not the matter by the number, nor by the severity of the punishment only or specially, but by the cause, by the order of justice in proceeding, by the laws of God and all Christian nations, and such other circumstances; whereby we can prove Queen Mary's doings to be commendable and most lawful, the other, towards us and our brethren, to be unjust and impious. The difference is in these points: You profess to put none to death for religion: you have no laws to put any man to death for his faith; you have purposely repealed by a special statute made in the first year and parliament of this Queen's reign, all former laws of the realm for burning heretics, which smelleth of something that I need not here express: you have provided at the same time that nothing shall be deemed or adjudged heresy, but by your parliament and Convocation: you have not yet set down by any new law what is heresy, or who is a heretic. Therefore you can neither adjudge of our doctrine as of heresy, nor of us as of heretics; nor have you any law left whereby to execute us: and so, to put any of us to death for religion, is against justice, law, and your own profession and doctrine.

But nevertheless you do torment and punish us, both otherwise intolerably, and also by death most cruel; and that (as we have proved) for *Agnus-deis* [literally, "lambs of God," wax discs stamped with an image of Jesus as a lamb bearing a cross, usually blessed by a bishop, priest, or pope, often worn round the neck on a chain], for ministering the holy Sacraments, for our obedience to the See Apostolic, for persuading our friends to the Catholic faith, for our priesthood, for studying in the Society or colleges beyond the seas, and such like, which you have ridiculously made treason; but afterwards (being ashamed of the foul absurdity) acknowledge them to be matters of religion and such as none shall die for. And therefore we most justly make our complaint to God and man, that you do us plain violence, and persecute us without all equity and order.

On the other side, Queen Mary against the Protestants executed only the old laws of our country, and of all Christendom made for punishment of heretics, by the canons and determination of all Popes, Councils, Churches and ecclesiastical tribunals of the world, allowed also and authorized by the civil and imperial laws, and received by all kingdoms Christian besides; and who then hath any cause justly to be grieved? Why should any man complain or think strange for executing the laws which are as ancient, as general, and as godly against heretics, as they are for the punishment of traitors, murderers, or thieves?

Secondly, we complain justly of persecution; for that our cause for which we suffer, is the faith of all our forefathers; the faith of our persecutors' own ancestors; the faith into which our country was converted, and by which we are called Christian; the faith of the Catholic Churches and Kingdoms round about us; the faith that we promised in our regeneration; and therefore cannot be forced from it, nor punished for it, by any law of God, nature, or nations. . . . So that, as no law of God or man can force us to be Protestants; no more can any reason be alleged, nor just excuse made, for either young or old, why being baptized or brought up amongst Arians or Calvinists, they may not be forced to return to the Catholic Church and faith again.

And we may marvel in what age or world those people were born, which the libeller noteth to have been burned in Queen Mary's time; having never heard (as he sayeth) of any other religion than that for which they suffered? For the sect which they pretended to die for was not extant in England above five or six years before in the short reign of King Edward the Sixth, or rather of his protector; for before that, in King Henry's days, the same profession was accounted heresy, and the professors thereof were burned for heretics, and that by public laws, no less than in the reign of Queen Mary. But the truth is, that because we Catholic Christian men do justly ground ourselves upon the former profession of our faith notoriously known to be, and to be called Catholic; these men apishly would imitate our phrase and argument in a thing as far differing as heaven and hell.

Thirdly we say that we have just cause to complain of this present persecution; for that the manner of it is such, and the proceeding so conformable to the old pagan, heretical, and apostatical fashion and dealing against God's Church and children that nothing can be more like. They hated all Catholics, and counted them traitors, so do you. They specially persecuted bishops, priests, and religious; so do you. They killed them indeed for their belief, but yet pretended other crimes more odious, and especially matters of conspiracy and rebellion against the civil magistrate; so do you. They drove the innocent, by captious interrogatories, into dangers of laws that never offended the laws; so do you. They pressed men by torments to deny their faith, under colour of trying their secret intents against the Prince; so do you. They punished and have put to death one Catholic for another man's fault of the same profession, and, upon general supposals common to all of the same faith, made away whom they list; so do you. I refer the indifferent readers to the persecution of Julian the Apostate; of the Goths and Vandals in Italy and Africa.

It is not only the slaughter of many, and them specially the priests of God, which is most proper to heretical persecution; but the other infinite spoil of Catholic men's goods, honours and liberty, by robbing them for receiving priests, hearing Mass, retaining Catholic schoolmasters, keeping Catholic servants; mulcting [penalizing and swindling] them by twenty pounds a month (which by their cruel account they make thirteen score a year) for not repairing to their damnable schismatical service. By which a number of ancient gentlemen fall to extremity, either of conscience, if for fear they obey, or of their undoing in the world, if they refuse. The taking of their dear children from them by force, and placing them for their seduction with heretics (which violence cannot be done by the law of God to Jews themselves); the burning of our priests in the ears; the whipping and cutting of the ears of others; carrying some in their sacred vestments through the streets; putting our chaste virgins into infamous places appointed for strumpets; and other unspeakable villianies, not inferior to any of the said heathenous persecutions.

They have pined and smothered in their filthy prisons above thirty famous prelates; above forty excellent learned men; of nobles, gentlemen, and matrons a number; whose martyrdom is before God as glorious as if they had by a speedy violent death been dispatched; every dungeon and filthy prison in England full of our priests and brethren; all provinces and princes Christian witnesses of our banishment. In all this we yield them our bodies, goods, country, blood and lives; and nothing will quench their hatred of our priesthood, faith, and profession. Thus in all causes we suffer, and yet they would not have us complain; they say all is sweet, clement, and merciful in this regiment. But as we said, we no otherwise complain of this persecution against us, but as it is exercised for that faith and quarrel which the laws of God and man approve and justify in us: That it is done by the sheep and subjects of God's Church against their own prelates and pastors, to whom in causes of religion they are bound to obey by the express word of God.

Source: William Allen and William Cecil. *The Execution of Justice in England. A True, Sincere, and Modest Defense of English Catholics* (St. Louis, MO: B. Herder, Publisher, 1914), 27–28; 48–54.

Further Readings

Asquith, Claire. *Shadowplay: The Hidden Beliefs and Coded Politics of William Shakespeare*. New York: Perseus Books, 2005.

Baker, Christopher. *Religion in the Age of Shakespeare*. Westport and London: Greenwood, 2008.

Beauregard, David N. *Catholic Theology in Shakespeare's Plays*. Newark: University of Delaware Press, 2008.

Cox, John D. "Was Shakespeare a Christian, and If So, What Kind of Christian Was He?" *Christianity and Literature* 55 (2006): 539–66.

Cressy, David, and Lori Ferrell, eds. *Religion and Society in Early Modern England*. London: Routledge, 1996.

De Groot, John Henry. *The Shakespeares and "The Old Faith."* Fraser, MI: Rel-View Books, 1995.

Enos, Carol Curt. *Shakespeare and the Catholic Religion*. Pittsburgh: Dorrance Publishing, 2000.

Graham, Kenneth J. E., and Philip D. Collington, eds. *Shakespeare and Religious Change*. Basingstoke and New York: Palgrave Macmillan, 2009.

Greenblatt, Stephen. *Hamlet in Purgatory*. Princeton, NJ: Princeton University Press, 2001.

Groves, Beatrice. *Texts and Traditions: Religion in Shakespeare 1592–1604*. Oxford: Clarendon Press, 2007.

Haigh, Christopher. *English Reformations: Religion, Politics, and Society under the Tudors*. Oxford: Oxford University Press, 1993.

Hamlin, Hannibal. *The Bible in Shakespeare*. Oxford: Oxford University Press, 2013.

Jackson, Ken, and Arthur F. Marotti. *Shakespeare and Religion: Early Modern and Postmodern Perspectives*. South Bend, IN: University of Notre Dame Press, 2011.

Kastan, David Scott. *A Will to Believe: Shakespeare and Religion*. Oxford: Oxford University Press, 2014.

Kaufman, Peter Iver. *Religion around Shakespeare*. University Park: Pennsylvania State University Press, 2013.

Knight, G. Wilson. *Shakespeare and Religion: Essays of Forty Years*. New York: Barnes and Noble, 1967.

Leithart, Peter J. *Brightest Heaven of Invention: A Christian Guide to Six Shakespeare Plays*. Moscow, ID: Canon Press, 1996.

Loewenstein, David, and Michael Witmore, eds. *Shakespeare and Early Modern Religion*. Cambridge: Cambridge University Press, 2015.

Marx, Steven. *Shakespeare and the Bible*. Oxford: Oxford University Press, 2000.

McCoy, Richard. *Faith in Shakespeare*. Oxford: Oxford University Press, 2013.

Milward, Peter, S. J. *Shakespeare the Papist*. Ann Arbor: Sapientia Press, 2005.

Milward, Peter, S. J. *Shakespeare's Religious Background*. Bloomington: Indiana University Press, 1973.

Noble, Richmond. *Shakespeare's Biblical Knowledge and Use of the Book of Common Prayer*. London: Macmillan, 2000.

Pearce, Joseph. *The Quest for Shakespeare: The Bard of Avon and the Church of Rome*. San Francisco: Ignatius Press, 2008.

Pearce, Joseph. *Through Shakespeare's Eyes: Seeing the Catholic Presence in the Plays*. San Francisco: Ignatius Press. 2010.

Rice, Colin. *Ungodly Delights: Puritan Opposition to the Theatre: 1576–1633*. Genoa, Italy: Edizioni dell'Orso, 1997.

Schoenbaum, Samuel. *William Shakespeare: A Documentary Life*. New York: Oxford University Press, 1975.

Shaheen, Naseeb. *Biblical References in Shakespeare's Plays*. Newark: University of Delaware Press, 1999.

Shell, Alison. *Shakespeare and Religion*. London: Methuen Drama, 2010.

Taylor, Dennis, and David N. Beauregard, eds. *Shakespeare and the Culture of Christianity in Early Modern England*. New York: Fordham University Press, 2003.

Todd, Margo. *Reformation to Revolution: Politics and Religion in Early Modern England.* London: Routledge, 1995.

Wiener, Carol Z. "The Beleaguered Isle: A Study of Elizabethan and Early Jacobean Anti-Catholicism." *Past and Present* 51 (1971): 27–62.

Wilson, Richard. *Secret Shakespeare: Studies in Theatre, Religion, and Resistance.* Manchester, UK: Manchester University Press, 2004.

4

Shakespeare Was Poorly Educated

What People Think Happened

As we saw in chapter 1 ("William Shakespeare Was Not the Author of the Works We Know as Shakespeare's"), when people propose that someone other than William Shakespeare of Stratford-upon-Avon wrote the works of Shakespeare, the candidate for "real author" is inevitably someone of higher social status and higher education—such as Francis Bacon or the Earl of Oxford. Even those who believe that the Stratford glover's son wrote the plays and poems may wrestle with the question of Shakespeare's education. Commonly, teachers introduce Shakespeare's life with a statement such as "he only had a grammar school education," which is almost certainly true. In the twenty-first century, a high school education through about age eighteen is considered a minimal standard in developed nations; children from lower-middle-class through upper-class backgrounds are almost universally expected to go to college or university—mostly for four-year degrees, with some continuing for graduate degrees. Even many children from less affluent backgrounds find pathways to higher education. To hear of someone stopping his or her education after "grammar school" sounds barbaric and rather tragic.

Thus begins the idea of Shakespeare as uneducated and virtually illiterate, leaving some readers to propose that someone else must have written all these poems and plays—works that certainly demonstrate a high degree of knowledge of numerous subjects and settings, from botany to law, from royal courts to sea vessels. Others imagine where and how William Shakespeare picked up his learning. As we will find in chapter 7 ("Shakespeare

Was a Solitary Genius Whose Talents Cannot Be Explained"), many view Shakespeare as naturally endowed with talents that required little to no development or tutelage.

In fact, we have no records that Shakespeare even received the ostensibly minimal level of education provided through grammar school, as the records from the King Edward VI Grammar School (the Stratford-upon-Avon Grammar School, also known as the King's New School) were lost, possibly due to a fire. The image of the undereducated Shakespeare goes hand in hand with the common perception that most people of Renaissance England were illiterate. In an age in which few people—most of them upper class—went to university, Shakespeare's own minimal education would fall within the norm. For the vast majority of people in William's time, the goal for women was to acquire adequate domestic skills to become a good housewife and mother—and for men, to learn a trade so as to join the workforce as soon as practicable. The fact of Shakespeare's minimal education would serve as no impediment to that aspiration—except, of course, for the miraculous anomaly of the uneducated young man who somehow decided to become a poet and playwright. And for that, Shakespeare somehow must have educated himself, whether through voraciously reading, and/or through carefully observing and mimicking the works of traveling theater companies in and around Stratford, and then later in London.

How the Story Became Popular

In 1592 a pamphlet was published in London under the name of Robert Greene, a modestly talented playwright who had died just two weeks before. *Greenes, Groats-worth of Witte, Bought with a Million of Repentance* bears the inscription "Written before his death and published at his dyeing request" and includes the notoriously cantankerous Greene's complaints about various figures and phenomena of London society. The pamphlet is best known for what clearly seems to be an attack on a young, upcoming playwright: William Shakespeare:

> Yes, trust them not: for there is an upstart Crow, beautified with our feathers, that with his *Tygers hart wrapt in a Players hyde,* supposes he is as well able to bombast out a blanke verse as the best of you: and being an absolute *Iohannes fac totum,* is in his owne conceit the onely Shake-scene in a countrey.

The passage is intended for reading by Greene's fellow established, university-educated writers. The line about the "Tygers hart" echoes and mocks a line from one of Shakespeare's early plays, *Henry VI, Part 3*, and "Shake-scene" gives us a thinly veiled identification of Greene's target for the rant. The piece clearly expresses resentment at a newcomer ("upstart Crow") who is "beautified with our feathers." This implies that the rookie writer is unworthy of his newfound fame, and is elevating himself by glomming onto the achievements of his more educated predecessors—such as Greene, who possessed a MA from Cambridge. The uneducated actor/would-be playwright from a small town "supposes he is as well able" to compose blank verse (unrhymed, iambic pentameter, the main form of lines for the plays of the time) as are his betters. Greene was likely writing mostly for a group that came to be called the "university wits." That term was not used until the nineteenth century, when critic George Saintsbury differentiated two separate branches of Elizabethan playwrights, with the university wits including John Lyly, Thomas Lodge, and George Peele from Oxford; and Greene, Thomas Nashe, and Christopher Marlowe—easily the most successful playwright of the time—from Cambridge. On the other side were the uneducated writers, including Anthony Munday, with Shakespeare as the paragon. The image of an uneducated country bumpkin thus began early in Shakespeare's career.

With the 1623 publication of the First Folio (collected works of Shakespeare), fellow poet-playwright Ben Jonson's poetic eulogy to Shakespeare included the famous line "thou hadst small Latine, and lesse Greeke," which some read as another dig against Shakespeare's lack of education. In a way, Jonson's line constitutes a backhanded compliment that perpetuates the idea of Shakespeare as a great writer in spite of his ignorance. However, unlike Robert Greene, Jonson clearly adored and admired Shakespeare, and the overall eulogy (found in chapter 7, "Shakespeare Was a Solitary Genius Whose Talents Cannot Be Explained") could not be more effusive in its praise of Shakespeare's brilliance. Jonson himself came from humble origins but was fortunate enough to attend London's Westminster School, a prestigious, private academy (or what in England would be called a "public school"). Jonson planned to go to Cambridge but instead became apprenticed to his bricklayer stepfather. Though he never attended university, Jonson's erudition far outshone Shakespeare's, and even as a great friend and fan, he could not help but refer in his eulogy to Shakespeare's perceived educational shortcomings.

Twenty-two years after Jonson's eulogy, John Milton referred to the pair of great playwrights in his pastoral poem "L'Allegro": "If *Jonsons* learned Sock be on, / Or sweetest *Shakespear* fancies child, / Warble his native Wood-notes wilde. . . ." Here the Cambridge MA–educated Milton—the great poet of the next generation—perpetuates the contrast between the "learned" writer Jonson and Shakespeare, who is associated with being "child"-like and "native"—that is, a natural, uneducated genius. Subsequent eras paid little attention to the question of Shakespeare's education, with people such as the Romantic poets of the nineteenth century tending rather to assume and embrace the image of Shakespeare as untutored and natural genius.

A few scholars posit that Shakespeare secretly went to university, though we have no records of that. Some speculate that during Shakespeare's "lost years" (~1585–92), he audited classes at Oxford University (without leaving a record) and/or traveled, particularly to Italian regions—thus giving him experiential learning that would allow him to depict so many characters and plots in Italianate settings.

Compounding the mystery of how a grammar school–educated lad could produce works that reflect broad (if not deep) knowledge of so many areas of life, we also lack evidence of Shakespeare's informal learning. That is, if he were minimally formally educated, one assumes that he either learned from mentors, or that he taught himself through substantial reading. Unfortunately we have no documentation of either. As for mentorship, if one follows the belief that Shakespeare was Catholic, one can speculate that he learned from various Catholics—both while he was in school (e.g., Stratford schoolmasters Simon Hunt, who would become a Jesuit priest, and Thomas Jenkins) and after he left school, when some speculate that he lived in a Catholic household in Lancashire, and where he could have learned, for example, Philosophy, Theology, and languages, from refugee Jesuit priests (see chapter 3, "Shakespeare Was Secretly Roman Catholic"). But speculation is about all we have. As for Shakespeare's reading, those who argue that someone else—such as the Earl of Oxford—is the true author of "Shakespeare's works" point to the fact that Shakespeare made no mention in his will of any books. How, they ask, could someone who wrote plays that clearly reflect familiarity with myriad written works ranging from classical to contemporary have left no books for us to peruse his marginal notes and otherwise confirm that, yes, this "Shakespeare" read a great deal? Again, conclusions drawn from this mysteriously absent library are flimsy. To counter that anti-Stratfordian argument, Stratfordians note that likely, Shakespeare had already passed along his books before death, likely to his daughter Susanna and her physician-husband, John Hall.

Ultimately, those who argue most strongly for Shakespeare's inadequate education are anti-Stratfordians who believe that Shakespeare was someone else—someone highly educated and of a higher social class. However, even if William Shakespeare received the seemingly minimal formal grammar school education of the time—which is almost certainly true—this gave him much more profound grounding than the myth of the "poorly educated lad" would suggest.

What Really Happened

To contemporary American ears, the term "grammar school" equates with "elementary school" as the lowest level of education, consisting of introductions to various subjects (including playground/recess) for children between the ages of six and eleven. When Shakespeare grew up in Elizabethan England, it meant something very different. For starters, students would generally attend grammar school until age fourteen, after which the lads would begin an apprenticeship or—more rarely—pursue further education at university. Girls would be educated at home in domestic skills, though girls from aristocratic households commonly received private tutelage in languages and the arts. School was free for any male citizen, and evidence suggests that the King Edward VI Grammar School in Stratford-upon-Avon, an easy walk from the Shakespeare family's Henley Street house, provided high-quality education. Though records of student enrollment are lost, it is reasonable to assume that Shakespeare attended between the ages of about seven and fourteen. We do have records demonstrating that Stratford's "King's New School" paid its teachers well and thus attracted good ones: salaries of £10 per year for a master (who would have taught the children aged seven through ten) and £40 per year for the headmaster (who taught the boys aged eleven through fourteen and oversaw the entire school) were highly respectable for the time, and they compared well with wages paid by renowned grammar schools. Several headmasters from the King's New School (such as Thomas Jenkins) had been to Oxford, and some went on to establish colleges. Richard Fox later became Bishop of Winchester and founded Corpus Christi College of Oxford; William Smyth founded Brasenose College.

Shakespeare and the other Stratford boys would have spent a great deal of time with such highly qualified instructors. The school day ran from 6:00 a.m. to 5:00 p.m., slightly shortened in winter, and with a two-hour break for lunch. Not only were the days far longer than those found in contemporary Western societies, but the school week consisted of five full days (Saturdays included), with Thursday as a half day. The school year ran for forty to forty-four weeks—compared, for instance, with current public school requirements in most U.S. states of about twenty-five to twenty-six weeks. Thus the overall time spent in school by boys such as Will Shakespeare would easily double that of the typical contemporary American student. Hence, perhaps it is no wonder that those who completed this arduous educational stretch were prepared to enter the work world or to begin university—at age fourteen.

As for the curriculum, the term "grammar school" gives away the foundation: the study of grammar, based in the Latin language. However, although a common myth holds that the long days of study involved stultifying rote memorization of Latin tense and mood declensions, actually Latin served as a basis from which teachers could incorporate many subjects, including rhetoric (speech and composition), philosophy, theology, rudimentary math and science, and arts such as music and drama. Since a 1552 decree of Henry VIII, the standard Latin text across England was William Lily's *Shorte Introduction of Grammar*. Following on Jonson's jibe about Shakespeare possessing "small Latin and less Greek," we don't know to what extent—if any—Greek was included in the curriculum. Whereas Latin texts could be printed with the same typeset characters as used for English, Greek would require special letters that were not commonly available in print shops. But likely Shakespeare was well schooled in Latin—and also in English. Some educators, such as Richard Mulcaster, whose essay "Elementarie" is excerpted below, had begun to emphasize English as bearing at least equal importance in education as Latin. Nonetheless, Latin's centrality in the English educational system stemmed from its universality—throughout Europe, it was the language of the educated. The curriculum prescribed not only that boys learn the grammar rules of the ancient language, but also that they be able to write it, translate passages from English to Latin and vice versa, and to converse in Latin throughout some of the day. Of course, progression was expected, with early years devoted to study of Latin rules and vocabulary and later years moving to reading, writing, and discussing the poetry and prose of classical writers such as Horace, Virgil, Cicero, and even more contemporary authors such as the humanists Erasmus and Thomas More.

Shakespeare's plays evince tremendous influence from some of these authors who wrote in Latin, particularly Ovid, Plautus, and Seneca, meaning that even if he didn't possess showy fluency in Latin or Greek, his grammar school studies deeply imprinted many of the ideas, stories, and techniques he had absorbed from the ancient writers. Shakespeare's early plays particularly show the degree to which he learned from Roman authors.

The Comedy of Errors closely follows the plot of two plays by Plautus: *The Menaechmi* and *The Amphitryon*. Early tragedies such as *Titus Andronicus* and *Richard III* show tremendous influence from the plays of Seneca (as do some later ones, such as *Hamlet* and *Macbeth*). *Titus Andronicus* also incorporates much from *The Metamorphoses*—Ovid's masterpiece— which also greatly influenced Shakespeare's *A Midsummer Night's Dream* and *A Winter's Tale*. And Shakespeare drew heavily from Plutarch's *Parallel Lives of the Noble Grecians and Romans* for his Roman plays *Julius Caesar, Antony and Cleopatra*, and *Coriolanus*. Some scholars argue that Shakespeare himself translated *The Metamorphoses* for his own use, though others suggest that he worked from existing English translations of this and other Latin works. In any event, Shakespeare's skill in incorporating these texts as sources for his own plays and poems demonstrates the deep impressions made by his Stratford grammar school education.

Some passages of Shakespeare's plays also demonstrate familiarity with French and Italian, which would not have been in the typical English grammar school curriculum. Thus we face the mystery of how he was able to create, for example, the touching, amusing, and lengthy scenes in *Henry V* wherein Catherine of Valois learns English from Alice, her lady-in-waiting—and when the victorious King Henry attempts to court Catherine using his limited French. Did Shakespeare pick up that much French somewhere along the line, or did he simply pick the brain or pen of a friend or colleague such as Christopher Marlowe (who could have studied French at Cambridge, although his attendance record was sketchy at best) to aid him with such scenes? The plot of *Othello* largely derives from a story by the Italian writer Cinthio (Giovanni Battista Giraldi) called "Un Capitano Moro" ("A Moorish Captain"), part of his 1565 novella *The Hecatommithi*. This story was not available in English when Shakespeare wrote his play (though there was a French translation), and thus we face the question of how he so masterfully integrated Cinthio's Italian tale into his great tragedy. Could Shakespeare read Italian and/or French, or did he utilize the expertise of a "better-educated" friend?

Along with the myth of Shakespeare as poorly educated comes the parallel notion that people in Renaissance England were generally illiterate and more concerned with putting children to work as early as possible than with educating them. In fact, the Renaissance period brought something akin to an education revolution. In the preceding (Medieval) period, likely fewer than 10 percent of children received any formal education. Only people destined for particular occupations qualified—for example, priests, lawyers, and merchant mariners who might need facility with reading, writing, and even foreign languages to conduct their business. As we have seen, in Shakespeare's sixteenth century, a robust grammar school education became the norm—with the notable exceptions that only boys received it, and typically only boys of at least middle-class status—though as time went on, more and more boys of lower economic backgrounds were able to attend school, through a great rise of charitable giving for education. Literacy rates are notoriously difficult to estimate, but they certainly soared during and after the Elizabethan and Jacobean periods. One main movement can be credited for most of the increased societal emphasis on education during the era: Renaissance humanism.

With its origins in the Italian city-states in the fourteenth century, humanism spread throughout Europe in the succeeding centuries, flourishing in England in the 1500s. The essence of humanism—as the name would imply—was an appreciation of the potential for human development and achievement. Whereas the medieval view of humanity—based on the model of the Great Chain of Being—emphasized the omnipotence of God, asserted the importance of life after death, placed man as a moderately important link, and encouraged conformity over individual aspiration and achievement, the Renaissance humanist model appreciated the aesthetic beauty of this world, elevated the significance of humans in the scheme of creation, and greatly valued learning. The exemplars and models for humanists came from the classical civilizations of ancient Greece and Rome, which is why Renaissance English education revolved around Latin texts.

Though some Renaissance humanists (such as Niccolo Machiavelli in Florence and Francis Bacon in England) promoted humanism as an alternative to traditional Christian beliefs, others, such as the Dutchman Desiderius Erasmus and England's own Sir Thomas More, espoused a Christian humanism that maintained traditional Christian beliefs while elevating the status of people in the order of the universe. To Christian humanists, when Jesus Christ—the Word of God who created the universe—descended to incarnate as a human being, he sanctified all of humanity, reestablishing human beings as the crown of God's creation despite their fall from grace in the Garden of Eden. It might seem odd that Christian humanists would place such paramount value in the writings and culture of pre-Christian writers. But people such as Erasmus and More did not abandon their belief in the importance of the afterlife and Christ as savior; rather, they found in the texts of Socrates, Cicero, and others valuable guidance for how to live a good, virtuous life on Earth. The humanist vision permeated the English Renaissance educational system and provided Shakespeare with the inspiration, tools, and vision to create literary masterworks—not bad for a grammar school–educated lad.

PRIMARY SOURCE DOCUMENTS

RICHARD MULCASTER, "ELEMENTARIE" (1582)

Born in 1539, Richard Mulcaster went to Cambridge and Oxford, and in 1561, he became the first headmaster of Merchant Taylors' School in London, the largest school in England. An Anglican priest and a humanist, Mulcaster was unconventional and innovative, introducing music, art, physical education, and drama into the curriculum and advocating for girls to receive education and for teachers to receive rigorous training. He was also a lexicographer who standardized the spelling of thousands of English words and argued that English should become as standardized as Latin. Spelling has been modernized.

First of all Plato a man . . . very well thought of among those that be learned examining . . . what things be needful for the first education of young children, finds out Gymnastics for the body and Music for the mind, where he construes Music a great deal larger than we commonly do, comprising under that name speech, and harmony: and therewith . . . he comprehends writing & reading for the benefit of speech, as singing and playing for the utterance of harmony. . . .

In the same place freeing poetry from fabulous and unseemly arguments, and picture [drawing] from wanton & lascivious resemblances, which he finds both he refuses neither: but as by cleansing poetry he proves grammar to be but an *Elementary* principle, so by clearing picture, he proves drawing to be another. . . . [D]rawing should be held for the first degree of liberal science in the training up of children, and that no bondman should be admitted to use the pencil. . . .

He spendeth also the most part . . . to clear *Music* from blame, and to prove it needed . . . for bettering of manners besides undoubted pleasure.

Quintilian, also a Rhetoric master among the Romans, and of no less account in his country then he was of cunning, and so esteemed of among us, in the framing of his best orator, first names *writing* and *reading*, and with some earnest challenge takes upon him the protection of *Music*, whose two arms *singing* and *playing* be. And in the same place using the same favor to *Arithmetic* and *Geometry*. . . .

Neither is there any other of either value or account, which handleth this argument of children . . . whether in Greek or Latin . . . whether Christian or profane writer. . . . The best appointed commonwealths also, in the best & most flourishing times for all kind of learning embraced the same train. . . . Neither is it any discredit for a Christian writer in cases of learning and education, such as these be, where Christianism may furnish the matter, though profanism yield the form, to follow the precedent of profane commonwealths, & to cite the testimony of old philosophers, from whence we set the most part of our learning. Neither can any Christian state, or any religious consideration though never so precise, but think very well of these Elementary principles.

[. . .] As for knowledge, whereby to increase the child's understanding, that is assigned to the teacher alone, as proper to his office without participation of any parent, though a wise and a learned parent be the very best part of the very best teacher. Now both to help parents in their virtuous performance, and to assist teachers in their learned direction . . . I proffered my service in general to them all, but first of them all to the elementary teacher and his tall scholar, as whose labor doth first call for aid, to whom I promised this Elementary institution, wherein I intend to handle all those things which young children are to learn of right, and may learn at ease, if their parents will be careful, a little more than ordinary. The things be five in number, infinite in use, principles in place, and these in name, *reading, writing, drawing, singing,* and *playing.* . . . [T]his is most true, that in the right course of best education to learning and knowledge, all these, & only these be Elementary principles, and most necessary to be dealt with. Whatsoever else besides these is required in that age, either to strengthen their bodies, or to quicken their wits, that is rather incident to exercise for health, than to Elementary for knowledge. Thus I have showed both why I begin at the Elementary, and wherein it consists.

Source: Richard Mulcaster. "The First Part of the Elementarie Which Entreateth Chefelie of the Right Writing of our English Tung, Set Furth by Richard Mulcaster." Available online at https://quod.lib.umich.edu/e/eebo/A07881.0001.001?view=toc

ROGER ASCHAM, *THE SCHOOLMASTER* (1570)

Roger Ascham lived from 1515 to 1568 and received his Cambridge MA in 1537, having distinguished himself as a lecturer in Greek. From 1548 to 1550, Ascham served as private tutor of languages to Princess Elizabeth (future queen) and praised her handwriting and her fluency in French, Italian, and Latin. He later served under King Edward, Queen Mary, and his former student Elizabeth I, proving adept at navigating or avoiding the dangerous, shifting religious allegiances under these various monarchs. His 1570 book The Schoolmaster *focuses on Latin and was aimed more at private tutors than at classroom teachers. Spelling has been modernized, but Ascham's sometimes eccentric capitalization (common for the time) has been preserved.*

In writing this book, I have had earnest respect to three special points, truth of Religion, honesty in living, right order in learning. In which three ways, I pray God, my poor children may diligently walk. . . .

For, seeing at my death, I am not like to leave them any great store of living, therefore in my lifetime, I thought good to bequeath unto them, in this little book, as in my Will and Testament, the right way to good learning: which if they follow, with the fear of God, they shall very well come to sufficiency of living.

[. . .] There is a way, touched in the first book of Cicero's *De Oratore,* which, wisely brought into schools, truly taught, and constantly used, would not only take wholly away this butcherly fear [of] Latin, but would also, with ease and pleasure . . . work a true choice and placing of words, a right ordering of sentences, an easy understanding of the tongue [language], a readiness to speak, a faculty to write, a true judgement, both of his own, and other men's doings, what tongue so ever he doth use.

The way is this. . . . Let the master read unto him the Epistles of *Cicero.* First, let him teach the child, cheerfully and plainly, the cause, and matter of the letter: then, let him construe [translate] it into English, so often, as the child may easily carry away the understanding of it: Last, parse it over perfectly. This done thus, let the child . . . both construe and parse it over again: so that . . . the child doubts in nothing. . . . After this, the child must take a paper book, and . . . let him translate into English his former lesson. Then . . . let the master take from him his Latin book, then let the child translate his own English into Latin again. . . . When the child brings it, turned into Latin, the master must compare it with *Tullie's* book, and lay them both together: and where the child doth well, either in choosing, or true placing of *Tullie's* words, let the master praise him, and say here you do well. For I assure you, there is no such whetstone, to sharpen a good wit and encourage a will to learning, as is praise.

But if the child miss, either in forgetting a word, or in changing a good with a worse, or misordering the sentence, I would not have the master, either frown, or chide with him, if the child have done his diligence, and used no truantship. . . . For I know by good experience, that a child shall take more profit of two faults, gently warned of, than of four things, rightly hit. For then, the master shall have good occasion to say unto him . . . *Tullie* would have used such a word, not this: *Tullie* would have placed this word here, not there: would have used this case, this number, this person, this degree, this gender: he would have used this mood, this tense, this simple, rather than this compound: this adverb here, not there: he would have ended the sentence with this verb, not with that noun or participle, etc.

In these few lines, I have wrapped up, the most tedious part of Grammar: and also the ground of almost all the Rules, that are so busily taught by the Master, and so hardily learned by the Scholar, in all common Schools: which after this sort, the master shall teach without all error, and the scholar shall learn without great pain: the master being led by so sure a guide, and the scholar being brought into so plain and easy a way. And therefore, we do not condemn Rules, but we gladly teach Rules: and teach them, more plainly, sensibly, and orderly, than they be commonly taught in common Schools. . . . This is a lively and fit way of teaching of Rules: where the common way, used in common Schools, to read the Grammar alone by itself, is tedious for the Master, hard for the Scholar, cold and uncomfortable for them both.

Let your Scholar be never afraid, to ask you any doubt, but use discreetly the best allurements you can, to encourage him to the same: lest, his overmuch fearing of you, drive him to seek some misorderly shift: as, to seek to be helped by some other book, or to be prompted by some other Scholar, and so go about to beguile you much, and himself more.

With this way, of good understanding the matter, plain construing, diligent parsing, daily translating, cheerful admonishing, and heedful amending of faults: never leaving behind just praise for well doing, I would have the Scholar brought up . . . till he had read, & translated [the] first book of Epistles . . . with a good piece of a Comedy of *Terence* also.

[. . .] Some wits, moderate enough by nature, be many times marred by over much study and use of some sciences, namely, Music, Arithmetic, and Geometry. These sciences, as they sharpen men's wits over much, so they change men's manners . . . if they be not moderately mingled, & wisely applied to some good use of life. Mark all Mathematical heads, which be only and wholly bent to those sciences, how solitary they be themselves, how unfit to live with others, & how unapt to serve in the world. . . .

And therefore, if you would speak as the best and wisest do, you must be conversant, where the best and wisest are: but if you be born or brought up in a rude country, you shall not choose but speak rudely: the rudest man of all knoweth this to be true.

Yet nevertheless, the rudeness of common and mother tongues, is no bar for wise speaking. For in the rudest country, and most barbarous mother language, many be found can speak very wisely: but in the Greek and Latin tongues, the two only learned tongues, which be kept, not in common talk, but in private books, we find always, wisdom and eloquence, good matter and good utterance, never or seldom asunder. For all such Authors, as be fullest of good matter and right judgment in doctrine, be likewise always most proper in words, most apt in sentence, most plain and pure in uttering the same.

You know not, what hurt you do to learning, that care not for words, but for matter, and so make a divorce between the tongue and the heart. For mark all ages: look upon the whole course of both the Greek and Latin tongue, and you shall surely find, that, when apt and good words began to be neglected, and properties of those two tongues to be confounded, then also began, ill deeds to spring: strange manners to oppress good orders, new and fond [foolish] opinions to strive with old and true doctrine, first in Philosophy: and after in Religion: right judgment of all things to be perverted, and so virtue with learning is condemned, and study left off: of ill thoughts comes perverse judgment: of ill deeds springs lewd talk. Which four misorders, as they mar man's life, so destroy the good learning withal.

But to return to *Imitation*. . . . There be three kinds of it in matters of learning. The whole doctrine of Comedies and Tragedies, is a perfect *imitation,* or fair lively painted picture of the life of every degree of man. . . .

The second kind of *Imitation,* is to follow for learning of tongues and sciences, the best authors. Here riseth, among proud and envious wits, a great controversie, whether, one or many are to be followed: and if one, who is that one: *Seneca,* or *Cicero: Salust* or *Cæsar,* and so forth in Greek and Latin.

The third kind of *Imitation,* belongs to the second: as when you be determined, whether you will follow one or more, to know perfectly, and which way to follow that one: in what place: by what means and order: by what tools and instruments you shall do it, by what skill and judgment, you shall truly discern, whether you follow rightly or no.

This . . . order and doctrine of *Imitation* would bring forth more learning, and breed up truer judgment, than any other exercise that can be used. . . . For surely the meanest painter uses more wit, better art, greater diligence, in his shop, in following the Picture of any mean man's face, than commonly the best students do, even in the university, for the attaining of learning itself.

Some ignorant, unlearned, and idle student: or some busy looker upon this little poor book, that has neither will to do good himself, nor skill to judge right of others, but can lustily condemn, by pride and ignorance, all painful diligence and right order in study, will perchance say, that I am too precise, too curious, in marking . . . thus about the imitation of others: and that the old worthy Authors did never busy their heads and wits, in following so precisely, either the matter what other men wrote, or else the manner how other men wrote. They will say, it were a plain slavery, & injury . . . to shackle and tie a good wit, and hinder the course of a man's good nature with such bonds of servitude, in following other.

Except such men think themselves wiser than *Cicero* for teaching of eloquence, they must be content to turn a new leaf.

Source: Roger Ascham. *The Schoolmaster* (London: Castle and Company, 1909). Available online at https://archive.org/details/schoolmaster00aschuoft/page/n7

Further Readings

Andrews, John F. *William Shakespeare: His World, His Work, His Influence.* Toronto: Collier Macmillan Canada, 1985.

Balmuth, Miriam. "Female Education in 16th & 17th Century England: Influences, Attitudes, and Trends." *Canadian Woman Studies/les cahiers de la femme* 9, 3–4 (1988): 17–20.

Brown, J. Howard. *Elizabethan Schooldays.* Oxford: Basil Blackwell, 1933.

Bushnell, Rebecca W. *A Culture of Teaching: Early Modern Humanism in Theory and Practice.* Ithaca: Cornell University Press, 1996.

Chamberline, E. R. *Everyday Life in Renaissance Times.* London: B. T. Batsford, 1967.

Charlton, Kenneth. *Education in Renaissance England.* London: Routledge & Kegan Paul, 1965.

Cressy, David. *Education in Tudor and Stuart England.* New York: St. Martin's Press, 1976.

Cressy, David. *Literacy and the Social Order: Reading and Writing in Tudor and Stuart England.* Cambridge: Cambridge University Press, 1980.

Enterline, Lynn. *Shakespeare's Schoolroom: Rhetoric, Discipline, Emotion.* Philadelphia: University of Pennsylvania Press, 2012.

Greene, Robert. *Groats-Vvorth of Witte, Bought with a Million of Repentance. The Repentance of Robert Greene, 1592.* Edinburgh: Edinburgh University Press, 1966.

Henry, John, Sarah Hutton, and Charles B. Schmitt. *New Perspectives on Renaissance Thought: Essays in the History of Science, Education and Philosophy: In Memory of Charles B. Schmitt.* London: Duckworth, 1990.

Leach, Arthur F. *English Schools at the Reformation 1546–8.* New York: Russell & Russell, 1968.

Martindale, Charles, and Michelle Martindale. *Shakespeare and the Uses of Antiquity.* London & New York: Routledge, 1990.

Nelson, William, ed. *A Fifteenth Century School Book.* Oxford: Clarendon Press, 1956.

Orme, Nicholas. *Education and Society in Medieval and Renaissance England.* London: The Hambledon Press, 1989.

Pincombe, Michael. *Elizabethan Humanisms: Literature and Learning in the Later Sixteenth Century.* New York: Longman, 2001.

Plimpton, George Arthur. *The Education of Shakespeare Illustrated from the Schoolbooks in Use in His Time.* London, New York: Oxford University Press, 1933.

Simon, Joan. *Education and Society in Tudor England.* Cambridge: Cambridge University Press, 1966.

Thompson, C. R. *School in Tudor England.* Ithaca, NY: Cornell University Press, 1958.

Watson, Foster. *The English Grammar Schools to 1660: Their Curriculum and Practice.* Cambridge: Cambridge University Press, 1908.

Whitaker, Virgil K. *Shakespeare's Use of Learning.* San Marino, CA: Huntington Library, 1953.

Woodward, William Harrison. *Desiderius Erasmus Concerning the Aim and Method of Education.* New York: Teacher's College, Columbia University, 1964.

5

Shakespeare Rejected His Wife and Family

What People Think Happened

In November 1582, near Stratford-upon-Avon, England, eighteen-year-old William Shakespeare married twenty-six-year-old Anne Hathaway, who was pregnant. In May of the following year, Anne delivered their first child, Susanna. Given the shotgun nature of the wedding and young William's lack of a career, the marriage never thrived. As was the common practice of the day, the couple and their newborn moved into Shakespeare's father's house on Henley Street in Stratford. William continued working for his father in his glovemaking business, for which he had neither heart nor ambition. In 1585, the family grew as Anne delivered the twins Hamnet and Judith.

William found himself in misery, cramped in a small house with his parents, his wife, and his three young children, plus William's four younger siblings. He wasn't sure what he wanted to do with his life, but glovemaking wasn't it. Will wondered if married life was even it. He had certainly felt desire and perhaps affection for the comely and more experienced Anne, but once the realities of their daily life together set in, William lost any romantic feeling for his wife.

Somewhere along the way—probably beginning in grammar school and augmented by his viewings of traveling companies that came through Warwickshire County—William had caught the theater bug. He didn't know what he could do with this newfound desire, but he wanted to be involved in the world of theater. He had ideas percolating inside him that involved telling stories—acting and writing plays. London, the center of the theatrical and cultural universe, lay barely eighty miles southeast, and Will heard it calling him.

There was no way for Will to move his family to London. He had no clear plan and no means of supporting himself, let alone his wife and three small children. His father had no extra funds to offer, and he wouldn't have understood or supported the move anyway. So sometime between 1585 and 1590—whether in secret or with open good-byes—Will left his family and rode off alone on horseback for London. Or perhaps he brought them along to see him off before sending them back to Stratford so he could embark on his new, uncharted adventure in the big city. Perhaps he promised to come home soon and often, once he'd made his mark. Possibly he received some travel allowance from an artistic benefactor and visited Italy and other European nations before settling in London and beginning his theatrical career. In any event, for the next twenty-five or so years, William lived apart from his wife and children, returning to Stratford to visit only a couple of times a year until he retired from the theater—having, improbably, succeeded wildly both artistically and financially. During those decades, William played the field, enjoying his London fame and fortune by carousing and sleeping with numerous women.

As he retired from the London theater scene, Shakespeare finally returned to Stratford in 1611 to live at New Place, the large estate he'd purchased in 1597 with his theatrical earnings and in which he'd long since installed his family from a distance. However, Shakespeare's homecoming constituted no warm reunion with his family. His son Hamnet had died in 1596. His daughter Susanna had married and moved in with her physician husband a few blocks from New Place. And Anne could never forgive William for abandoning her and the children all those years ago. William died only five years after returning to Stratford, and the coldness of his relationship with his wife is reflected in the clause of his will in which he leaves Anne "the second-best bed."

How the Story Became Popular

"Item: I give unto my wife my second best bed with the furniture." Along with the fact of Shakespeare's working in London while his family lived in Stratford-upon-Avon, this single clause from Will's will forms the basis for the common narrative regarding Shakespeare's estrangement from his family and especially from his wife, Anne. In the upcoming section, "What Really Happened," we will discuss in detail the question of where William actually made his home during the years between 1585 and 1611. We begin here by addressing the question of William Shakespeare's last will and testament, which is how the story got started.

On March 25, 1616,—working with his longtime lawyer Francis Collins (who had assisted with Shakespeare's 1613 purchase of Blackfriars Gatehouse, among other transactions)—Shakespeare produced the document that still exists today, preserved in the London suburb of Kew, in England's National Archives. Shakespeare would die less than a month after drawing the will, and handwriting analysis suggests that the hand that wrote William's three signatures—one for each page of the document— was shaky, suggesting severe illness. Commonly, people of Renaissance England did not write their wills until death was on the horizon; although we do not know for certain the cause of Shakespeare's death, evidently he knew it was imminent.

Scholars agree that the document we have—though complete and final—was a redrafting of a version presumably drawn up a couple of months earlier, and for reasons unknown, a "fair copy" (meaning a clean version absent blots, cross-outs, inserts, and so forth) was never produced. For example, we know about the will's revision schedule because at the top of the first page, "January" is crossed out and "March" written in. The chief reason for the redrafting was evidently the February 10 marriage of Shakespeare's daughter Judith to the Stratford vintner Thomas Quiney—a man who quickly brought scandal to the family and about whom Judith's father could not have been thrilled. First came a minor scandal: for whatever reason, the couple married during Lent, which was prohibited without a special license that should have been issued by the bishop. This breach may thus have been more the fault of the local priest who married them. Nonetheless, Quiney was summoned to church court to answer for the infraction, and he failed to appear—which technically brought him (and possibly Judith) a temporary excommunication. The much more serious scandal was Quiney's recent affair with and impregnation of another woman, who died in childbirth, as did the baby. Thomas was called to "bawdy court"—a church-run venue specifically for alleged offenses of the sexual nature—and confessed to "carnal copulation." For punishment, Quiney ultimately had only to wear a white sheet in church for three Sundays and to pay the modest fine of five shillings. His larger, informal penalty may have been his demotion from Shakespeare's will. Though the stillbirth of the baby and the death of Quiney's mistress took place just after Shakespeare's own death, clearly the affair and pregnancy were known among the family and the Stratford community at the time Shakespeare revised his will. In fact, some scholars have speculated that the shock of the public scandal associated with his new son-in-law contributed to Shakespeare's untimely death.

The will deals first with Judith. After the standard phrase, "I give and bequeath unto my," the words "son in law" are crossed out and replaced with "daughter Judith." Shakespeare bequeaths to Judith £150 but places some interesting stipulations and creates incentives such that if Thomas stays married to Judith and provides worthy lands for her, he would have claim to the £150. On the second page, a clause that would provide for Judith "until her marriage" is crossed out, confirming that she had married between the first and last drafts of the document. On the third and last page, Shakespeare also bequeaths to Judith a silver gilt bowl.

One could not argue that anything in the will's text reflects the style or spirit of perhaps the greatest poet and dramatist the world has ever known. There is no humor; there is no literary flair; one senses no sentiment, love, or warmth in any of the clauses. The document formulaically and matter-of-factly distributes Shakespeare's possessions. His sister Joan receives £20, all of William's clothing, and the right to live in her Stratford house (owned by her brother) for 12 pence per year (that is, essentially rent-free) in perpetuity. The will allocates the almost absurdly specific amount of 26 shillings plus 8 pence for several friends to buy mourning rings—including his "fellows" from the King's Men John Heminge, Richard Burbage, and Henry Condell; these bequests to his theatrical buddies were evidently a late remembrance, as they were squeezed in between two lines. The will tersely bequeaths £10 to the poor of Stratford—quite a miserly sum for a man of Shakespeare's means. The bulk of the estate (including New Place and all of William's other properties) went to his oldest daughter, Susanna, who—along with her husband, Dr. John Hall—was also named executor of the will. Shakespeare clearly had more confidence in the marriage and perhaps the judgment of his first daughter than in those of Judith. Susanna and Dr. Hall—already well off—were rendered instantly wealthy by her father's will.

There remains only Anne. The document's only reference to Shakespeare's wife—which was inserted between lines, suggests that it was a late addition, almost an afterthought. And that sentence—"Item: I leave unto my wife my second best bed with the furniture"—forms the crux of the notion that Shakespeare detested and rejected Anne. Throughout the centuries and decades, scholars have lined up on either side of the debate.

Do these casual, minimal words demonstrate bitter coldness, a slap in the face to Will's wife of thirty-four years, who bore him three children? In 1780, Shakespeare scholar and editor Edmund Malone stated: "His wife had not wholly escaped his memory; he had forgot her,—he had recollected her,—but so recollected her, as more strongly to mark how little he esteemed her; he had already (as is vulgarly expressed) cut her off, not indeed with a shilling, but with an old bed" (Schoenbaum 1975, 248). Nineteenth-century biographer Charles Knight concurred, arguing that the will "clearly proved . . . the unhappiness of his marriage" and the reference to the bed demonstrating "bitter sarcasm" and "unfriendly feeling" (Knight 1865). More recent biographer Stephen Greenblatt agreed, seeing the "second best bed" clause as an "eloquently hostile gesture" and adding that "Shakespeare had found his trust, his happiness, his capacity for intimacy, his best bed elsewhere. . . . So much for the dream of love" (Greenblatt 2004, 146–47).

But many scholars interpret the passage—and the fact that it constitutes the will's only mention of Anne—completely differently. For starters, English common law clearly held that the wife of the deceased would receive one third of the estate. To mention that third as a bequest would have been superfluous at best and potentially confusing at worst. As Shakespeare well knew, Anne was set for life—argue historians and scholars who interpret the will more benignly. Obviously when Susanna Hall became the owner of New Place upon her father's death, she would hardly eject her mother—in fact, Susanna would likely continue to live with her husband at their nearby home, Hall's Croft, and allow Anne not only to live at New Place but to continue running that large household as long as she was able.

With regard to the notorious and specific phrasing of the "second best bed," historians have searched for contemporaneous wills and have found several examples of similar language. The second best bed bequest should not be seen as a window into William and Anne's marriage but as a way to distinguish one bed from another, such that his wife received the right one. Terms such as "best" and "second best" were used as objective, nonsentimental descriptors to clarify which item was being designated for whom. Commonly, affluent English households such as Shakespeare's would reserve the "best bed" for guests, and thus the "second best bed" would have been the marital one. It is tempting for us to project our contemporary desire for emotional expression onto our reading of William's sole expressed bequest to Anne, but given the consistently unsentimental tone of the entire will, we might allow that the phrase "my second best bed" is merely consistent with the objective, matter-of-fact nature of this most pragmatic and unpoetic of Shakespearean texts. It could even be read as tongue-in-cheek, with the idea that Shakespeare is well aware of the inadequacy of this single, clinical phrase; husband and wife know full well what they have shared (though we can still only speculate), and this document is not the place where William would attempt to express that intimacy for posterity.

PRIMARY SOURCE DOCUMENTS

SHAKESPEARE'S WILL (1616)

Shakespeare's will appears in its entirety. Explanatory notes have been inserted in brackets, and punctuation and spelling have been modernized.

March 25, in the 14th year of the reign of James now king of England and the 49th year of Scotland, 1616

William Shakespeare

In the name of God, Amen. I, William Shakespeare of Stratford upon Avon in the county of Warwick, gent. [*indicates his status as a gentleman, as Shakespeare had purchased a coat of arms for his father and family in 1596*], in perfect health and memory, God be praised, do make and ordain this my last will and testament in manner and form following, that is to say, first I commend my soul into the hands of God my creator, hoping and assuredly believing through the only merits of Jesus Christ my Saviour to be made partaker of life everlasting, and my body to the earth whereof it is made.

Item: I give and bequeath unto my daughter Judith one hundred and fifty pounds of lawful English money to be paid unto her in manner and form following, that is to say, one hundred pounds in discharge of her marriage portion within one year after my decease, with consideration after the rate of two shillings in the pound, for so long time as the same shall be unpaid unto her after my decease, and the fifty pounds residue thereof upon her surrendering of, or giving of, such sufficient security as the overseers of this my will shall like of to surrender or grant all her estate and right that shall descend or come unto her after my decease or that she now hath of in or to one Copyhold tenement with the appurtenances lying and being in Stratford upon Avon aforesaid in the said county of Warwick, being parcel or holden of the manor of Rowington unto my daughter Susanna Hall and her heirs forever.

Item: I give and bequeath unto my said daughter Judith one hundred and fifty pounds more if she or any issue of her body living at the end of three years next ensuing the day of the date of this my will, during which time my executors to pay her consideration from my decease according to the rate aforesaid.

And if she die within the said term without issue of her body then my will is and I do give and bequeath one hundred pounds thereof to my niece Elizabeth Hall [*actually Shakespeare's granddaughter*], and fifty pounds to be set forth by my executors during the life of my sister Joan Hart and the use and profit thereof coming shall be paid to my said sister Joan, and after her decease the said 50 pounds shall remain amongst the children of my said sister equally to be divided amongst them.

But if my said daughter Judith be living at the end of the said three years, or any issue of her body, then my will is, and so I devise and bequeath the said hundred and fifty pounds to be set out by my executors and overseers for the best benefit of her and her issue, and the stock not to be paid unto her so long as she shall be married and covert baron [*a legal term meaning "with husband"*] but my will is that she shall have the consideration yearly paid unto her during her life and after her decease the said stock and consideration to be paid to her children if she have any and if not to her executors or assigns, she living the said term after my decease, provided that if such husband as she shall at the end of the said three years be married unto or attain after, do sufficiently assure unto her and the issue of her body, lands answerable to the portion by this my will given unto her, and to be adjudged so by my executors and overseers then my will is that the said £150 shall be paid to such husband as shall make such assurance to his own use.

Item: I give and bequeath unto my said sister Joan 20 pounds and all my wearing apparel to be paid and delivered within one year after my decease. And I do will and devise unto her the house with the appurtenances in Stratford wherein she dwelleth for her natural life under the yearly rent of 12 pence.

Item: I give and bequeath unto her three sons William Hart, _____ Hart, [*blank line in the original; evidently Shakespeare forgot the first name of his nephew Thomas*] and Michael Hart five pounds a piece to be paid within one year after my decease unto her.

Item: I give and bequeath unto the said Elizabeth Hall all my plate (except my broad silver and gilt bowl) that I now have at the date of this my will.

Item: I give and bequeath unto the poor of Stratford aforesaid ten pounds; to Mr. Thomas Combe, my sword; to Thomas Russell, Esquire, five pounds; and to Francis Collins of the borough of Warwick in the county of Warwick, gent., thirteen pounds, six shillings, and eight pence, to be paid within one year after my decease.

Item: I give and bequeath to Hamlett Sadler [Shakespeare's friend is actually named Hamnet Sadler, he for whom Will and Anne named their son; his name is spelled correctly below as one of the witnesses to this will.] 26s 8d to buy him a ring; to William Reynolds, gent., 26s 8d to buy him a ring; to my godson William Walker 20s in gold; to Anthony Nash, gent., 26s 8d; to Mr. John Nash, 26s 8d; and to my fellows John Heminge, Richard Burbage, and Henry Condell 26s 8d a piece to buy them rings.

Item: I give, will, bequeath, and devise unto my daughter Susanna Hall, for better enabling of her to perform this my will and towards the performance thereof:

All that capital messuage or tenement [*both terms for a house*] with the appurtenances in Stratford aforesaid called the New Place, wherein I now dwell, and two messuages or tenements with the appurtenances situate, lying and being in Henley Street within the borough of Stratford aforesaid.

And all my barns, stables, orchards, gardens, lands, tenements, and herediments whatsoever, situate, lying, and being, or to be had, received, perceived, or taken within the towns and hamlets, villages, fields, and grounds of Stratford upon Avon, Old Stratford, Bishopton, and Welcombe, or in any of them in the said county of Warwick.

And also all that messuage or tenement with the appurtenances wherein one John Robinson dwelleth, situate, lying and being in the Blackfriars in London near the Wardrobe, and all other my lands, tenements and hereditaments whatsoever.

To have and to hold all & singular the said premises with their appurtenances unto the said Susanna Hall for and during the term of her natural life and after her decease to the first son of her body lawfully issuing, and to the heirs males of the body of the said first son lawfully issuing and for default of such issue to the second son of her body lawfully issuing and to the heirs males of the body of the said second son lawfully issuing and for default of such heirs to the third son of the body of the said Susanna lawfully issuing and of the heirs males of the body of the said third son lawfully issuing. And for default of such issue the same so to be and remain to the fourth, fifth, sixth, and seventh sons of her body lawfully issuing, one after another, and to the heirs males of the bodies of the said fourth, fifth, sixth, and seventh sons lawfully issuing in such manner as it is before limited to be and remain to the first, second and third sons of her body and to their heirs males. And for default of such issue the said premises to be and remain to my said niece Hall and the heirs males of her body lawfully issuing for default of such issue to my daughter Judith & the heirs males of her body lawfully issuing. And for default of such issue to the right heirs of me the said William Shakespeare forever.

Item: I give unto my wife my second best bed with the furniture.

Item: I give and bequeath to my said daughter Judith my broad silver gilt bowl.

All the rest of my goods, chattel, leases, plate, jewels, and household stuff whatsoever, after my debts and legacies paid and my funeral expenses discharged, I give, devise, and bequeath to my son in law John Hall, gent., and my daughter Susanna, his wife, whom I ordain and make executors of this my last will and testament.

And I do entreat and appoint the said Thomas Russell, Esquire, and Francis Collins, gent., to be overseers hereof. And do revoke all former wills and publish this to be my last will and testament. In witness whereof I have hereunto put my hand the day and year first above written.

By me William Shakspeare (signed)

Witness to the publishing hereof

Francis Collins
Julius Shawe
John Robinson
Hamnet Sadler
Robert Whattcott
Probatum coram Magistro Willielmo Byrde
legum doctore Commissario etc. xxijd die

mensis Junij Anno domini 1616 Juramento
Johannis Hall unius executorum etc. Cui etc.
de bene etc. Jurati Reservata potestate
etc. Sussanne Hall alteri executorum etc. cum
venerit etc petitur

Source: E. K. Chambers. *William Shakespeare, a Study of Facts and Problems*, Vol. 2. (Oxford: Clarendon Press, 1930). Used by permission of Oxford University Press through PLSClear.

SHAKESPEARE PLAY EXCERPTS INVOLVING MARRIAGE

Shakespeare's plays present often competing views of myriad subjects, including marriage and family. On the whole it is inadvisable to read the lines of a character created by Shakespeare and assume, "Ah, that's what Shakespeare says." Rather, Shakespeare presents a grand panoply of voices and views, expressing what Peter Sellers's Inspector Clouseau and the band R. E. M. called "life's rich pageant." With that caveat, nonetheless, we analyze Shakespeare's lines to try to glean common themes and perspectives. In that spirit, there follow several quotes from the plays regarding marriage.

Get thee a good husband,
and use him as he uses thee.
(*All's Well That Ends Well* 1.1.212–13)

If men could be contented to be what they are, there were no fear in marriage.
(*All's Well That Ends Well* 1.3.54)

A young man married is a man that's marr'd.
(*All's Well That Ends Well* 2.3.297)

Men are April when they woo, December when they wed: maids are May when they are maids, but the sky changes when they are wives.
(*As You Like It* 4.1.130–2)

The fittest time to corrupt a man's wife is when she's fallen out with her husband.
(*Coriolanus* 4.3.30–2)

The instances that second marriage move
Are base respects of thrift, but none of love.
(*Hamlet* 3.2.185–6)

Marriage is a matter of more worth
Than to be dealt in by attorneyship.
(*1 Henry VI* 5.5.50–1)

For what is wedlock forced but a hell,
An age of discord and continual strife?
Whereas the contrary bringeth bliss,
And is a pattern of celestial peace.
(*1 Henry VI* 5.5.63–6)

Hasty marriage seldom proveth well.
(*3 Henry VI* 4.1.19)

Hanging and wiving goes by destiny.
(*The Merchant of Venice* 2.9.85)

In love the heavens themselves do guide the state;
Money buys lands, and wives are sold by fate.
(*The Merry Wives of Windsor* 5.5.225–6)

In time the savage bull doth bear the yoke.
(*Much Ado About Nothing* 1.1.243–4)

Thou art sad; get thee a wife, get thee a wife!
(*Much Ado About Nothing* 5.4.126)

I have thrust myself into this maze,
Haply to wive and thrive as best I may.
(*The Taming of the Shrew* 1.2.56–7)

Thy husband is thy lord, thy life, thy keeper,
Thy head, thy sovereign; one that cares for thee,
And for thy maintenance commits his body
To painful labour both by sea and land,
To watch the night in storms, the day in cold,
Whilst thou liest warm at home, secure and safe;
And craves no other tribute at thy hands
But love, fair looks and true obedience;
Too little payment for so great a debt.
(*The Taming of the Shrew* 5.2.145–53)

Fools are as like husbands as pilchards are to
herrings, the husband's the bigger.
(*Twelfth Night* 3.1.35–6)

JOHN MANNINGHAM'S DIARY (1601)

Our only evidence of Shakespeare's supposed infidelity and putative cocksmanship comes from an anecdote recorded in a 1601 diary entry of law student John Manningham.

Upon a time when Burbage played Richard III. There was a citizen grown so far in liking with him, that before she went from the play, she appointed him to come that night unto her by the name of Richard the Third. Shakespeare, overhearing their conclusion, went before, was entertained and at his game, ere Burbage came. Then message being brought that Richard the Third was at the door, Shakespeare caused return to be made that William the Conqueror was before Richard the Third. (Shakespeare's name William.)

Source: John Bruce, ed. *Diary of John Manningham.* Westminster: J.B. Nichols and Sons, 1868, 39.

What Really Happened

Some 2.5 million people each year journey to Stratford-upon-Avon, with one overwhelming draw: Shakespeare. Travelers to the charming town can take in plays at the Royal Shakespeare Company; can visit Holy Trinity Church to see William's final resting place; can sit in King Edward VI School, where William received his formal education; and can tour at least five other key destinations associated with the world's most renowned writer: Hall's Croft, the home of Dr. John Hall and his wife, Shakespeare's daughter Susanna; Anne Hathaway's Cottage, childhood home of Shakespeare's wife; Mary Arden's farm, childhood home of Shakespeare's mother; Henley Street house, where Shakespeare was born and lived; and New Place, a recreation of the site where Shakespeare lived his final years and died.

New Place has been open to the public only since 2016, but long before then, historians, scholars, and archaeologists had been exploring the site where Shakespeare's home once stood. Evidence that they have uncovered suggests that some of our common, long-standing impressions of Shakespeare's life are fictitious. As we have seen, the standard view of Shakespeare's biography holds that William abandoned his wife and family in Stratford-upon-Avon, settled in London, and lived there full time as a writer, actor, and theater company shareholder from sometime in the late 1580s until his retirement in 1611–12. Often when we speak of investigating the biography of a long-dead author such as Shakespeare, we use archaeological metaphors; we speak of "digging into" the historical records and hoping to "unearth" a text or document that will shed new light on the writer's life. In the case of Shakespeare, actual archaeological excavations were undertaken at New Place beginning in 2010, and the findings have dramatically shifted the evidence regarding where Shakespeare actually spent most of his time during those decades. It now seems probable that Shakespeare was not a London denizen who occasionally journeyed home to little Stratford-upon-Avon, but quite the reverse: throughout those years, he lived most of the time in Stratford, in his large and impressive family home (New Place) and stayed in various rented lodgings in London when his career and company obligations called him to do so. New Place holds the key to this new understanding that contradicts the fiction that has held sway for centuries regarding Shakespeare's life and family relations.

One can understand why for centuries people overlooked and underestimated the importance of New Place in Shakespeare's biography. Whereas the other Stratford-upon-Avon sites associated with Shakespeare (Holy Trinity Church, King Edward School, Hall's Croft, Anne Hathaway's Cottage, Mary Arden's farm, and Shakespeare's Henley Street birthplace) have all stood since the end of Shakespeare's life, New Place was demolished in 1759. Thus, although we were well aware of the exact location of the home, and while the site was preserved as a sort of memorial garden in Shakespeare's honor, there were no rooms to examine, crawlspaces to explore, or any other physical reifications of the importance of New Place. When the Shakespeare's Birthplace Trust conceived the plan to (re) create a New Place site that tourists could visit, they began by digging. Before we explore what these archaeologists discovered, let us consider a few simple facts that perhaps should long ago have called into question the legend of Shakespeare as a Londoner who only returned to Stratford upon retirement, to live out the last four or five years of his life. First, we should consider the dates. Shakespeare didn't buy New Place in 1608 or 1610, when presumably he had begun to conceive the plan to retire from the world of the theater. He purchased the estate in 1597, well before the midpoint of his thriving career and when he had just turned thirty-three years old. Standing since the 1480s, on the next block from the Guildhall (town government hall) and grammar school, New Place was the second-largest house in Stratford-upon-Avon; Shakespeare had achieved wealth and success (and/or patronage) through his theater work that allowed him to purchase the home for what scholars estimate at around £120. It seems illogical that he would buy—and expand and remodel—such a grand, conspicuous home just for his family to live in while he stayed in London, coming to Stratford only on rare occasions, as the common myth would have it. It is quite possible that three of William's brothers, his sister, and even perhaps John and Mary, Shakespeare's parents, also came to live at New Place—which bore the family's coat of arms (acquired through William's efforts) to signify their newly acquired gentry status.

The archaeological findings at New Place demonstrate that there were extensive gardens, at least one study, and probably up to thirty rooms. Historical records also suggest that although Shakespeare was an occasional actor with his theater company, as time went on, he concentrated foremost or wholly on writing—for which New Place would serve as an ideal setting. Add to that the fact that the years between 1603 and 1609 were "plague years," during which public theaters were closed far more often than they were open. People of means would flee London to avoid contamination by the Black Death—which was (erroneously) believed to be spread by airborne means. New Place would afford Shakespeare the ideal retreat from which he could continue to create his masterworks while also enjoying the love of family.

Whereas Shakespeare owned perhaps the finest home in Stratford, he never purchased a house in London—oddly, until after his retirement and departure from the city in 1612. Why would Shakespeare buy property in London after he'd finished his theatrical career there? In March 1613, Will and some friends purchased "Blackfriars Gatehouse," which evidently had for decades been a hotbed of underground Catholic activity. Shakespeare immediately leased the house to John Robinson. Robinson's father had been reported in 1599 for sheltering a priest, Father Richard Dudley. By the time of Shakespeare's acquisition of the Gatehouse, Robinson's brother was studying for the priesthood in Rome. Shakespeare was certainly aware that he was leasing the Blackfriars to a Catholic recusant, one who would not just happen to live there but who would continue to run the property as an underground safe house for Catholic priests. John Robinson also visited his landlord in Stratford and signed as a witness to Shakespeare's will, demonstrating that he was no random acquaintance/tenant but rather a close friend. Thus, it is clear that the only London house Shakespeare ever bought was meant not as a home but rather perhaps as an investment property—or most likely as a haven for Catholic recusants (see chapter 3, "Shakespeare Was a Secret Catholic").

Leaving aside the question of how Shakespeare's possible Catholic sympathies affected his real estate transactions, the records we have (business and archaeological) defy the long-standing and dominant belief that Shakespeare made himself into a Londoner, simultaneously abandoning his hometown roots and family. In the two decades prior to his purchase of the Blackfriars Gatehouse, Shakespeare rented various accommodations in London. As with many aspects of Shakespeare's life, we work mostly from a few legal and religious records (lawsuits, marriage and baptismal records, and documents of other legal proceedings) and try to fill in the often enormous gaps. For example, we know of two of William's London lodgings because he was twice cited for tax evasion.

Shakespeare's name appears in the records of St. Helen's/Bishopsgate parish from 1596. We have no idea of the precise address, though this was (and remains) a small parish, and we can thus narrow a radius of several blocks where the playwright had residence at the time; recently, London has erected two landmark buildings in that area, uniquely shaped structures known as the Gherkin (completed in 2003) and the Cheesegrater (completed in 2014). A second brush with the law tells us that Shakespeare had moved from St. Helen's/Bishopsgate by 1599, when he was cited for tax trouble as a resident of the area called Liberty of the Clink. Unlike the City of London and Bishopsgate, Liberty of the Clink no longer exists today as a district. The area was located in Southwark, near the Clink (from where we get the slang term "clink" for prison) and the home of several theaters. From 1575 on, public theatrical performances had been prohibited within city limits, though frequently those laws were flouted on the grounds that the company was practicing for a performance at court. Even today, there exists a legal distinction between the City of London and the surrounding boroughs and districts that make up the metropolis. The City of London was founded in 43 CE as Londinium by the Romans, who built a wall around approximately the same one-square-mile area known as the City of London in Shakespeare's time and still today (the wall had crumbled by Shakespeare's time, and a few remnants can still be seen today). London City still stands as a separate jurisdiction from the other boroughs—and from the rest of England. For example, if the queen wishes to visit the City of London, technically, she needs permission. In Shakespeare's time, the districts south of the Thames and outside city limits—Southwark, including Bankside and Liberty of the Clink—became home to what were viewed as unwholesome entertainments, from brothels to bear-baiting arenas to theaters, including the newly built (1599) Globe.

Yet another legal proceeding gives us our record for Shakespeare's residence in 1604, by which time he'd moved back north of the river. This time Will wasn't in tax trouble, but he would appear as a witness in a marriage dispute. The proceeding actually didn't take place until 1612, but Shakespeare was called based on having lived in the household of Christopher and Marie Mountjoy, a French family living on Silver Street, which stood in an area near St. Paul's Cathedral. In 1604, their daughter Mary married Stephen Bellott, who had served as an apprentice for Mary's father. At the behest of Marie Mountjoy, Shakespeare had encouraged and even made the match. Mrs. Mountjoy, who had encouraged her husband to be more generous to the young couple (he had given them quite a paltry dowry), died in 1606. The couple moved back into the Silver Street home to help run the family business of fancy wigmaking. But the couple argued with Mr. Mountjoy over money, and the Bellotts again moved out. Mr. Mountjoy declared that he would never leave the couple "a groat" in his will. Bellott alleged that his father-in-law had thus reneged on an agreement to support the couple, first by a dowry of £60 and/or a bequest of £200 through his will. In the 1612 proceeding, Shakespeare testified that Stephen "did well and honestly behave himself" and was "a very good and industrious servant." According to Shakespeare, Mr. Mountjoy "did bear and show great good will and affection" to Stephen Bellott. However, Shakespeare could not recall any specifics as to the financial arrangements agreed upon by the now warring parties.

Thus through legal records we find that Shakespeare bounced around a good bit in London, always renting his lodgings and never owning a house until he purchased the Blackfriars Gatehouse in 1613, which—even if one holds to the theory of Shakespeare having lived primarily in London and not Stratford for twenty-fiveish years—was clearly not intended for him to live in, as nobody disputes that he spent his last few years in Stratford. Especially with the fairly recent excavations at New Place, the preponderance of the evidence suggests that the notion of Shakespeare having abandoned his wife, children, and Stratford to become a London dweller is more fiction than fact.

Further Readings

Bell, Ilona. *Elizabethan Women and the Poetry of Courtship*. Cambridge: Cambridge University Press, 1998.

Boose, Lynda E. "The Father and the Bride in Shakespeare." *PMLA* 97 (1982): 325–47.

Carlson, Eric Josef. *Marriage and the English Reformation*. Cambridge, MA: Blackwell, 1994.

Clark, Cumberland. *Shakespeare and Home Life*. London: Williams & Norgate, 1935.

Cook, Ann Jennalie. *Making a Match: Courtship in Shakespeare and His Society*. Princeton, NJ: Princeton University Press, 1991.

Cook, Ann Jennalie. "The Mode of Marriage in Shakespeare's England." *Southern Humanities Review* 2 (1977): 126–32.

Cook, Ann Jennalie. "Wooing and Wedding: Shakespeare's Dramatic Distortion of the Customs of His Time." In *Shakespeare's Art from a Comparative Aspect*. Edited by Wendell M. Aycock. Lubbock: Texas Tech Press, 1981.

Cressy, David. *Birth, Marriage, and Death: Ritual, Religion, and the Life-Cycle in Tudor and Stuart England*. New York: Oxford University Press, 1997.

Duncan-Jones, Katherine. *Shakespeare: An Ungentle Life*. London: Methuen Drama, 2010.

Edmonson, Paul, Kevin Colls, and William Mitchell. *Finding Shakespeare's New Place: An Archaeological Biography*. Manchester: Manchester University Press, 2016.

Emmison, F. G. *Elizabethan Life: Morals and the Church Courts*. Chelmsford: Essex County Council, 1973.

Frye, Roland M. "The Teachings of Classical Puritanism on Conjugal Love." *Studies in the Renaissance* 2 (1955): 148–59.

Greenblatt, Stephen. *Will in the World: How Shakespeare Became Shakespeare*. New York: Norton, 2004.

Halleck, Reuben Post. *Halleck's New English Literature*. New York: American Book Company, 1913. *Shakespeare Online*, February 20, 2011. http://www.shakespeare-online.com/theatre/newdocumentsshk.html

Haller, William, and Malleville. "The Puritan Art of Love." *Huntington Library Quarterly* 5 (1942): 235–72.

Honigmann, E. A. J. *Shakespeare: The "Lost Years."* Manchester: Manchester University Press, 1998.

Houlbrooke, Ralph. *The English Family 1450–1700*. London & New York: Longman, 1984.

Ingram, Martin. *Church Courts, Sex, and Marriage in England, 1570–1640*. Cambridge: Cambridge University Press, 1987.

Klein, Joan Larsen. *Daughters, Wives, and Widows: Writings by Men about Women and Marriage in England, 1500–1640*. Urbana: University of Illinois Press, 1992.

Knight, Charles. *William Shakespeare: a Biography*. London: G. Routledge, 1865.

Laslett, Peter. *Family Life and Illicit Love in Earlier Generations*. Cambridge: Cambridge University Press, 1977.

MacFarlane, Alan. *Marriage and Love in England: Modes of Reproduction, 1300–1840*. New York: Blackwell, 1986.

Meader, William Granville. *Courtship in Shakespeare: Its Relation to the Tradition of Courtly Love*. New York: King's Crown Press, Columbia University, 1954.

Pearson, Lu Emily. *Elizabethans at Home*. Stanford, CA: Stanford University Press, 1957.

Quaife, G. R. *Wanton Wenches and Wayward Wives: Peasants and Illicit Sex in Early Seventeenth Century England*. London: Croom Helm, 1979.

Rowse, A. L. *Simon Forman: Sex and Society in Shakespeare's Age*. London: Weidenfeld and Nicolson, 1974.

Schoenbaum, Samuel. *William Shakespeare: A Documentary Life*. New York: Oxford University Press, 1975.

Singman, Jeffrey L. *Daily Life in Elizabethan England*. Westport, CT: Greenwood Press, 1995.

Stone, Lawrence. *The Family, Sex, and Marriage in England 1500–1800*. London: Weidenfeld Press, 1977.

"Where in London Did Shakespeare Live?" *The Londonist* online, February 27, 2017. https://londonist.com/london/history/where-in-london-did -shakespeare-live

6

Shakespeare's Plays Were All Recycled and Not Original

What People Think Happened

William Shakespeare authored dozens of plays that have enjoyed popularity from their first productions through today. However, none of his works contains an original plot; rather, Shakespeare crafted his plays by freely borrowing, stealing, cutting, and pasting from various existing sources. As such, his accomplishments as an author are less impressive than to warrant his reputation as the greatest writer ever to live.

English Renaissance playwrights had a difficult task as secular drama had essentially ceased to exist between Roman times and theirs—a span of over a thousand years. Writers such as Christopher Marlowe, Ben Jonson, and William Shakespeare had to determine and create what a play could be—what plots to use, what genres to inhabit, and what structures to employ. The era immediately preceding the English Renaissance—the medieval period—thoroughly lacked nonreligious drama, so Shakespeare and his colleagues largely looked back for models in ancient Roman plays. From there, they gleaned features such as the chorus, the five-act structure, and the genres of comedy and tragedy. In addition to these technical and structural elements, Shakespeare also more or less directly borrowed the plots of six plays (*Titus Andronicus, Julius Caesar, Antony and Cleopatra, Timon of Athens, Coriolanus*, and *Troilus and Cressida*) from Greco-Roman sources, and he included classical elements in various other plays. In some cases, Shakespeare lifted lines almost directly from ancient sources.

Even when Marlowe and Shakespeare created a new genre—the English history play—the plot events, characters, and, in some cases, lines of dialogue came straight from historical chronicles of events and figures with which English Renaissance audiences would be familiar, such as the Wars of the Roses. Thus some of Shakespeare's very earliest works were the three parts of *Henry VI*, to which he added the historical play *Richard III* to constitute perhaps the first of what we would now call a "franchise"—similar to contemporary superhero film series. Enjoying the success of those plays, Shakespeare went back to the well of English history to craft a second tetralogy—this one involving an earlier historical period and plucked from the pages of the same historical chronicles that served as sources for the first tetralogy. Those plays also became great hits for Shakespeare: *Richard II*; *Henry IV, Part 1*; *Henry IV, Part 2*; and *Henry V*. Even in historically based plays set outside England, Shakespeare relied on existing chronicles. Two plays considered among his greatest—*Hamlet* and *Macbeth*—take their plot outlines respectively from historical sources regarding a Danish prince and a Scottish king.

The plots of Shakespeare's plays derive from a huge variety of sources, including ancient (e.g., *The Comedy of Errors* is based on *The Menaechmi*, a comedy by the Roman author Plautus) and more recent texts. For example, *As You Like It* relies heavily on a 1590 pastoral romance novel by English author Thomas Lodge. Shakespeare borrowed heavily from the Italian writer Giovanni Boccaccio, whose fourteenth-century series of novellas gave him ideas, characters, and plot points for *The Two Gentlemen of Verona, All's Well That Ends Well,* and *Cymbeline*. Some works, such as *The Taming of the Shrew* and *King Lear*—are versions of then recent English plays with unknown authors; thus, Shakespeare's plays could—using the vocabulary of contemporary films—be called "reboots." Very little of what Shakespeare created was truly original; his greatest talent may have been recycling.

How the Story Became Popular

In 1691 Gerald Langbaine published *An Account of the English Dramatic Poets*, the first work to investigate the authorship of the plays of the English Renaissance. He closely critiqued the works of Shakespeare and was the first to demonstrate how freely Shakespeare and other writers borrowed—and "plagiarized," a favorite word of Langbaine—from various existing texts. For example, Shakespeare's famous speech describing

Cleopatra's glorious appearance closely mirrors the passage from Plutarch's *Lives of the Noble Grecians and Romans*:

[S]he came sailing up the river Cydnus, in a barge with gilded stern and outspread sails of purple, while oars of silver beat time to the music of flutes and fifes and harps. She herself lay all along under a canopy of cloth of gold, dressed as Venus in a picture, and beautiful young boys, like painted Cupids, stood on each side to fan her. Her maids were dressed like sea nymphs and graces, some steering at the rudder, some working at the ropes. The perfumes diffused themselves from the vessel to the shore, which was covered with multitudes, part following the galley up the river on either bank, part running out of the city to see the sight.

The barge she sat in, like a burnish'd throne, / Burn'd on the water: the poop was beaten gold; / Purple the sails, and so perfumed that / The winds were love-sick with them; the oars were silver, / Which to the tune of flutes kept stroke, and made / The water which they beat to follow faster, / As amorous of their strokes . . . she did lie / In her pavilion—cloth-of-gold of tissue— / O'er-picturing that Venus where we see / The fancy outwork nature: on each side her / Stood pretty dimpled boys, like smiling Cupids, / With divers-colour'd fans, whose wind did seem / To glow the delicate cheeks which they did cool, / And what they undid did.

[. . .]

Her gentlewomen, like the Nereides, / So many mermaids, tended her i' the eyes, / And made their bends adornings: at the helm / A seeming mermaid steers: the silken tackle / Swell with the touches of those flower-soft hands, / That yarely frame the office. From the barge / A strange invisible perfume hits the sense / Of the adjacent wharfs. The city cast / Her people out upon her. . . .

Though Shakespeare's version clearly expands the description, the passages use strikingly similar language; Shakespeare clearly immersed himself in Plutarch and had no qualms about mining that and other sources, classical and contemporary, to produce his plays.

Throughout the centuries, scholars have delved deeper into documenting Shakespeare's sources, culminating in Geoffrey Bullough's eight-volume *Narrative and Dramatic Sources of Shakespeare*, first published in 1957 and augmented and republished several times through 1975. With such scholarship often illuminating Shakespeare's molding of material from various sources, it gradually became commonplace for teachers, scholars, and critics to issue statements such as "None of Shakespeare's plays is original." Any Shakespeare anthology or single play edition has for decades included a section on the sources for each play. Students assigned class presentations are often required to research and discuss sources, and scholars carved out a subfield of Shakespeare studies devoted to investigating and proposing new textual candidates for sources of and influences on various plays. In some cases—as with *Antony and Cleopatra* or with the English history plays—the borrowings and the sources are clear and undeniable; for other plays, the suggested influences of "source" texts on the Shakespearean play seem tenuous, but scholars nonetheless make the case. How can readers actually know from where—and to what extent—Shakespeare gleaned his material?

As we have seen, in some cases a play's sources are fairly obvious—as with the ten English history plays. But let us take for example a play usually cited as Shakespeare's only truly original plot: *The Tempest*. For this 1611 play—probably the last one Shakespeare composed solo—editors often seem chagrined not to be able to point to a significant source. Even in an early twentieth-century edition, we find a sense of editorial frustration over *The Tempest*'s elusiveness as far as sources:

> Whence Shakespeare derived the story which forms the basis of the simple plot of *The Tempest* we do not yet know. Since in all but one or two cases definite sources for his plots have been found, the likelihood is that he did not invent this one. But the stories brought forward as bearing some resemblance to the present play can at most be regarded as belonging to the same family of tales, not as direct ancestors. (Neilson 1914)

Absent actual plot parallels with texts that might be labeled as sources, scholars comb *The Tempest*—and all the plays—for lines that seem to allude to recent historical events. This process also helps us to narrow down a play's date of composition, as clearly a work can't have been written before a documented historical event to which it refers. Thus, for example, the beginning of *The Tempest* seems to be influenced by the shipwreck of the *Sea Venture* in the Bermudas in 1609. After this event, several survivors wrote tales of their experiences, both of the shipwreck and the subsequent survival on the island for nine months. However, even here we face ambiguity as to the degree of influence. The most famous of these accounts—by William Strachey—was written in 1610 but not published until 1625, after Shakespeare's death. If we wish to claim Strachey's "True Repertory of the Wreck and Redemption of Sir Thomas Gates, July 15,

1610" as a source for *The Tempest*—as many do—we can only speculate that Shakespeare knew Strachey, perhaps read his narrative in manuscript, or that tales of this famous adventure were shared far and wide, at least orally, before publication. Shakespeare's character Caliban in *The Tempest* may have been influenced by Michel de Montaigne's essay "Of the Cannibals" ("Caliban" seeming like a sort of anagram for "cannibal"), which was translated and published in English in 1603, and from Ovid's *Metamorphoses*, with which Shakespeare was greatly familiar from his grammar school days and from which he drew elements for several of his plays—including *Titus Andronicus*, *A Midsummer Night's Dream*, and *A Winter's Tale*. But these connections are tenuous at best. Thus, even for plays whose plots seem almost wholly created by Shakespeare, the zeal for proposing possible "sources" for his works continues apace—though sometimes with scanty evidence.

PRIMARY SOURCE DOCUMENTS

WILLIAM STRACHEY, *A TRUE REPORTORY* (1625)

Strachey's account of the voyage of the Sea Venture—*destined for Jamestown, Virginia*—*begins with a vivid depiction of a devastating tempest hitting the ship. Shakespeare's play begins on a ship similarly besieged by a powerful storm, but Shakespeare's tempest comes not from nature but from the conjurings of the magician Prospero. Strachey's scene is much longer than is that of Shakespeare, who is only concerned with the storm as a brief pretext to launch the plot of his play; Prospero uses his powers to wreck the ship carrying his enemies, so that they will be brought (unharmed and magically dry) onto the island where he reigns. Spellings have been modernized.*

I. *A most dreadful tempest, the manifold deaths whereof are here to the life described*—*Their wrack on Bermuda, and the description of those islands.*

EXCELLENT LADY—

KNOW THAT upon Friday late in the evening [2 June 1609], we broke ground out of the sound of Plymouth, our whole fleet then consisting of seven good ships and two pinnaces, all which from the said second of June unto the twenty—three of July kept in friendly consort together, not a whole watch at any time losing the sight each of other. Our course . . . we declined to the northward, and . . . found the wind to this course indeed as friendly as . . . it is upon a more direct line, and by Sir George Summers, our admiral, had been likewise in former time sailed—being a gentleman of approved assuredness and ready knowledge in seafaring actions, having often carried command and chief charge in many ships royal of Her Majesty's, and in sundry voyages made many defeats and attempts in the time of the Spaniard's quarreling with us upon the islands and Indies, etc.

We had followed this course so long as now we were within seven or eight days at the most, by Captain Newport's reckoning, of making Cape Henry upon the coast of Virginia, when on Saint James day, July 24 . . . preparing for no less all the black night before—the clouds gathering thick upon us, and the winds singing and whistling most unusually . . . a dreadful and hideous storm began to blow from out the northeast, which swelling and roaring . . . did beat all light from heaven, which like an hell of darkness turned black upon us, so much the more fuller of horror, as in such cases horror and fear . . . overrun the troubled and overmastered senses of all, which, taken up with amazement . . . as who was most armed and best prepared was not a little shaken. For surely . . . as death comes not so sudden nor apparent, so he comes not so elvish and painful to men, especially even then in health and perfect habitudes of body, as at sea. . . . For indeed death is accompanied at no time nor place with circumstances every way so uncapable of particularities of goodness and inward comforts as at sea. . . . And the manner of the sickness it lays upon the body, being so unsufferable, gives not the mind any free and quiet time to use her judgment and empire. . . .

For four and twenty hours the storm in a restless tumult had blown so exceedingly as we could not apprehend in our imaginations any possibility of greater violence. Yet did we still find it not only more terrible but more constant, fury added to fury, and one storm urging a second more outrageous than the former . . . .

Sometimes strikes in our ship amongst women and passengers not used to such hurly and discomforts made us look one upon the other with troubled hearts and panting bosoms. . . . Prayers might well be in the heart and lips, but drowned in the outcries of the officers, nothing heard that could give comfort, nothing seen that might encourage hope.

[. . .] Our sails, wound up, lay without their use . . . six and sometimes eight men were not enough to hold the whipstaff in the steerage and the tiller below in the gunner room, by which may be imagined the strength of the storm in which the sea swelled above the clouds and gave battle unto heaven.

It could not be said to rain. The waters like whole rivers did flood in the air . . . whereas upon the land when a storm hath poured itself forth once in drifts of rain, the wind . . . not long after endureth. Here the glut of water, as if throttling the wind . . . was no sooner a little emptied and qualified but instantly the winds, as having gotten their mouths now free and at liberty, spake more loud, and grew more tumultuous and malignant. . . . Winds and seas were as mad as fury and rage could make them. . . . I had been in some storms before. . . . Yet all that I had ever suffered gathered together might not hold comparison with this. There was not a moment in which the sudden splitting or instant oversetting of the ship was not expected.

[. . . T]his was not all. It pleased God to bring a greater affliction yet upon us, for in the beginning of the storm we had received likewise a mighty leak, and the ship in every joint almost having spewed out her oakum before we were aware . . . was grown five foot suddenly deep with water above her ballast, and we almost drowned within whilst we sat looking when to perish from above. This imparting no less terror than danger ran through the whole ship . . ., startled and turned the blood . . . of the most hardy mariner of them all. . . .

There might be seen master, master's mate, boatswain, quartermaster, coopers, carpenters . . . with candles in their hands, creeping along the ribs . . . searching every corner, and listening in every place, if they could hear the water run. Many a weeping leak was this way found and hastily stop'd, and at length one in the gunner room made up with . . . pieces of beef. But all was to no purpose: The leak . . . which drunk in our greatest seas and took in our destruction fastest could not then be found, nor ever was. . . .

[. . . T]o me this leakage appeared as a wound given to men that were before dead. The Lord knoweth I had . . . little hope . . . of life in the storm, and . . . it went beyond . . . my reason why we should labor to preserve life. Yet we did, either because so dear are a few ling'ring hours of life in all mankind or that our Christian knowledges taught us how much we owed to the rites of nature, as bound not to . . . neglect the means of our own preservation, the most despairful things amongst men being matters of no wonder nor moment with Him who is the rich fountain . . . of all mercy.

[. . .] Then men might be seen to labor . . . for life, and the better sort, even our governor and admiral themselves, not refusing their turn . . . to give example to other. The common sort stripped naked . . . with tired bodies and wasted spirits, three days and four nights destitute of . . .

comfort and . . . of any deliverance, testifying how mutually willing they were yet by labor to keep each other from drowning. . . .

Once, so huge a sea brake upon the poop and quarter upon us as it covered our ship from stern to stem. Like a . . . vast cloud, it filled her brim full . . . within from the hatches up to the spar deck. This . . . confluence of water was so violent as it rush'd and carried the helm—man from the helm, and . . . so tossed him from starboard to larboard as it was God's mercy it had not split him. . . .

Our governor was . . . heartening every man unto his labor. It struck him from the place where he sat and groveled him, and all us about him on our faces, beating . . . all thoughts from our bosoms else than that we were now sinking. . . . One thing . . . it pleased God to be gracious unto us: There was not a passenger, gentleman or other, after he began to stir and labor but was able to relieve his fellow . . . such as in all their lifetimes had never done hours' work before . . . were able twice forty—eight hours together to toil with the best.

During all this time, the heavens look'd so black upon us that it was not possible the elevation of the Pole might be observed, nor a star by night, not sunbeam by day was to be seen. Only upon the Thursday night, Sir George Summers, being upon the watch, had an apparition of a little round light like a faint star, trembling and streaming along with a sparkling blaze half the height upon the mainmast, and shooting sometimes from shroud to shroud, tempting to settle as it were upon any of the four shrouds. And for . . . half the night it kept with us, running sometimes along the main yard to the very end, and then returning; at which Sir George Summers called divers about him and showed them the same, who observed it with much wonder and carefulness. . . .

The superstitious seamen make many constructions of this sea fire. . . . The Spaniards call it Saint Elmo, and have an authentic and miraculous legend for it. . . .

East and by south we steered away . . . which was no small carefulness nor pain to do . . . we . . . threw overboard much luggage, many a trunk and chest . . . and staved many a butt of beer, hogsheads of oil, cider, wine, and vinegar, and heaved away all our ordnance . . . and had now purposed to . . . cut down the mainmast the more to lighten her, for . . . our men so weary as their strengths together failed them with their hearts, having travailed now from Tuesday till Friday morning . . . without either sleep or food. For the leakage taking up all the hold, we could neither come by beer nor fresh water; fire we could keep none in the cookroom to dress any meat, and carefulness, grief, and our turn at the pump or bucket were sufficient to hold sleep from our eyes.

And surely . . . it is most true there was not any hour . . . all these days in which we freed not twelve hundred barricoes of water . . . besides three deep pumps continually going . . . so . . . every four hours we quitted one hundred tons of water. And from Tuesday noon till Friday noon, we bailed and pumped two thousand ton, and yet . . . when our ship held least in her . . . she bore ten foot deep. . . . And it being now Friday, the fourth morning . . . there had been a general determination to have shut up hatches, and commending our sinful souls to God, committed the ship to the mercy of the sea. Surely that night we must have done it, and that night had we then perished.

But see the goodness . . . by our merciful God given unto us: Sir George Summers, when no man dreamed of such happiness, had discovered and cried LAND! Indeed the morning . . . had won a little clearness from the days before, and it being better surveyed, the very trees were seen to move with the wind upon the shore side. . . . The boatswain sounding at the first found it thirteen fathom, and when we stood a little in, seven fathom; and . . . the third time had ground at four fathom. And by this we had got her within a mile under the southeast point of the land, where we had somewhat smooth water. But having no hope to save her by coming to an anchor . . . we were enforced to run her ashore as near the land as we could, which brought us within three quarters of a mile offshore; and by the mercy of God . . . making out our boats, we had ere night brought all our men, women, and children, about the number of one hundred and fifty, safe into the island.

We found it to be the dangerous and dreaded island, or rather islands, of the Bermuda . . . they be so terrible to all that ever touched on them, and such tempests, thunders, and other fearful objects are seen and heard about them that they be called commonly "the Devil's Islands," and are feared and avoided of all sea travelers alive above any other place in the world. Yet it pleased our merciful God to make even this hideous and hated place both the place of our safety and means of our deliverance.

Source: William Strachey. "A True Reportory of the Wreck and Redemption of Sir Thomas Gates, July 15, 1610." Available online at http://fas-history.rutgers.edu /clemens/Jamestown/StracheyReportoryI.html

What Really Happened

The word "plagiarism" evidently first appeared in English language usage in 1621, around five years after Shakespeare's death. Plays during the English Renaissance lacked the benefit of copyright laws; being written primarily for their performance value and not for literary purchase, these works were highly malleable, collaborative, and unprotected from unauthorized printings by whomever might recreate a version. Some texts we have of Shakespearean plays seem to have been generated from memorial reconstruction; that is, someone involved with a production—say, an actor—dictated his memory of the dialogue to a publisher, and that version (often skewed toward the part played by that actor) was published and circulated as Shakespeare's work.

In fact, we have no play to which we can point and say with any certainty, "That's exactly what Shakespeare wrote; that's the *correct* version." The pursuit of such a "pristine text" or "master text" leads nowhere. For many of the plays, we have two or more valid, competing versions from which to choose, or cull, a contemporary edition. Such was the climate in the burgeoning theater scene of Renaissance London. Playwrights, actors, poets, producers, and publishers freely collaborated, competed, borrowed, and stole in order to get dramatic works produced—and sometimes published. Nobody cared *how or from where* a playwright came up with a play that might entertain the public—just that he or she did so. Thus, Shakespeare's drawing from various sources to create the plots of his plays was no more a demerit in terms of his creative achievement than is, say, the creation of a 2019 movie from a Marvel or D.C. franchise—drawing from existing characters, plot lines, and, often, other films already produced (sequels upon sequels). In fact, it is a great oversimplification to assert that Shakespeare's plays lack originality.

First, we should note the way Shakespeare wrote his dramas—through the defining characteristic of all plays: dialogue. That is, even if he had entirely stolen a play's plot, Shakespeare nonetheless wrote from scratch thousands of words of dialogue that constitute the body of each work. And he did so largely in iambic pentameter, meaning that not only did he create thousands of lines of powerful dialogue that drives the plots, but he also wrote the bulk of the plays as grand, enormous poems. Even in those few cases where Shakespeare took some actual words from historical sources—as in the case of Enobarbus's description of Cleopatra, above—those lines constitute a miniscule fraction of the total dialogue of the play. The rest is completely invented by the mind of Shakespeare, who, in creating the words, brings to life the characters and produces the drama. We'll examine two popular plays—one history and one tragedy—to discover the facts of how much astonishing creativity Shakespeare displayed even as he borrowed from sources.

Shakespeare's most used source was Raphael Holinshed's *Chronicles of England, Scotland, and Ireland*, published in 1577 and revised for 1587.

Over a third of Shakespeare's plays owe something to Holinshed's *Chronicles*, including all ten English history plays plus *King Lear*, *Macbeth*, and *Cymbeline*. Even though all the history plays revolve around actual events and real people, Shakespeare creates worlds nowhere near those suggested by Holinshed or the other historical chronicles Shakespeare likely consulted, such as Edward Hall's 1548 work, *The Union of the Two Noble and Illustre Families of Lancastre and Yorke*, commonly known as *Hall's Chronicle*. The playwright also freely deviates from those sources to suit his dramatic purposes. For example, in the histories, Shakespeare commonly "telescopes" time for dramatic compression; thus, the *Henry IV* plays feature battles and rebellions that historically spanned a decade but that, in the plays, occur immediately after each other. The rebel character Hotspur (Harry Percy) historically was older than was King Henry IV, but in *Henry IV, Part 1*, Shakespeare depicts him as around the same age of young Prince Hal (the future Henry V) so as to accentuate their rivalry and parallel positions as sons of powerful and demanding fathers. In *Henry V*, the new king woos and wins the French Princess Katherine immediately after his victory in the battle of Agincourt (1415), whereas according to Holinshed, their match had been proposed when they were children, and their marriage took place in 1420, five years after Agincourt. In addition to adapting and reshaping some of the main historical events outlined in the historical chronicles (such as battles and killings), Shakespeare created and amplified subplots, often creating new characters and worlds. One of Shakespeare's most beloved characters, Sir John Falstaff—who appears in three different plays—is entirely original, as is the rogue's gallery with whom Shakespeare surrounds Sir John and Prince Hal.

Though classified as a tragedy, *Hamlet* derives to some extent from a historical source: Saxo Grammaticus's twelfth-century *Historia Danica* (History of Denmark), which was translated and adapted into the French chronicle *Histoires Tragiques* by François de Belleforest in 1572. No English translation of Belleforest existed during the time of Shakespeare's composition of *Hamlet*, and we don't know that Shakespeare understood any French. Nonetheless, most editors and scholars cite *Histoires Tragiques* as a principal source for *Hamlet*. Even assuming that Shakespeare did draw from Belleforest or from Saxo—which requires speculation as to his access to an unpublished translation or to an unknown French speaking friend—his *Hamlet* vastly deepens and expands upon any possible source. Just to cite a few examples of Shakespeare's alterations and elaborations, he creates and fleshes out the characters of Polonius, Laertes, Ophelia, and Rosencrantz and Guildenstern; Horatio—a key character in Shakespeare's play—was only minimally hinted at in the sources, in the character of a "gentleman" who warns the prince about the King's duplicity. Shakespeare gives him a name and identity as Hamlet's bosom friend, with whom the prince shares wonderfully deep philosophical and theological dialogues and debates. He also creates the most profound psychological explorations in the history of literature through Hamlet's soliloquies, none of which are remotely suggested by Shakespeare's sources.

Shakespeare also significantly alters the plot of the Hamlet story. In the sources, the new king (Shakespeare's Claudius, called "Feng" in Saxo and "Fengon" in Belleforest) publicly admits to having killed his brother, father of the Hamlet ("Amleth" in the Saxo version) character. In both source versions, the Hamlet character burns down the palace, killing many. Unlike Shakespeare's character, who wrestles throughout the play with the morality of revenge, in Saxo, the prince exults in the slaughter, and in Belleforest, he at least justifies it. Most notably, in Shakespeare's and Saxo's versions, virtually everyone dies in the end, including the prince; in Belleforest's version, Hamlet survives to tell his tale to the people, who enthusiastically embrace him as their new king.

Ultimately, the notion of Shakespeare as shameless borrower and plagiarizer from sources far and wide—though not inaccurate—in no way diminishes the greatness of his achievement in creating timeless and original plays.

PRIMARY SOURCE DOCUMENT

FRANÇOIS DE BELLEFOREST, "THE HISTORY OF HAMLET," FROM *HISTOIRES TRAGIQUES* (1572)

Fengon [Hamlet's Uncle Claudius in Shakespeare's version], brother to this prince Horvendile [Hamlet Senior in Shakespeare], who [not] only fretting and despiting in his heart at the great honor and reputation won by his brother in warlike affairs but . . . provoked by a foolish jealousy, or rather desiring to be only governor, determined . . . to kill him; which he effected in such sort that no man once so much as suspected him. . . . Fengon . . . suddenly set upon him, where he slew him as traitorously, as cunningly he purged himself of so detestable a murder to his subjects; for that before he had any violent or bloody hands, or once committed parricide upon his brother, he had incestuously abused his wife. . . .

[He] covered his boldness and wicked practice . . . under a veil of mere simplicity, that . . . for the honest love that he bare to his sister-in-law, for whose sake . . . he had . . . murdered his brother, that his sin found excuse among the common people, and of the nobility was esteemed for justice; for that Geruth, being as courteous a princess as any then living in the north parts . . . this adulter and infamous murderer slandered his dead brother that he would have slain his wife, and that he, by chance finding him upon the point ready to do it, in defense of the lady had slain him. . . .

Fengon, boldened and encouraged by such impunity, durst venture to couple himself in marriage with her whom he used as his concubine during good Horvendile's life . . . and that the unfortunate and wicked woman, that had received the honor to be the wife of one of the valiantest and wiseth princes in the north, embased herself in such vile sort as to falsify her faith unto him, and, which is worse, to marry him that had been the tyrannous murderer of her lawful husband; which made divers men think that she had been the causer of the murder, thereby to live in her adultery without control.

[. . .] Prince Hamlet perceiving himself to be in danger of his life, as being abandoned of his own mother and forsaken of all men, and assuring himself that Fengon would not detract the time to send him the same way his father Horvendile was gone . . . counterfeiting the madman with such craft and subtle practices that he made show as if he had utterly lost his wits. . . . For every day being in the Queen's palace . . . he rent and tore his clothes, wallowing and lying in the dirt and mire . . . running through the streets like a man distraught, not speaking one word but such as seemed to proceed of madness and mere frenzy . . . But the young prince noted them well enough, minding one day to be revenged. . . .

Hamlet, in this sort counterfeiting the madman, many times did divers actions of great and deep consideration . . . for that standing by the fire and sharpening sticks like poniards and pricks, one . . . asked him wherefore he made those little staves so sharp at the points? "I prepare," saith he, "piercing darts and sharp arrows to revenge my father's death." Fools . . . esteemed . . . his words as nothing; but men . . . as had a deeper reach began to suspect somewhat, esteeming that under that kind of folly there lay hidden a great and rare subtlety. . . . For which cause they counseled the King to try and know . . . how to discover the intent and meaning of the young Prince . . . to entrap him . . . set some fair and beautiful woman in a secret place that, with flattering speeches and all the craftiest means she could use, should purposely seek to allure his mind to have his pleasure of her. . . .

To this end certain courtiers were appointed to lead Hamlet into a solitary place within the woods, whither they brought the woman, enciting him to take their pleasures together, and to embrace one another. . . . And surely the poor Prince . . . had been in great danger, if a gentleman that in Horvendile's time had been nourished with him had not shown himself more affectioned to the bringing up he had received with Hamlet than desirous to please the tyrant. . . . This gentleman bare the courtiers . . . company; . . . by certain signs he gave Hamlet intelligence in what danger he was like to fall. . . . The Prince in this sort having both deceived the courtiers and the lady's expectation, that affirmed and swore that he never once offered to have his pleasure of the woman . . . so that . . . Fengon's practice took no effect. . . .

Among the friends of Fengon, there was one that above all the rest doubted of Hamlet's practices in counterfeiting the madman; . . . he said he knew a fit way and a most convenient mean to . . . entrap Hamlet in his subtleties, and cause him of his own accord to fall into the net prepared for him. . . . King Fengon should make as though he were to go some long voyage concerning affairs of great importance, and that in the meantime Hamlet should be shut up alone in a chamber with his mother . . . and withal offered himself to be the man that should stand to hearken and bear witness of Hamlet's speeches with his mother. . . . This invention pleased the King . . . the counselor [Shakespeare's Polonius] entered secretly into the Queen's chamber and there hid himself behind the arras, not long before the Queen and Hamlet came thither, who . . . doubting [suspecting] some treason, and fearing if he should speak . . . to his mother touching his secret practices he should be understood and by that means intercepted . . . began to crow like a cock, beating with his arms in such manner as cocks use to strike with their wings, upon the hangings of the chamber; . . . feeling something stirring under them, he cried, "A rat, a rat," and presently drawing his sword thrust it into the hangings, which done, pulled the counselor half dead out by the heels, made an end of killing him . . . cut his body in pieces, which he caused to be boiled and then cast it into an open vault or privy, that so it might serve for food to the hogs.

[. . . H]e came again to his mother, who . . . esteeming that the gods sent her that punishment for joining incestuously in marriage with the tyrannous murderer of her husband . . . she sat tormenting herself, Hamlet . . . [said]:

"What treason is this, O most infamous woman, of all that ever prostrated themselves to the will of an abominable whoremonger, who, under the veil of a dissembling creature, covereth the most wicked and detestable crime that man could ever imagine . . . ? Now may I be assured to trust you, that . . . runs spreading forth her arms joyfully to embrace the traitorous villainous tyrant that murdered my father, and most incestuously receivest the villain into the lawful bed of your loyal spouse. . . . Is this the part of a queen and daughter to a king?"

[. . . T]he Queen overcome and vanquished with his honest passion, and weeping most bitterly

. . . at the last embracing him in her arms . . . spake unto him . . . :

"I know well, my son, that I have done thee great wrong in marrying with Fengon, the cruel tyrant and murderer of thy father and my loyal spouse. But when thou shalt consider the small means of resistance, and the treason of the palace . . . thou wouldest rather excuse than accuse me of lasciviousnes or inconstancy, much less offer me that wrong to suspect that ever thy mother Geruthe once consented to the death and murder of her husband; swearing unto thee, by the majesty of the gods, that if it had lain in my power to have resisted the tyrant, although it had been with the loss of my blood, yea, and my life, I would surely have saved the life of my lord and husband. . . . I am in hope to see an easy means invented for the revenging of thy father's death . . . beseeching the gods, my good son, that they guiding thy heart, directing thy counsels, and prospering thy enterprise, I may see thee possess and enjoy . . . the crown of Denmark by the tyrant taken from thee; . . . and therewith content myself, seeing with what courage and boldness thou shalt take vengeance upon the murderer of thy father. . . ."

"Madam," said Hamlet, "I will put my trust in you, and from henceforth mean not to meddle further with your affairs, beseeching you . . . that you will from henceforth no more esteem of the adulterer . . . whom I surely kill or cause to be put to death. . . .

[. . .] But if I lay hands upon Fengon, it will neither be felony nor treason, he being neither my king nor my lord, but I shall justly punish him as my subject, that hath disloyally behaved himself against his lord and sovereign prince. . . .

After this, Fengon, as if he had been out some long journey . . . asked for him that had received the charge to play the intelligencer to entrap Hamlet in his dissembled wisdom. . . . The Prince . . . answered and said that the counselor he sought for was gone down through the privy, where, being choked by the filthiness of the place, the hogs meeting him had filled their bellies.

[. . .] Fengon . . . determined to find the means to do it by the aid of a stranger, making the King of England minister of his massacring resolution . . . to whom he purposed to send him, and by letters desire him to put him to death.

[. . .] Now, to bear him company were assigned two of Fengon's faithful ministers, bearing letters . . . that contained Hamlet's death. . . . But the subtle Danish Prince (being at sea) whilst his companions slept . . . razed out the letters that concerned his death, and instead thereof graved others, with commission to the King of England to hang his two companions. . . . And so arriving in England the messengers presented themselves to the King, giving him Fengon's letters, who, having read the contents, said nothing as then, but stayed convenient time to affect Fengon's desire. . . .

The King . . . the next day caused the two servants of Fengon to be executed, to satisfy, as he thought, the King's desire. But Hamlet, although the sport pleased him well, and that the King of England could not have done him a greater favor, made as though he had been much offended, threatening the King to be revenged. But the King, to appease him, gave him a great sum of gold, which Hamlet caused to be molten and put into two staves, made hollow for the same purpose.

[. . .] Hamlet in that sort sailing into Denmark . . . entered into the palace of his uncle the same day that they were celebrating his funerals. . . . Their amazement at the last being turned into laughter, all that as then were assistant at the funeral banquet of him whom they esteemed dead mocked each at other for having been so simply deceived . . . and Hamlet's arrival provoked them more to drink and carouse, the Prince . . . played the butler and a gentleman attending on the tables . . . whereby he gave the noblemen such store of liquor that all of them, being full laden with wine and gorged with meat . . . lay themselves down in the same place where they had supped, so much their senses were dulled . . . which when Hamlet . . . seeing those drunken bodies filled with wine, lying like hogs upon the ground, some sleeping, others vomiting the over-great abundance of wine which without measure they had swallowed up, made the hangings about the hall to fall down and cover them all over, which he nailed to the ground, being boarded, and at the ends thereof he stuck the brands . . . by him sharpened, which served for pricks, binding and tying the hangings in such sort that, what force soever they used to loose themselves, it was unpossible to get from under them; and presently he set fire in the four corners of the hall in such sort that all that were as then therein not one escaped away but were forced to purge their sins by fire and dry up the great abundance of liquor by them received into their bodies, all of them dying in the inevitable and merciless flames of the . . . fire.

Which the Prince . . . knowing that his uncle . . . had withdrawn himself into his chamber . . . went thither and . . . laid hand upon the sword of his father's murderer . . . and . . . said: "I wonder, disloyal king, how thou canst sleep here at thine ease, and all thy palace is burnt, the fire thereof having burnt the greatest part of thy courtiers and ministers of thy cruelty and detestable tyrannies; and . . . seeing Hamlet so near thee armed with the shafts by him prepared long since, and at this present is ready to revenge the traitorous injury by thee done to his lord and father."

Fengon, as then knowing the truth of his nephew's subtle practice, and hearing him speak with staid mind, and . . . perceived a sword naked in his hand, which he already lifted up to deprive him of his life, leaped quickly out of the bed, taking hold of Hamlet's sword, that was nailed into the scabbard, which, as he sought to pull out, Hamlet gave him such a blow upon the chine of the neck that he cut his head clean from his shoulders, and as he fell to the ground said, "This . . . death is a just reward for such as thou art. Now go thy ways, and when thou comest in hell, see thou forget not to tell thy brother, whom thou traitorously slewest, that it was his son that sent thee thither with the message, to the end that being comforted thereby, his soul may rest among the blessed spirits, and quit me of the obligation that bound me to pursue his vengeance upon mine own blood. . . ."

The next morning the towns bordering thereabouts, desiring to know from whence the flames of fire proceeded the night before they had seen, came thither, and perceiving the King's palace burnt to ashes, and many bodies . . . lying among the ruins of the house, all of them were much abashed. . . . But they were much more amazed to behold the body of the King all bloody, and his head cut off lying hard by him; whereat some began to threaten revenge, yet not knowing against whom; . . . others lamenting the death of their prince, but the greatest part, calling Horvendile's murder to remembrance, acknowledging a just judgment from above that had thrown down the pride of the tyrant. . . .

[. . .] Hamlet . . . spake unto them . . . : "If there be any among you, good people of Denmark, that as yet have fresh within your memories the wrong done to the valiant King Horvendile, let him not be moved, nor think it strange to behold the confused, hideous, and fearful spectacle of this present calamity. . . . For the hand that hath done this justice could not effect it by any other means . . . thereby to preserve the memory of so just a vengeance. . . . I see well, my good friends . . . that you are sorry before your eyes to see Fengon so murdered and without a head . . . but I pray you remember this body is not the body of a king, but of an execrable tyrant and a parricide most detestable. O Danes! The spectacle was much more hideous when Horvendile your king was murdered by his brother. . . . [Y]ou . . . saw Horvendile's members massacred, his body disfigured, hurt in a thousand places, and misused in ten times as many fashions. . . . And it was one hand only that, murdering Horvendile, cruelly dispoiled him of life, and by the same means unjustly bereaved you of your ancient liberties. . . . And what madman is he that delighteth more in the tyranny of Fengon than in the clemency and renewed courtesy of Horvendile? . . . Remember . . . what love and amity Horvendile showed unto you, . . . and with what humanity and courtesy he defended and cherished you, and . . . the simplest man among you will . . . acknowledge that he had a most peaceable, just, and righteous king taken from him, to place in his throne a tyrant and murderer of his brother . . . . And should you now be sorry to see the end of your mischiefs, and that this miserable wretch . . . payeth the usury of the parricide committed upon the body of his brother. . . . [H]e sought to deprive of mine inheritance, taking from Denmark a lawful successor, to plant a wicked stranger. . . .

I have taken vengeance for the violence done unto my lord and father, and for the . . . servitude that I perceived in this country, whereof I am the just and lawful successor. . . . I alone . . . have done this piece of work, whereunto you ought to have lent me your hands . . . I have burnt the bodies of the courtiers to ashes, being companions in the . . . of the tyrant; but I have left Fengon whole, that you might punish his dead carcass . . . to accomplish the punishment and vengeance due unto him, and so satisfy your choler [anger] upon the bones of him that filled his greedy hands and coffers with your riches and shed the blood of your brethren and friends. . . . Burn his abominable body, boil his lascivious members, and cast the ashes of him that hath been hurtful to the world into the air; . . . to the end that neither silver nor crystal cup nor sacred tomb may be the restful habitation of the relics and bones of so detestable a man. . . . [Y]ou are innocent of all treason and never defiled your hands, spirits, nor desires with the blood of the great and virtuous King Horvendile. Take pity upon the Queen, sometime your sovereign lady and my right honorable mother, forced by the tyrant, and rejoice to see the . . . extinguishing of the object of her dishonor. . . .

This oration of the young prince so moved the hearts of the Danes and won the affections of the nobility that some wept for pity, others for joy, to see the wisdom and gallant spirit of Hamlet; and having made an end of their sorrow, all with one consent proclaimed him King of Jute and Chersonnese, at this present the proper country of Denmark.

Source: Israel Gollancz. *The Sources of* Hamlet: *With An Essay on the Legend* (London: Humphrey Milford, 1926). Used by permission of David Gollancz.

Further Readings

Bate, Jonathan. *Shakespeare and Ovid*. Oxford: Oxford University Press, 1994.

Bate, Jonathan. "Shakespeare's Ovid." In *Ovid's Metamorphoses: The Arthur Golding Translation of 1567*. Edited by John Frederick Nims. Philadelphia: Paul Dry Books, 2000.

Bevington, David. "*Hamlet*: Sources and Analogues." Internet Shakespeare Editions, January 11, 2019. http://internetshakespeare.uvic.ca/doc/Ham_Sources/complete/

Bullough, Geoffrey. *Narrative and Dramatic Sources of Shakespeare*. New York: Routledge, 1996.

Hosley, Richard, ed. *Shakespeare's Holinshed*. New York: Capricorn, 1968.

Jones, Emrys Maldwyn. *The Origins of Shakespeare*. Oxford: Clarendon Press, 1977.

Kewes, Paulina, ed. *Plagiarism in Early Modern England*. London: Palgrave Macmillan, 2014.

Langbaine, Gerald. *An Account of the English Dramatick Poets*. Oxford: Printed by L. L. for George West and Henry Clements, 1691. https://archive.org/details/anaccountenglis00langgoog/page/n7

Leahy, William, ed. *Shakespeare and His Authors*. London and New York: Continuum/Bloomsbury, 2010.

Martindale, Charles, and A. B. Taylor. *Shakespeare and the Classics*. Cambridge: Cambridge University Press, 2004.

Miola, Robert. *Shakespeare and Classical Comedy: The Influence of Plautus and Terence*. Oxford: Clarendon Press, 1995.

Miola, Robert. *Shakespeare and Classical Tragedy: The Influence of Seneca*. Oxford: Clarendon Press, 1992.

Monmouth, Geoffrey of. *History of the Kings of Britain*. Trans. Lewis Thorpe. Harmondsworth, England: Penguin, 1988.

Muir, Kenneth. *The Sources of Shakespeare's Plays.* Abingdon-on-Thames: Routledge, 2008.

Nameri, Dorothy E. *Three Versions of the Story of King Lear (Anonymous Ca. 1594–1605, William Shakespeare 1607–1608, Nahum Tate 1681) Studied in Relation to One Another.* Salzburg, Austria: Institut für Englische Sprache und Literatur, 1976.

Orgel, Stephen. "The Renaissance Artist as Plagiarist." *English Literary History* 48, 3 (1981): 476–95.

Phillips, Andrew, and Patrick Hunt. "Shakespeare and the Classics: Plutarch, Ovid, and Inspiration." *Electrum Magazine: Why the Past Matters,* December 21, 2010. http://www.electrummagazine.com/2010/12/shakespeare-and-the-classics-plutarch-ovid-and-other-sources/

Rackin, Phyllis. *Stages of History: Shakespeare's English Chronicles.* Ithaca, NY: Cornell University Press, 1990.

Saccio, Peter. *Shakespeare's English Kings: History, Chronicle, and Drama.* Oxford: Oxford University Press, 2000.

Seneca, Lucius A. *Anger, Mercy, Revenge (The Complete Works of Lucius Annaeus Seneca).* Trans. and ed. Robert A. Kastner and Martha C. Nussbaum. Chicago: University of Chicago Press, 2012.

Shakespeare, William. *The Tempest.* Edited by William Allan Neilson. New York: Scott, Foresman & Company, 1914.

Spencer, T. J. B. "Shakespeare and the Elizabethan Romans." *Shakespeare Survey* 10 (1957): 27–38.

Spencer, T. J. B., ed. *Shakespeare's Plutarch.* Harmondsworth, UK: Penguin, 1968.

Taylor, Marion A. *A New Look at the Old Sources of Hamlet.* The Netherlands: Mouton & Co, 1968.

7

Shakespeare Was a Solitary Genius Whose Talents Cannot Be Explained

What People Think Happened

In films, novels, and biographies throughout the years, we find images of the young man who has abandoned his family in Stratford, taken humble lodgings in London, and works alone by candlelight, dashing off his masterworks. How did this Shakespeare learn how to write such magnificent plays? History gives us no evidence that Shakespeare received formal education beyond grammar school (see chapter 4, "Shakespeare Was Poorly Educated"). Indeed, we do not even have records from the Stratford-upon-Avon grammar school where we assume William was educated—though it is extremely likely that he did attend. Thus we confront the mystery of how this apparently inexperienced and undereducated man produced dozens of plays and hundreds of poems that many believe are the greatest literary works ever written. The simplest explanation is that one can't account for genius. Whatever his experiences or lack thereof in education and life, William Shakespeare was born with the unique, solitary talent to write brilliant poems and plays considered perhaps the greatest literary works in history. And when the moment was ripe, he moved from the countryside to the big city and did just that. Sometime during the "lost years" of 1585–92, between the births of his children in Stratford-upon-Avon and the first records of his appearance in London, Shakespeare developed the experiences, desire, and abilities that would allow him to revolutionize public entertainment and forever change history through his genius. Though he didn't actually spend time at court or voyage to foreign countries, he educated himself through solitary and voracious reading and study of humanity.

Within the span of the next twenty-five years, William produced thirty-eight plays, 154 sonnets, and five long, narrative poems, and then he concluded his career with a highly autobiographical play, *The Tempest*, which constitutes his farewell to art and the theater. After putting *The Tempest* onstage in 1611, Shakespeare left London and returned to Stratford-upon-Avon, where he lived in his house called New Place and spent his remaining seven years in quiet retirement.

This natural genius Shakespeare gave us the great works still read, discussed, and performed four hundred–plus years later, and he left in the dust the other playwrights of his day, such as Christopher Marlowe, Ben Jonson, and John Fletcher. Shakespeare's death brought the end of the great English theatrical renaissance, an era often seen as the second "golden age" of Western drama—the first being the period of its invention in the Athens of the fifth century BCE and the masterworks of Sophocles, Aeschylus, and Euripides.

Shakespeare almost single-handedly created western drama, which had been abandoned for over a thousand years. At this pivotal moment in history—which paved the way for today's theater, opera, television, and film—William Shakespeare not only created the plays but acted in them, directed them, and owned a share of the theater company and the theater itself. Shakespeare learned none of these skills through education or even apprenticeship; rather, he followed the light of his own solitary muse to produce and promulgate the masterworks that will forever be enjoyed throughout the world.

How the Story Became Popular

In 1623, seven years after Shakespeare's death, John Heminge and Henry Condell, two of Will's actor-shareholder-colleagues from The King's Men theater company, compiled and published *Mr. William Shakespeare's Comedies, Histories, & Tragedies*. Commonly known throughout history as the First Folio and constituting the first collected edition of Shakespeare's plays, this volume features prefatory dedications and eulogies by several writers, including Shakespeare's fellow poet-playwright Ben Jonson. Jonson extravagantly praises his friend as possessing a singular and unfathomable genius: "Soule of the Age! The applause! delight! the wonder of our Stage / My Shakespeare, rise." Jonson compares Shakespeare's individual brilliance with other great authors of the recent English past and finds him superior to all: "I will not lodge thee by / Chaucer, or Spenser, or bid Beaumont lye / A little further, to make thee a roome." He notes that the Folio itself will guarantee Shakespeare's individual immortality: "Thou art a Moniment, without a tombe, / And art alive still, while thy Booke doth live, / And we have wits to read, and praise to give." Jonson asks forgiveness for any possible mixing of Shakespeare's reputation with those of other authors:

> That I not mixe thee so, my braine excuses;
> I meane with great, but disproportion'd Muses:
> For, if I thought my judgement were of yeeres,
> I should commit thee surely with thy peeres.

But so transcendent is Shakespeare that he should not be mixed or even compared with other writers: "And tell, how farre thou dist our Lily out-shine, / Or sporting Kid or Marlowes mighty line." Only the legendary masters of ancient Athenian tragedy should be mentioned in the same breath as Shakespeare's name: "[T]o honour thee, I would . . . call forth . . . Euripides, and Sophocles to us." In the most famous lines from Jonson's poem, he locates Shakespeare as transcending the bounds of time and place, so as to become England's most precious treasure:

> Triumph, my Britaine, thou hast one to showe,
> To whom all scenes of Europe homage owe.
> He was not of an age, but for all time !

Jonson's heartfelt and effusive eulogy expressed and advanced a phenomenon later called "bardolatry"—the near worshipful pedestal-placement of William Shakespeare as the peerless and singular author of the greatest works ever written. Implied in the bardolatrous view is the image of a solitary genius, in touch with a muse inaccessible to mere mortal playwrights who must slog through the muck in order to create their works.

Aside from the occasional doubters that William Shakespeare even *was* the author of Shakespeare's works (see chapter 1, "William Shakespeare Was Not the Author of the Works We Know as Shakespeare's"), throughout history the view of Shakespeare as solitary, untouchable genius has dominated. Not only has Shakespeare been seen as the greatest writer of all time, but because of the power and depth of his works, he has also been upheld as a visionary, a psychologist, a prophet, and, to some, practically a deity. The earliest references to the idolizing of Shakespeare occur in an anonymous play, *The Return from Parnassus*, written during the poet's lifetime. A poetry-loving character says he will obtain a picture of Shakespeare for his study and that "I'll worship sweet Mr. Shakespeare and to honour him will lay his *Venus and Adonis* under my pillow, as we read of . . . a king [who] slept with Homer under his bed's head." During Shakespeare's time, poetry was viewed as a more weighty and respectable form of authorship than was playwrighting, which would account for this play's reference not to, say, *Hamlet*, but to *Venus and Adonis*. Even though the scene pokes fun at a shallow and worshipful reverence for Shakespeare, it demonstrates that the view of Shakespeare as transcendent genius was common enough to be parodied.

Not long after Shakespeare's death, England experienced its Civil Wars (1642–51), overlapping with and followed by the eras of the Commonwealth and Protectorate (1649–60). During these decades of Puritan dominance, theater was essentially dead in England, with no public performances and no new plays produced. Upon the Restoration of the English monarchy in 1660, the theaters were reopened, and a new generation of playwrights started producing fresh works. But eager theater owners and producers also looked to the recent past for material, and the legendarily popular plays of Shakespeare immediately regained favor; however, some theater practitioners believed that although Shakespeare was a genius, he had lived in an uncivilized era and so his plays must be sanitized and refined for the more cultured Restoration age. Thus, for example, the Restoration version of *King Lear* as revised by Nahum Tate—which was to be the dominant version of that play across the world for over 150 years—removed several of the bleaker, more tragic scenes and inserted a happy ending onto arguably the most devastating of Shakespeare's tragedies. Although Shakespearean plays were popular in the Restoration era, those of other Jacobean writers such as Francis Beaumont and John Fletcher were even more so, until the great Restoration playwright and critic John Dryden took up the cause for Shakespeare's transcendence. In a 1668 essay, Dryden argued that Shakespeare was incomparable, a natural genius, and the keenest revealer of human nature.

Despite the prevalence of such bowdlerizations as Tate's sanitized version of *King Lear*, Shakespeare's worshipful status increased over the next two centuries. By the mid-eighteenth century, English writer and critic Samuel Johnson spent years compiling and editing Shakespeare's complete works, and he famously noted, "Shakespeare is above all writers, at least above all modern writers, the poet of nature; the poet that holds up to his readers a faithful mirrour of manners and of life" (Johnson 2004, par. 8). Similarly, the nineteenth-century literary critic William Hazlitt stated that "every single character in Shakespeare is as much an Individual as those in Life itself" (Hazlitt 2016, Preface).

The eighteenth century also featured tremendous numbers of live Shakespearean productions and the rise of the Shakespearean actor as public celebrity. The most famous of these figures was English actor David Garrick, who contributed much to the growth of bardolatry. Garrick starred in numerous Shakespearean plays and also (like Shakespeare) shared in the management and ownership of his theater company. Garrick proposed and organized a "Shakespeare Jubilee" to be held in Stratford-upon-Avon in 1769. The three-day event featured nearly a thousand high-society people descending on tiny Stratford for dinners, readings, pageants, and the unveiling of a new statue of Shakespeare. With choral and musical accompaniment, Garrick performed an ode he'd written, including lines such as:

> 'Tis he! 'tis he! "The god of our idolatry!" . . .
> SHAKESPEARE! SHAKESPEARE! SHAKESPEARE!

Shakespeare's worldwide popularity only grew in the nineteenth century, when the image of the solitary genius in touch with his personal muse deeply resonated with the Romantics, including German poet Johann Wolfgang von Goethe, as well as English poets Samuel Taylor Coleridge, John Keats, and Percy Shelley. In his classic 1823 essay "On the Knocking at the Gate in *Macbeth*," critic Thomas De Quincey invokes Shakespeare as a force of nature before which humans should simply submit their rational powers:

> O, mighty poet! Thy works are not as those of other men, simply and merely great works of art; but are also like the phenomena of nature, like the sun and the sea, the stars and the flowers,—like frost and snow, rain and dew, hail-storm and thunder, which are to be studied with entire submission of our own faculties. (De Quincey 2015)

The vision of Shakespeare as an unparalleled freak of nature continued apace through the Victorian era, with writers such as Thomas Carlyle upholding his works as sacred scripture:

> That King Shakespeare, does not he shine, in crowned sovereignty, over us all, as the noblest, gentlest, yet strongest of rallying signs; indestructible. . . .
> Of this Shakespeare of ours, perhaps the opinion one sometimes hears a little idolatrously expressed is, in fact, the right one; I think the best judgment not of this country only, but of Europe at large, is slowly pointing

to the conclusion, that Shakespeare is the chief of all Poets hitherto; the greatest intellect who, in our recorded world, has left record of himself in the way of Literature. On the whole, I know not such a power of vision, such a faculty of thought, if we take all the characters of it, in any other man. Such a calmness of depth; placid joyous strength; all things imaged in that great soul of his so true and clear, as in a tranquil unfathomable sea! (Carlyle 1968, 95–96)

In reaction to such effusiveness, Irish playwright George Bernard Shaw would later coin the derogatory term "bardolatry." Shaw—whose life and career bridged the nineteenth and twentieth centuries—was fascinated with Shakespeare and wrote three plays based on his works, but he also detested what he saw as overly worshipful treatment of Shakespeare by various nineteenth-century critics and fellow writers such as Carlyle and Coleridge. Shaw sought to demythologize Shakespeare, identifying him as a gifted but flawed writer; he saw Shakespeare as capable of both profundity and banality.

Through the twentieth century and into the twenty-first, some have continued to view Shakespeare as a singular wonder whose genius cannot be explained. Despite living in a more cynical, post-modern age, some critics—such as Harold Bloom—have analyzed Shakespeare's works and suggested that we have only begun to appreciate his brilliance. In his 1998 book *Shakespeare and the Invention of the Human*, Bloom argues that Shakespeare personally invented what it means to be human, that through his creation of characters so alive in their capacity for introspection— such as Hamlet and Falstaff—Shakespeare developed insights into human psychology that would not be scientifically explored (the field of psychology/psychiatry did not exist in Shakespeare's time) for almost three hundred years after Shakespeare's death. Bloom reifies the characters of Shakespeare, regarding them as "real people," and suggests:

Bardolatry, the worship of Shakespeare, ought to be even more a secular religion than it already is. The plays remain the outward limit of human achievement: aesthetically, cognitively, in certain ways morally, even spiritually. They abide beyond the end of the mind's reach; we cannot catch up to them. Shakespeare will go on explaining us, in part because he invented us. (Bloom 1999, xix–xx)

Aside from any individual critic's advocacy for or against bardolatry, the phenomenon has become so entrenched worldwide that even many having little familiarity with Shakespeare's works perceive him as a godlike figure demanding awe and reverence.

Bardolatry can be dangerous, particularly as it infests our educational systems. Along with the idea of Shakespeare's transcendent greatness often comes a sense that he is unapproachable, highbrow, and unable to be understood by mere mortals. This positioning of Shakespeare on a pedestal can engender what scholar/director Ralph Alan Cohen calls "ShakesFear" (Cohen 2018). Due to ShakesFear, many people believe that Shakespeare is so grave and deep that only high-level students and grown-ups *might* barely have a chance to understand and appreciate—let alone actually enjoy and engage with—the characters and situations. In the American educational system, Shakespeare is rarely taught until high school, which reinforces the notion of his unapproachability. We face a cyclical situation wherein we have generations of teachers who themselves were introduced to Shakespeare by a teacher who didn't particularly like Shakespeare but gritted his/her teeth to proclaim him the greatest of all writers.

The view of Shakespeare as a solitary, transcendent genius began during his lifetime and shows no signs of abating. Chapter 9 ("Shakespeare's Plays are Elite and His Old English is Incomprehensible for Contemporary Readers and Audiences") will explore in depth Shakespeare's accessibility and will provide some directions for combatting excessive bardolatry and ShakesFear.

PRIMARY SOURCE DOCUMENTS

AMERICA'S SHAKESPEARE (2016)

In 2016, the Folger Shakespeare Library in Washington, D.C., mounted an exhibition called "America's Shakespeare: Connections Between the Bard and the Founding Fathers." Some excerpts from the accompanying text appear below.

[Thomas Jefferson] "haunted the playhouses" of Williamsburg, Virginia, in the spring of 1768, most likely attending (among other plays) the Virginia Company of Comedians' production of *The Merchant of Venice*. Later in life, he went to *The Merchant of Venice* and *Macbeth* in London.

In a letter to a friend, Jefferson recommends Shakespeare for reading in the evening, explaining that "Shakespeare must be singled out by one who wishes to learn the full powers of the English language."

When a friend asked him to recommend books to buy, Jefferson encouraged him to include some works of fiction, like Shakespeare's plays, as a guide to virtue, arguing that "a lively and lasting sense of filial duty is more effectually impressed on the mind of a son or daughter by reading King Lear, than by all the dry volumes of ethics, and divinity that were ever written."

While in England in 1786, Jefferson went on a trip with John Adams that included Shakespeare's childhood home at Stratford-upon-Avon. Although Adams described this tourist site as "small and mean," Jefferson simply noted the costs of going there, including entry fees to see the birthplace and the tomb. He and Adams also followed the custom of other visitors by cutting a souvenir piece of wood from a chair where Shakespeare had supposedly sat. In 2006, Jefferson's home at Monticello exhibited this memento, along with a wry note by Jefferson: "A chip cut from an armed chair in the chimney corner in Shakespeare's house at Stratford on Avon said to be the identical chair in which he usually sat. If true like the relics of the saints it must miraculously reproduce itself."

Jefferson and Adams's diaries certainly suggest the visit was disappointing (one biographer pictures Jefferson's "teeth obviously grating" as he jotted down the fees). Many years later, however, a very different version of these events—perhaps apocryphal—was suggested by Abigail Adams. She wrote in an 1815 letter that when Thomas Jefferson first reached Stratford, he kissed the ground.

John Adams read and quoted from Shakespeare's plays throughout his life. From his earliest years as a colonial teacher and a lawyer, Adams filled his diaries with references to Shakespeare's plays—including *King Lear, Romeo and Juliet, Henry VIII, The Merry Wives of Windsor*, and *Timon of Athens*—as well as other literary references and accounts of the people he met. "Let me search for the clue which led great Shakespeare into the labyrinth of human nature," he wrote. "Let me examine how men think."

Source: Shakespeare & Beyond. "America's Shakespeare: Connections between the Bard and the Founding Fathers." June 28, 2016. Folger Shakespeare Library. Available online at https://shakespeareandbeyond.folger.edu/2016/06/28/americas-shakespeare-founding-fathers/. Used by permission.

"ODE TO SHAKESPEARE" BY DAVID GARRICK (1769)

To what blest genius of the isle,
Shall Gratitude her tribute pay,
Decree the festive day,
Erect the statue, and devote the pile?
Do not your sympathetic hearts accord,
To own the "bosom's lord"?
'Tis he! 'tis he!—that demi-god!
Who Avon's flow'ry margin trod,

While sportive *Fancy* round him flew,
Where *Nature* led him by the hand,
Instructed him in all she knew,
And gave him absolute command!
'Tis he! 'tis he!
"The god of our idolatry!"
To him the song, the Edifice we raise,
He merits all our wonder, all our praise!
Yet ere impatient joy break forth,
To tell his name, and speak his worth,
And to your spell-bound minds impart
Some faint idea of his magic art;
Let awful silence still the air!
From the dark cloud, the hidden light
Bursts tenfold bright!
Prepare! prepare! prepare!
Now swell at once the choral song,
Roll the full tide of harmony along;
Let Rapture sweep the trembling strings,
And Fame expanding all her wings,
With all her trumpet-tongues proclaim,
The lov'd, rever'd, immortal name!
SHAKESPEARE! SHAKESPEARE! SHAKESPEARE!
Let th' inchanting sound,
From Avon's shores rebound;
Thro' the Air,
Let it bear,
The precious freight the envious nations round!
Swell the choral song,
Roll the tide of harmony along,
Let Rapture sweep the strings,
Fame expand her wings,
With her trumpet-tongues proclaim,
The lov'd, rever'd, immortal name!
SHAKESPEARE! SHAKESPEARE! SHAKESPEARE!
I.
Sweetest bard that ever *sung,*
Nature's *glory,* Fancy's *child;*
Never sure did witching tongue,
Warble forth such wood-notes wild!

II.

Come each Muse, *and sister* Grace,
Loves *and* Pleasures *hither come*;
Well you know this happy place,
Avon's *banks were once your home.*

III.

Bring the laurel, bring the flow'rs,
Songs of triumph to him raise;
He united all your pow'rs,
All uniting, sing his praise!
When Nature, smiling, hail'd his birth,
To him unbounded pow'r was given;
The whirlwind's wing to sweep the sky,
"The frenzy-rowling eye,
To glance from heav'n to earth,
From earth to heav'n!"
O from his muse of fire
Could but one spark be caught,
Then might these humble strains aspire,
To tell the wonders he has wrought.
To tell,—how sitting on his magic throne,
Unaided and alone,
In dreadful state,
The subject passions round him wait;
Who tho' unchain'd, and raging there,
He checks, inflames, or turns their mad career;
With that superior skill,
Which winds the fiery steel at will,
He gives the aweful word—
And they, all foaming, trembling, own him for their Lord.
Ye guilty, lawless tribe,
Escap'd from punishment, by art or bribe,
At *Shakespeare's* bar appear!
No bribing, shuffling there—
His genius, like a rushing flood,
Cannot be withstood,

I.

Thou soft-flowing Avon, *by thy silver stream,*
Of things more than mortal, sweet Shakespeare *would dream,*
The fairies by moonlight dance round his green bed,
For hallow'd the turf is which pillow'd his head.

IV.

Flow on, silver Avon, *in song ever flow,*
Be the swans on thy bosom still whiter than snow,
Ever full be thy stream, like his fame may it spread,
And the turf ever hallow'd which pillow'd his head.
Tho' bards with envy-aching eyes,
Behold a tow'ring eagle rise,
And would his flight retard;
Yet each to *Shakespeare's* genius bows,
Each weaves a garland for his brows,
To crown th' heaven-distinguish'd Bard.
Nature had form'd him on her noblest plan,
And to the genius join'd the feeling man.
What tho' with more than mortal art,
Like *Neptune* he directs the storm,
Lets loose like winds the passions of the heart,
To wreck the human form;
Tho' from his mind rush forth, the Demons to destroy,
His heart ne'er knew but love, and gentleness, and joy.
To him the first of poets, best of men?
"We ne'er shall look upon his like again!"
Sing immortal *Shakespeare's* praise!
The song will cease, the stone decay,
But his Name,
And undiminish'd fame,
Shall never, never pass away.

Source: *The Town and Country Magazine*, September 1769. London: Printed for A. Hamilton Jr., 493–96.

What Really Happened

As the twentieth century evolved and the twenty-first unfolded, schol-ars and critics have grown generally less reverent of Shakespeare, and at least since the 1980s have sought to see Shakespeare less as a timeless and singular genius and more as a product of his time, place, and social group. The dominant schools of such recent literary scholarship and criticism bear names such as "new historicism" and "cultural materialism," pointing to their interest in exploring the historical and cultural forces that shaped and formed Shakespeare and thus his works. Contrary to the famous line from Ben Jonson's bardolatrous eulogy of Shakespeare ("He was not of an age, but for all time!"), such contemporary critics view Shakespeare as very much of his age.

Renaissance London featured a lively and complex theater scene, with concepts of authorship, ownership, and copywriting quite different than in our times. Playwrights made little to no money from the publication of their works; they had absolutely no copyright protection or owner-ship of print sales, and essentially anyone could go to a printer with a version of a play to get it published. Playwrights were paid by theater companies to produce plays, which then succeeded or failed at the box office. The reality of Shakespeare's work life stands in stark contrast to the view of him as isolated, solitary genius dashing off fully formed master-pieces; William got his hands dirty—and not just from wearing his quill pens to the nubs by candlelight. Shakespeare filled various roles, includ-ing playwright, occasional actor, and—most important from the financial perspective—shareholder in the company. In 1594, a new company called the Lord Chamberlain's Men began performing at a venue simply called the Theater—London's oldest playing space—which had stood since 1576 in the Shoreditch district. Shakespeare either was one of the eight original company shareholders or soon became one. The Lord Chamberlain's Men saw many changes, including the 1599 dismantling of the physical build-ing due to a lease battle between land owner Giles Allen and the company members; Shakespeare and friends eventually moved the Theater's materi-als to Southwark—the area south of the Thames River and free from Lon-don city regulations—to construct the Globe (popular stories of the men sliding the heavy timbers across the frozen Thames constitute romanticized fiction; the thin ice would have been far too dangerous for such a crossing, and rather the men transported the materials to a friend's warehouse until they could be ferried across in the spring). In 1603, newly crowned King James I took over patronage, and the company became the King's Men, with Shakespeare the principal playwright as well as shareholder.

Through all these twists and turns, we know that Shakespeare acted, participated in the company's debts and profits, and attended many a shareholders' meeting to hash out plans for how to keep the company solvent, particularly during the period of homelessness with the loss of their lease. The notion of Shakespeare as director is erroneous, for the company had no such position—and neither did their rival companies. Also fictitious is the image of a solitary genius who spent most of his time communing with a heavenly muse; Shakespeare kept busy with nearly all aspects of the troupe's functioning.

Obviously, history most remembers that Shakespeare composed over three dozen plays that were performed by the company, with popular and enduring success. But about his actual writing process we know little to nothing. For instance, we have no extant manuscripts in Shakespeare's hand. For nineteen of the plays, we have differing texts—sometimes as many as nine versions, including the ones in the 1623 First Folio, the collected works of Shakespeare compiled by John Heminge and Henry Condell, Shakespeare's mates and fellow shareholders; this plethora of textual versions adds to the unsolvable mystery of how and what William Shakespeare actually wrote.

Through the decades, textual scholars have analyzed myriad plays in efforts to determine which ones belong to the "canon"—that set of works that most people agree to have been authored by William Shakespeare. In recent decades, some plays have been removed and some added to the canon, with opinions often varying among scholars. And for several of the plays, evidence points to collaborative authorship, a very common Renaissance practice and one that contradicts the narrative of Shakespeare as solitary and transcendent author. The number and list of plays that we can assign as Shakespearean remains open to debate. If we begin with the First Folio—actually titled *Mr. William Shakespeare's Comedies, Histories, & Tragedies*—we have thirty-six plays. However, several of those have long been seen as bearing collaborative authorship; meanwhile, an additional three plays are often added to that list of thirty-six.

The three plays most scholars would add to the *Folio* group are *Pericles, Prince of Tyre*; *The Two Noble Kinsmen*; and *Edward III*. But each play gives us different strength of evidence of collaborative authorship. For example, people almost universally agree that *Pericles* is Shakespearean, but speculate that someone else may have had a hand, due to some passages that seem stylistically choppy and atypical of Shakespeare. By contrast, from the first publication of *The Two Noble Kinsmen* in 1634 (well after Shakespeare's death), it has been credited to Shakespeare and John Fletcher—his successor as chief playwright for the King's Men; that attribution has seen little debate or controversy. As the most tenuous candidate, *Edward III* has only recently been argued as bearing (partial) Shakespearean authorship, and a few recent editions of Shakespeare's collected plays have included it.

Even for the thirty-six plays published in the First Folio, scholars find evidence that Shakespeare worked with other authors—but without a clear picture of whom or to what degree. Early plays such as the three parts of *Henry VI* and *Titus Andronicus* contain parts that have long seemed un-Shakespearean. In 2018, *The New Oxford Shakespeare* became the first collected works to credit Christopher Marlowe as co-author of *Henry VI*, Parts 1, 2, and 3. That edition also credits various coauthors for fourteen other plays, radically increasing the proposed number of collaborative plays and number of collaborators. The editors *The New Oxford Shakespeare* boast of employing computer-aided analysis of linguistic patterns across databases of early modern plays—though such technology still involves interpretation, has led to faulty attributions, and is far from definitive.

Along with early works such as the *Henry VI* plays and *Titus Andronicus*, some of Shakespeare's late plays (for example, *Timon of Athens* and *Cymbeline*) also present issues and speculation as to collaboration. However, within the most renowned Shakespearean plays—those generally believed to be masterpieces—we find very little argument that anyone else had a hand, with the possible exception of *Macbeth*, for which playwright Thomas Middleton (who wrote a similarly themed play called *The Witch*) may have added a few songs about ten years after Shakespeare originally wrote the play.

Given people's perpetual and powerful fascination with the question of how and what Shakespeare actually wrote, ironically, the only words we *seem to have* in Shakespeare's own hand—aside from his signatures on various legal documents—come from *Sir Thomas More*, a play that scholars suggest was produced and/or revised by a team of playwrights led by Anthony Munday, with Shakespeare's possible contribution being a mere three pages of dialogue. The attribution of even that scene is based merely on some perceived similarities between the writing and that of some of the existing signatures, and again, stands as a tantalizing possibility rather than a proven fact.

Even for plays that everyone agrees are solely Shakespearean, we face the problem of not knowing what he actually wrote. Because of the lack of Renaissance copyright protection and the lack of manuscripts in Shakespeare's hand, we simply cannot know with any certainty, for example, which of the six printed versions of *Hamlet* is the "authentic" one. In fact, many modern editions of any play for which we have multiple versions will conflate parts from different available texts or will at least include notes or appendices showing the textual variations. What has been called "the dream of the master text" amounts to an impossible quest.

The image of Shakespeare as solitary genius whose sources of inspiration and composition methods are unknowable has been challenged by much speculation and some actual evidence that he collaborated with other writers to produce his works. However, for the majority of the plays considered part of the Shakespeare canon, there exists neither evidence nor grounds for questioning the sole authorship of William Shakespeare.

Ultimately, we still lack any better explanation than that Shakespeare did indeed produce these great works largely through his own unfathomable and solitary genius.

PRIMARY SOURCE DOCUMENTS

INTRODUCTION TO *MR. WILLIAM SHAKESPEARE'S COMEDIES, HISTORIES, & TRAGEDIES* ("FIRST FOLIO," 1623)

This introduction was written by Shakespeare's friends and company mates John Heminge and Henry Condell. Spelling has been largely modernized; eccentric punctuation, spacing, and capitalization have been left as written.

It had been a thing, we confess, worthy to have been wished, that the author himself had lived to have set forth, and overseen his own writings; but since it hath been ordained otherwise, and he by death departed from that right, we pray you do not envy his Friends, the office of their care, and pain, to have collected & published them; and so to have published them, as where (before) you were abused with diverse stolen, and surreptitious copies, maimed, and deformed by the frauds and stealths of injurious impostors, that exposed them: even those, are now offered to your view cured, and perfect of their limbs; and all the rest, absolute in their numbers as he conceived them.

Who, as he was a happy imitator of Nature, was a most gentle expresser of it. His mind and hand went together: And what he thought, he uttered with that easiness, that we have scarce received from him a blot in his papers. But it is not our province, who only gather his works, and give them you, to praise him. It is yours that read him. And there we hope, to your diverse capacities, you will find enough, both to draw, and hold you: for his wit can no more lie hidden, than it could be lost. Read him, therefore; and again, and again: And if then you do not like him, surely you are in some manifest danger, not to understand him. And so we leave you to other of his Friends, whom if you need, can be your guides: if you need them not, you can lead yourselves, and others, and such readers we wish him.

John Heminge.

Henrie Condell

Source: *Mr. William Shakespeares Comedies, Histories, & Tragedies,* Published according to the True Originall Copies (London: Printed by Isaac Jaggard and Ed. Blount, 1623).

BEN JONSON'S EULOGY TO SHAKESPEARE, FROM THE FIRST FOLIO: "TO THE MEMORY OF MY BELOVED, THE AUTHOR, MR. WILLIAM SHAKESPEARE."

For the eulogy to accompany the publication of the First Folio, Heminge and Condell called upon one of the leading playwrights of the era: Ben Jonson. We know that Shakespeare acted in at least two of Jonson's plays—Sejanus and Every Man in His Humor, and the two most significant playwrights of the early Jacobean era were friends and rivals. Jonson's eulogy gives us oft-quoted lines that demonstrate both Jonson's tendency to satirize and his ability to give high praise for an artist whose greatness he exalted. First, he gives the backhanded compliment/dig at Shakespeare's lack of education compared with Jonson's own—"though thou hadst small Latin, and less Greek . . ."—then goes on to bardolatrously declare: "Triumph, my Britain, thou hast one to show, / To whom all scenes of Europe homage owe. / He was not of an age, but for all time!" Spelling has been modernized and the text abridged, with occasional notes in brackets.

To draw no envy (Shakespeare) on thy name,
Am I thus ample to thy Book, and Fame;
While I confess thy writings to be such,
As neither Man, nor Muse, can praise too much.
'Tis true, and all men's suffrage. But these ways
Were not the paths I meant unto thy praise;
For seeliest [silliest] Ignorance on these may light,
Which, when it sounds at best, but echoes right;
Or blind Affection, which doth never advance
The truth, but gropes, and urges all by chance;
Or crafty Malice, might pretend this praise,
And thine to ruin, where it seemed to raise.
These are, as some infamous Baud, or Whore,
Should praise a Matron. What could hurt her more?
But thou art proof against them, and indeed
Above the ill fortune of them, or the need.
I, therefore will begin. Soul of the Age!
The applause ! delight ! the wonder of our Stage !
My Shakespeare, rise; I will not lodge thee by
Chaucer, or Spenser, or bid Beaumont lie
A little further, to make thee a room:
Thou art a Monument, without a tomb,

And art alive still, while thy Book doth live,
And we have wits to read, and praise to give.
That I not mix thee so, my brain excuses;
I mean with great, but disproportioned Muses:
For, if I thought my judgement were of years,
I should commit thee surely with thy peers,
And tell, how far thou did our Lily out-shine,
Or sporting Kid or Marlowe's mighty line.
And though thou hadst small Latin, and less Greek,
From thence to honour thee, I would not seek
For names; but call forth . . .
Euripides, and Sophocles to us
[. . .]
And shake a stage : Or, when thy socks were on,
Leave thee alone, for the comparison
Of all, that insolent Greece, or haughty Rome
Sent forth, or since did from their ashes come.
Triumph, my Britain, thou hast one to show,
To whom all scenes of Europe homage owe.
He was not of an age, but for all time!
And all the Muses still were in their prime,
When like Apollo he came forth to warm
Our ears, or like a Mercury to charm!
Nature herself was proud of his designs,
And joyed to wear the dressing of his lines!
Which were so richly spun, and woven so fit,
As, since, she will vouchsafe no other Wit.
The merry Greek, tart Aristophanes,
Neat Terence, witty Plautus, now not
please; But antiquated, and deserted lie
As they were not of Nature's family.
Yet must I not give Nature all: Thy Art,
My gentle Shakespeare, must enjoy a part;
For though the Poets matter, Nature be,
His Art doth give the fashion. And, that he,
Who casts to write a living line, must sweat,
(Such as thine are) and strike the second heat
Upon the Muse's anvil : turn the same,
(And himself with it) that he thinks to frame;
Or for the laurel, he may gain a scorn,

For a good Poet's made, as well as borne.
And such wert thou. Look how the father's face
Lives in his issue, even so, the race
Of Shakespeare's mind, and manners brightly shines
In his well toned, and true-filed lines:
In each of which, he seems to shake a Lance,
As brandished at the eyes of Ignorance.
Sweet swan of Avon! what a fight it were
To see thee in our waters yet appear,
And make those flights upon the banks of Thames,
That so did take Eliza, and our James!
But stay, I see thee in the Hemisphere
Advanced, and made a Constellation there!
Shine forth, thou Star of Poets, and with rage,
Or influence, chide, or cheer the drooping Stage;
Which, since thy flight from here, hath mourned like night,
And despairs day, but for thy Volumes light.
BEN JONSON

Source: Mr. William Shakespeares Comedies, Histories, & Tragedies, Published according to the True Originall Copies (London: Printed by Isaac Jaggard and Ed. Blount, 1623).

SPEECH FROM *SIR THOMAS MORE* (CA. 1592)

"Hand D" is hypothesized as the only surviving text we have from the hand of William Shakespeare, based on purported stylistic similarities, nonconclusive handwriting analysis, and perhaps wishful thinking. The lines are spoken by the title character.

You'll put down strangers,
Kill them, cut their throats, possess their houses,
And lead the majesty of law in lyam [leash]
To slip him like a hound; alas, alas, say now the King,
As he is clement if th'offender mourn,
Should so much come too short of your great trespass
As but to banish you: whither would you go?
What country, by the nature of your error,
Should give you harbour? Go you to France or Flanders,
To any German province, Spain or Portugal,

Nay, anywhere that not adheres to England,
Why, you must needs be strangers, would you be pleased
To find a nation of such barbarous temper
That breaking out in hideous violence
Would not afford you an abode on earth.
Whet their detested knives against your throats,
Spurn you like dogs, and like as if that God
Owed not nor made not you, not that the elements
Were not all appropriate to your comforts,
But chartered unto them? What would you think
To be used thus? This is the strangers' case
And this your mountainish inhumanity.

Source: British Library, Harley MS 7368. *The Booke of Sir Thomas Moore*. Available online at https://www.bl.uk/collection-items/shakespeares-handwriting-in-the-book -of-sir-thomas-more

Further Readings

Bate, Jonathan. *The Genius of Shakespeare*. London: Picador, 1997.

Bloom, Harold. *Shakespeare: The Invention of the Human*. New York: Riverhead, 1999.

Carlyle, Thomas. *Carlyle on Heroes, Hero-Worship, and the Heroic in History*. London: Oxford University Press, 1968.

Clare, Janet. *Shakespeare's Stage Traffic: Imitation, Borrowing and Competition in Renaissance Theatre*. Cambridge: Cambridge University Press, 2014.

Clark, Cumberland. *The Eternal Shakespeare*. London: Williams & Norgate, 1930.

Cohen, Ralph Alan. *ShakesFear and How to Cure It: The Complete Handbook for Teaching Shakespeare*. London: Arden Shakespeare/Bloomsbury Publishing, 2018.

De Quincey, Thomas. "On the Knocking at the Gate, in *Macbeth*." First published in *Blackwood's Magazine*, 1823. Ebook: The University of Adelaide, 2015. https://ebooks.adelaide.edu.au/d/de_quincey/thomas /on-the-knocking-at-the-gate-in-macbeth/

Dobson, Michael. *The Making of the National Poet: Shakespeare, Adaptation and Authorship, 1660–1769*. Oxford: Clarendon Press, 1992.

Hazlitt, William. *Characters of Shakespeare's Plays (1817)*. Ebook: The University of Adelaide, 2016. https://ebooks.adelaide.edu.au/h/hazlitt /william/characters-of-shakespeares-plays/index.html

Holbrook, Peter. *Shakespeare's Individualism*. Cambridge: Cambridge University Press, 2010.

Hope, Jonathan. *The Authorship of Shakespeare's Plays: A Socio-Linguistic Study*. Cambridge: Cambridge University Press, 1994.

Johnson, Samuel. *The Preface to Shakespeare. From his annotated edition of Shakespeare's Plays, published in 1765*. Ebook: University of Adelaide Library, 2004. https://ebooks.adelaide.edu.au/j/johnson/samuel/preface/

Kinney, Arthur F., ed. *The Oxford Handbook of Shakespeare*. Oxford: Oxford University Press, 2012.

Laporte, Charles. "The Devotional Texts of Victorian Bardolatry." In *Shakespeare, the Bible, and the History of the Material Book: Contested Scriptures*. Edited by Travis DeCook and Alan Galey. Abingdon-on-Thames: Routledge, 2012: 143–59.

Levin, H. "The Primacy of Shakespeare." *Shakespeare Quarterly* 26, 2 (1975): 99–112.

Marino, James J. *Owning William Shakespeare: The King's Men and Their Intellectual Property*. Philadelphia: University of Pennsylvania Press, 2011.

Masten, Jeffrey. "Playwrighting: Authorship and Collaboration." In *A New History of Early English Drama*. Edited by John D. Cox and David Scott Kastan. New York: Columbia University Press, 1997: 357–82.

Pollack-Pelzner, Daniel. "The Radical Argument of the New Oxford Shakespeare." *The New Yorker*, February 19, 2017. https://www.newyorker.com/books/page-turner/the-radical-argument-of-the-new-oxford-shakespeare

Vickers, Brian. *Shakespeare, Co-Author: A Historical Study of Five Collaborative Plays*. Oxford: Oxford University Press, 2002.

Wells, Stanley. *Shakespeare: For All Time*. Oxford: Oxford University Press, 2003.

8

Shakespeare, His Colleagues, and His Audiences Saw Tragedies as More Important Than Comedies

What People Think Happened

People who know little about Shakespeare's plays—or about theater in general—nonetheless likely recognize the masks signifying the two main theatrical genres: comedy and tragedy. If asked to name a Shakespearean play, no doubt most people would think first of *Hamlet*, *Romeo and Juliet*, and/or *Macbeth*. Though we have no solid data with which to measure, in American high schools those same plays clearly top the list of most commonly taught Shakespeare plays. The Folger Shakespeare Library Editions are the most popular Shakespeare texts used in American high school classrooms. Among those, in 2014 and 2015, *Romeo and Juliet* was the top seller, followed by *Hamlet*, *Macbeth*, *A Midsummer Night's Dream*, *Othello*, and *Julius Caesar* (five out of the six being tragedies). Typically students are introduced to Shakespeare in ninth grade with *The Tragedy of Romeo and Juliet*; beyond that, they are most likely to encounter *The Tragedy of Julius Caesar*; *The Tragedy of Hamlet, Prince of Denmark*; and/or *The Tragedy of Macbeth*.

Ask people around the world to share any memories or images they have of Shakespeare's plays, and most likely one will get "Romeo, oh Romeo, wherefore art thou Romeo" (often with a comma/pause added after "thou," following the erroneous belief that "wherefore" means "where" rather than "why"). Or people may recall something about a man (Hamlet) holding a skull, or some chanting witches from *Macbeth*. Tragedies dominate people's perception‾ and reception of Shakespeare; they have always been viewed as Shakespeare's most significant plays, with comedies following as amusing but less important cousins.

The original Renaissance English audiences for Shakespeare's plays loved to see the rises and especially the tragic falls of great characters whose lives and deaths provided the viewers with welcome distraction from their own difficult lives. In an era in which outbreaks of the Black Death (bubonic plague) regularly claimed the lives of thousands of people per year, month, or even week in London, seeing kings and queens and generals brought down from their lofty positions must have provided some small consolation for the common people. Shakespeare's tragedies succeeded and still succeed because they reflect the power of the genre pioneered by the ancient Athenians in the fifth century BCE and as Aristotle outlined in *The Poetics*.

Following in the footsteps of the ancient Greek tragedians (Aeschylus, Sophocles, and Euripides), Shakespeare's tragedies allowed his early audiences to experience what Aristotle described as the *catharsis* (purgation) through the emotions of pity and fear as they witnessed the myriad betrayals, bloodshed, and horrors that characterize plays such as *Hamlet*, *King Lear*, and *Macbeth*. Audiences have always loved seeing such things befall people outside their own worlds. Then as now, a play's success or failure depended on box office, and Renaissance English audiences flocked to see comedies and histories—but most of all tragedies. The tragedies that today stand as Shakespeare's best known and most popular plays have succeeded over the centuries because they were hits when first produced, and their preeminence has not diminished over the ages.

How the Story Became Popular

Of the ninety-two winners of the Academy Award for Best Picture, only seven to ten (depending on classification) have been comedies. Out of seventy winners, the Tony Award for Best Play has gone ten times to a comedy (again, depending on classification). Such disproportionate numbers perhaps demonstrate that—whether in theater or its offspring, film—people have long valued tragedies as more significant and important than comedies. This tendency to view tragic stories as more valuable than comic ones can be traced to ancient Athenian theater. Although the Athenians of the fifth century BCE held competitions for comedic as well as tragic plays—and although both genres evidently were popular, through the vicissitudes of history, we know more about the tragedies than we do the comedies. Unfortunately, most plays of both genres are lost; we have records of the existence of hundreds of plays but not the plays themselves. However, we have complete texts (many plays in both genres exist only in fragments) of about thirty-two tragedies by the three great known Greek masters: Aeschylus, Sophocles, and Euripides. For complete comedies, we have only the eleven plays of Aristophanes. Similarly, while we have the volume of Aristotle's *Poetics*—the first work of literary criticism, and highly influential throughout history—devoted to tragedy, we know that he also wrote an entire volume on comedy, but that work is lost. Thus, although we don't know for certain that the ancient Athenians valued tragic over comedic plays, the accidents of history give us much material that seems to reinforce the preeminence of tragedies. The effect throughout the centuries is such that the phrase "Greek tragedy" commonly evokes a sense of tremendous loss and sorrow, whereas "Greek comedy" would likely register little to nothing for most people.

Fast-forward some two thousand years to Renaissance England, when Shakespeare and a small group of playwrights reinvented Western drama, which essentially had been lost and forgotten in those intervening centuries. In their search for models, Shakespeare and his colleagues found some inspiration from late medieval drama—morality plays and mystery cycle dramas. However, those works were religious through and through, and in their desire to write secular plays, the authors looked further back to the plays of classical Greece and Rome—primarily the latter, given that none of the Greek plays had been translated into English as had the Roman ones. From the second century BCE into the first century CE, Roman authors mined much of the same material as had the Athenian dramatists before them; Roman playwrights created their own variations of the Greek legends and tales. The Roman plays to which Shakespeare and colleagues had access no doubt swayed them toward the preeminence of tragedy, as easily the most significant Roman dramatic figure for the writers of the English Renaissance was the tragedian Lucius Annaeus Seneca (4 BCE–65 CE), known as Seneca the Younger or simply Seneca.

Beginning in the 1550s, scholar-writers such as Jasper Heywood and Thomas Newton had begun translating Seneca's works, culminating in Newton's 1581 publication of Seneca's *Ten Tragedies*, which was enormously influential on Shakespeare and all other English Renaissance tragedians. In plays such as *Thyestes*, Seneca gave these writers wonderfully gory and entertaining tragedies, particularly in what would become the most popular subgenre for the London playwrights: the revenge tragedy. Scholars today often use the term "Senecan" to describe works such as Thomas Kyd's hugely influential *The Spanish Tragedy*, as well as Shakespearean tragedies such as *Hamlet*, *Macbeth*, and especially the early and wildly Senecan work *Titus Andronicus*—which features a plot similar to that of *Thyestes*, including a climactic banquet scene in which one of a pair of feuding brothers feeds the other his butchered children before revealing their heads on a platter and informing him what he has just consumed.

By the time Shakespeare wrote *Hamlet* around 1600–01, he and other playwrights had produced many plays reflecting the influence of the Greco-Roman revenge tragedy tradition. Along with Christopher Marlowe, the innovative Shakespeare even transposed characteristics of the revenge tragedy onto a new, specifically English genre: the history play. Shakespeare wrote at least ten plays dealing with English history, a genre closely entwined with tragedy, dealing as it always did with the bloody rises and falls of monarchs. For example, *Richard III*, written early in Shakespeare's career, contains many elements of Senecan revenge tragedy; though it is/was classified as a history play, the printed title of the first printed version (1597) is *The Tragedy of Richard III*. The play contains vast bloodshed, betrayal, injustice, corruption, ghostly visitations, curses, and long speeches of rhetorical flourish—all inheritances of Seneca.

The subjects and plots of tragedies—and histories, which one could argue are a permutation of tragedy—held great appeal for Shakespeare and for his audiences. Then as now, people loved watching the rises and falls of larger-than-life figures of wealth and power (such as Richard III, King Lear, Julius Caesar, Marc Antony, and Cleopatra) as well as the trials and tribulations of great characters of less high estate (such as Romeo, Juliet, Othello, and Desdemona). The special popularity of Shakespeare's tragedies continued after his death in 1616. As we can infer from the statistics regarding Tony and Oscar award winners, the perception of tragedies as the preeminent artistic form—which perhaps began with accidents of ancient Athenian history and continues through today—is deeply ingrained in many people and cultures.

PRIMARY SOURCE DOCUMENT

ARISTOTLE, *POETICS* (~335 BCE)

Aristotle's Poetics *is the earliest surviving work of literary and dramatic criticism. Though his fuller treatment of the genre of comedy is lost, nonetheless in the "Preliminary Discourse," or Introduction, the philosopher discusses the three genres of comedy, tragedy, and epic poetry. He notes that comedy "was not at first treated seriously" as an art form. Though Aristotle does not directly proclaim tragedy as superior to comedy, he does rank it as potentially greater than epic poetry, to which it is closely related.*

Comedy is . . . an imitation of characters of a lower type—not, however, in the full sense of the word bad, the ludicrous being merely a subdivision of the ugly. It consists in some defect or ugliness which is not painful or destructive. To take an obvious example, the comic mask is ugly and distorted, but does not imply pain.

The successive changes through which Tragedy passed, and the authors of these changes, are well known, whereas Comedy has had no history, because it was not at first treated seriously. . . . Comedy had already taken definite shape when comic poets, distinctively so called, are heard of. Who furnished it with masks, or prologues, or increased the number of actors—these and other similar details remain unknown.

[. . .] Tragedy endeavors, as far as possible, to confine itself to a single revolution of the sun, or but slightly to exceed this limit, whereas the Epic action has no limits of time. . . . All the elements of an Epic poem are found in Tragedy, but the elements of a Tragedy are not all found in the Epic poem.

[. . .] Tragedy, then, is an imitation of an action that is serious, complete, and of a certain magnitude; in language embellished with each kind of artistic ornament, the several kinds being found in separate parts of the play; in the form of action, not of narrative; through pity and fear effecting the proper purgation of these emotions. By "language embellished," I mean language into which rhythm, "harmony" and song enter. By "the several kinds in separate parts," I mean that some parts are rendered through the medium of verse alone, others again with the aid of song.

[. . .] Tragedy is the imitation of an action; and an action implies personal agents, who necessarily possess certain distinctive qualities both of character and thought; for it is by these that we qualify actions themselves, and these—thought and character—are the two natural causes from which actions spring, and on actions again all success or failure depends. Hence, the Plot is the imitation of the action—for by Plot I here mean the arrangement of the incidents.

[. . .] Every Tragedy . . . must have six parts . . . namely, Plot, Character, Diction, Thought, Spectacle, Song.

[. . .] But most important of all is the structure of the incidents. For Tragedy is an imitation, not of men, but of an action and of life, and life consists in action, and its end is a mode of action, not a quality. Now character determines men's qualities, but it is by their actions that they are happy or the reverse. Dramatic action, therefore, is not with a view to the representation of character: character comes in as subsidiary to the actions. Hence the incidents and the plot are the end of a tragedy. . . . [W]ithout action there cannot be a tragedy; there may be without character. The tragedies of most of our modern poets fail in the rendering of character. . . . [I]f you string together a set of speeches expressive of character, and well finished in point of diction and thought, you will not produce the essential tragic effect nearly so well as with a play which, however deficient in these respects, yet has a plot and artistically constructed incidents. [T]he most powerful elements of emotional interest in Tragedy—Peripeteia or Reversal of the Situation, and Recognition scenes—are parts of the Plot. . . .

The Plot, then, is the first principle, and . . . the soul of a tragedy; Character holds the second place. . . . Third in order is Thought—that is, the faculty of saying what is possible and pertinent in given circumstances. . . . Character is that which reveals moral purpose, showing what kind of things a man chooses or avoids. Speeches . . . in which the speaker does not choose or avoid anything whatever, are not expressive of character. . . .

Fourth among the elements enumerated comes Diction; by which I mean . . . the expression of the meaning in words. . . . Song holds the chief place among the embellishments. The Spectacle has . . . an emotional attraction of its own, but, of all the parts, it is the least artistic, and connected least with the art of poetry. . . . [T]he production of spectacular effects depends more on the art of the stage machinist than on that of the poet.

[. . . L]et us now discuss the proper structure of the Plot, since this is the first and most important thing in Tragedy. . . . Tragedy is an imitation of an action that is complete, and whole, and of a certain magnitude. . . . A whole is that which has a beginning, a middle, and an end. A beginning is that which does not itself follow anything by causal necessity, but after which something naturally is or comes to be. An end . . . is that which itself naturally follows some other thing, either by necessity, or as a rule, but has nothing following it. A middle is that which follows something as some other thing follows it. A well constructed plot, therefore, must neither begin nor end at haphazard, but conform to these principles.

[. . . A] beautiful object, whether it be a living organism or any whole composed of parts, must not only have an orderly arrangement of parts, but must also be of a certain magnitude; for beauty depends on magnitude and order. Hence a very small animal organism cannot be beautiful; for the view of it is confused, the object being seen in an almost imperceptible moment of time. Nor, again, can one of vast size be beautiful; for as the eye cannot take it all in at once, the unity and sense of the whole is lost for the spectator. . . . As, therefore, in the case of animate bodies and organisms a certain magnitude is necessary . . . so in the plot, a certain length is necessary, and a length which can be easily embraced by the memory. . . . [W]e may say that the proper magnitude is comprised within such limits, that the sequence of events, according to the law of probability or necessity, will admit of a change from bad fortune to good, or from good fortune to bad.

[. . .] The poet and the historian differ not by writing in verse or in prose. . . . The true difference is that one relates what has happened, the other what may happen. Poetry, therefore, is a more philosophical and a higher thing than history: for poetry tends to express the universal, history the particular. . . . In Comedy this is already apparent: for here the poet first constructs the plot on the lines of probability, and then inserts characteristic names. . . . But tragedians still keep to real names, the reason being that what is possible is credible: what has not happened we do not at once feel sure to be possible; but what has happened is manifestly possible. . . . Still there are even some tragedies in which there are only one or two well-known names, the rest being fictitious . . . and yet they give none the less pleasure. We must not, therefore, at all costs keep to the received legends, which are the usual subjects of Tragedy. . . . [T]he poet or "maker" should be the maker of plots rather than of verses; since he is a poet because he imitates, and what he imitates are actions. And even if he chances to take a historical subject, he is none the less a poet. . . .

[. . .] Tragedy is an imitation not only of a complete action, but of events inspiring fear or pity. Such an effect is best produced when the events come on us by surprise; and the effect is heightened when, at the same time, they follow as cause and effect. The tragic wonder will then be greater than if they happened of themselves or by accident; for even coincidences are most striking when they have an air of design. We may instance the statue of Mitys at Argos, which fell upon his murderer while he was a spectator at a festival, and killed him.

[. . .] Plots are either Simple or Complex. . . . An action which is one and continuous . . . , I call Simple, when the change of fortune takes place without Reversal of the Situation and without Recognition.

A Complex action is one in which the change is accompanied by such Reversal, or by Recognition, or by both. These last should arise from the internal structure of the plot, so that what follows should be the necessary or probable result of the preceding action.

Reversal of the Situation is a change by which the action veers round to its opposite. . . . Thus in the *Oedipus*, the messenger comes to cheer Oedipus and free him from his alarms about his mother, but by revealing who he is, he produces the opposite effect. . . .

Recognition, as the name indicates, is a change from ignorance to knowledge, producing love or hate between the persons destined by the poet for good or bad fortune. The best form of recognition is coincident with a Reversal of the Situation, as in the *Oedipus*. . . . This recognition, combined with Reversal, will produce either pity or fear. . . . Thus Iphigenia is revealed to Orestes by the sending of the letter; but another act of recognition is required to make Orestes known to Iphigenia.

Two parts, then, of the Plot—Reversal of the Situation and Recognition—turn upon surprises. A third part is the Scene of Suffering. The Scene of Suffering is a destructive or painful action, such as death on the stage, bodily agony, wounds, and the like.

[. . .] A perfect tragedy should . . . be arranged not on the simple but on the complex plan. It should, moreover, imitate actions which excite pity and fear, this being the distinctive mark of tragic imitation. It follows . . . that the change of fortune presented must not be the spectacle of a virtuous man brought from prosperity to adversity: for this moves neither pity nor fear; it merely shocks us. Nor, again, that of a bad man passing from adversity to prosperity: for nothing can be more alien to the spirit of Tragedy. . . . Nor, again, should the downfall of the utter villain be exhibited. A plot of this kind would, doubtless, satisfy the moral sense, but it would inspire neither pity nor fear; for pity is aroused by unmerited misfortune, fear by the misfortune of a man like ourselves. Such an event, therefore, will be neither pitiful nor terrible. There remains, then, the character between these two extremes—that of a man who is not eminently good and just, yet whose misfortune is brought about not by vice or depravity, but by some error or frailty. He must be one who is highly renowned and prosperous—a personage like Oedipus, Thyestes, or other illustrious men of such families.

A well-constructed plot should . . . be single in its issue, rather than double as some maintain. . . . At first the poets recounted any legend that came in their way. Now, the best tragedies are founded on the story of a few houses—on the fortunes of . . . Oedipus, Orestes . . . Thyestes . . . and those others who have done or suffered something terrible. . . .

In the second rank comes the kind of tragedy which some place first. Like the *Odyssey*, it has a double thread of plot, and also an opposite catastrophe [outcome] for the good and for the bad. It is accounted the best because of the weakness of the spectators; for the poet is guided in what he writes by the wishes of his audience. The pleasure, however, thence derived is not the true tragic pleasure. It is proper rather to Comedy, where those who . . . are the deadliest enemies—like Orestes and Aegisthus—quit the stage as friends at the close, and no one slays or is slain.

Fear and pity may be aroused by spectacular means; but they may also result from the inner structure of the piece, which is the better way, and indicates a superior poet. For the plot ought to be so constructed that, even without the aid of the eye, he who hears the tale told will thrill with horror and melt to pity at what takes place. This is the impression we should receive from hearing the story of the Oedipus. But to produce this effect by the mere spectacle is a less artistic method, and dependent on extraneous aids. Those who employ spectacular means to create a sense not of the terrible but only of the monstrous, are strangers to the purpose of Tragedy. . . .

Let us then determine what are the circumstances which strike us as terrible or pitiful. . . . If an enemy kills an enemy, there is nothing to excite pity either in the act or the intention—except so far as the suffering in itself is pitiful. . . . But when the tragic incident occurs between those who are near or dear to one another—if, for example, a brother kills, or intends to kill, a brother, a son his father, a mother her son, a son his mother . . . these are the situations to be looked for by the poet. He may not . . . destroy the framework of the received legends—the fact, for instance, that Clytemnestra was slain by Orestes—but he ought to . . . skillfully handle the traditional material. . . . It is thus too that Euripides makes Medea slay her children. Or . . . the deed of horror may be done, but done in ignorance, and the tie of kinship or friendship be discovered afterwards. The *Oedipus* of Sophocles is an example. . . . This, then, is why a few families only . . . furnish the subjects of tragedy. It was not art, but happy chance, that led the poets in search of subjects to impress the tragic quality upon their plots.

[. . .] In respect of Character there are four things to be aimed at. First, and most important, it must be good. Now any speech or action that manifests moral purpose of any kind will be expressive of character: the character will be good if the purpose is good. . . . Even a woman may be good, and also a slave; though the woman may be said to be an inferior being, and the slave quite worthless. The second thing to aim at is propriety. There is a type of manly valor; but valor in a woman, or unscrupulous cleverness is inappropriate. Thirdly, character must be true to life: for this is a distinct thing from goodness and propriety, as here described. The fourth point is consistency . . . [a]s an example of motiveless degradation of character, we have Menelaus in the *Orestes*; of inconsistency, the *Iphigenia at Aulis*—for Iphigenia the suppliant in no way resembles her later self.

[. . . T]he unraveling of the plot . . . must arise out of the plot itself, it must not be brought about by the Deus ex Machina [literally, "god from a machine"—a device Aristotle criticizes as a cheap and unartistic way for a writer to end a play by having a god come down to resolve the situation]— as in the *Medea*. . . . Deus ex Machina should be employed only for events external to the drama—for antecedent or subsequent events, which lie beyond the range of human knowledge . . . for to the gods we ascribe the power of seeing all things.

[. . . S]ince Tragedy is an imitation of persons who are above the common level, the example of good portrait painters should be followed. They, while reproducing the distinctive form of the original, make a likeness which is true to life and yet more beautiful. So too the poet, in representing men who are irascible or indolent, or have other defects of character, should preserve the type and yet ennoble it.

Source: Aristotle. *Poetics*. Translated by S. H. Butcher (London: Macmillan and Co., 1895).

What Really Happened

A well-known epigram, variously attributed to seventeenth-century French writers Jean Racine and Jean de La Bruyère, and eighteenth-century English author Horace Walpole, goes something like: "Life is a comedy to those who think, a tragedy to those who feel." And generic classification of plays is also tricky and often subjective. As per the divisions set out in the (1623) First Folio, William Shakespeare wrote in three genres: comedies, histories, and tragedies. However, we immediately face some classifications that seem arbitrary and potentially confusing; for example, Shakespeare's works dealing with English kings are all classified as histories despite some being originally titled, for example, *The Tragedy of Richard III*. Meanwhile the plays dealing with Roman rulers—such as *Julius Caesar*—all fall under the heading of tragedy, despite their plots deriving from Roman historical sources such as Plutarch's *Parallel Lives of the Noble Grecians and Romans*, which had recently been translated and published in English by Thomas North (1579). The First Folio listed fourteen comedies, ten histories, and twelve tragedies. Since its first publication, people have argued over some of those classifications. For example, *The Winter's Tale*—now listed among the "late romances" (a category added in the twentieth century, often seen as a subgenre of comedy)—was listed with the First Folio comedies, and *Cymbeline*—generally considered another late romance—originally came under the tragedies. Depending on whom you ask, the overall list of Shakespearean plays has also expanded to include the two late romances *Pericles* and *The Two Noble Kinsmen*—on the latter of which Shakespeare collaborated with John Fletcher. More recently, some scholars and editors have concluded that Shakespeare had enough of a hand in the history play *Edward III* to attribute authorship (for discussion of collaborative authorship, see chapter 7, "Shakespeare Was a Solitary Genius Whose Talents Cannot be Explained"). Perhaps the most perplexing play to classify is *Troilus and Cressida*, which is included in the First Folio but not listed on the Contents page. So immediately we lack clarity as to whether and where the editors (Shakespeare's friends and fellow company members John Heminge and Henry Condell) thought it belonged; in fact, in the printing, it falls in between the histories and tragedies. Throughout the years, *Troilus and Cressida* has been classified as a romance, a comedy, or a tragedy. This and a few other plays that tend most to challenge generic classification are sometimes called "problem plays." Just as we find with contemporary films and plays, often Shakespeare crossed and defied genres—to the point where scholars and critics still debate whether certain plays should be classified as comedy or tragedy, described with other terms such as tragicomedy, or simply listed as problem plays. Even within plays of clear generic pedigree, Shakespeare always blended comedic parts into the tragedies and included darker tones in the comedies.

This difficulty of labeling plays and the blurring of genres calls up the question of definitions: What makes a Shakespearean play—or any play—a comedy or a tragedy? The word "comedy" might suggest that the defining feature of the genre is humor. However, the more accurate distinction between a comedy and a tragedy lies in the nature of the outcome. As most people will recall from basic literary study, every story contains a problem or conflict. If through the course of the narrative, that dramatic conflict/problem is successfully resolved, one has a happy ending. That harmonious resolution defines the story—for our purposes, the play—as a comedy.

In a Shakespearean comedy, the problems to be solved revolve primarily around one subject: love. A comedy begins with people wanting love and finding obstacles to the fruition of that desire. For example, in

A Midsummer Night's Dream, Hermia loves Lysander, and her best friend Helena loves Demetrius. The play quickly presents several impediments to those matches. For starters, Hermia's father Egeus forbids her from marrying her beloved Lysander and in fact demands that she marry Demetrius . . . or be put to death according to Athenian law. *Midsummer's* myriad confusions and complications involve thwarted love within the parallel realm of the fairy king and queen, but to simplify, we will focus just on the quartet described above. The main plot of the play will involve how those four lovers can find their way through, past, around, and/or beyond the obstacles to their desired expressions of love. The play ends with the imminent marriages of Hermia with Lysander and Helena with Demetrius—plus that of the fairy king and queen, Oberon and Titania. The resolution of a Shakespearean comedy always involves celebration and festivity—specifically the celebration of marriage. At the end of a comedy, we can count the marriages (*As You Like It* tops the list with four); by contrast, the end of a tragedy brings us a body count. The death toll in a Shakespearean tragedy may be as small as just the main character (*Timon of Athens*), or it may rise to eight (*King Lear*), ten (*Macbeth*), or fourteen (*Titus Andronicus*). Of course, none of these counts takes into account myriad unnamed characters who may be killed in various wars associated with the actions of the main characters.

Though this comedy/marriage versus tragedy/death equation may seem to starkly define very different genres, often the outcome of a play depends on one or two twists. For example, *Romeo and Juliet* is definitively a tragedy, and *Much Ado about Nothing* undeniably a festive comedy. Yet their plots closely parallel each other. The outcome of each play hinges on a plot by a Catholic cleric to fake the death of a young woman in love. In *Romeo and Juliet*, Friar Laurence concocts a potion that will create the appearance that Juliet has died, thus freeing her from her father's command to marry Count Paris and allowing her to slip away to live with her beloved and banished Romeo—to whom she is already married. The plot goes awry when the friar's message fails to get through to Romeo—who finds Juliet in the Capulet family tomb, thinks her truly dead, and kills himself by drinking poison. Upon waking from her simulated death, Juliet finds her Romeo dead and stabs herself to join him in death.

In *Much Ado about Nothing*, the virtuous character Hero finds herself wrongly accused of promiscuity before her planned marriage to the soldier Claudio, who publicly and harshly spurns and condemns her. The religious brother Friar Francis comes up with a plan to fake Hero's death, not through botanical/pharmaceutical means as does Friar Laurence, but simply by proclaiming that she has died from the shock of her disgrace and hiding her away until the truth of her virtue can be reasserted. Unlike Friar Laurence's scheme, Francis's plot works. When the moment arrives for Hero's "resurrection," Claudio embraces her, she forgives him, and the play's conflicts are resolved with their marriage, along with that of the main characters Beatrice and Benedick.

Until the moment when by a weird twist of plotting, Friar Laurence's message to Romeo fails to reach him (the messenger is stopped by a quarantine order caused by an outbreak of disease—presumably the Black Death), *Romeo and Juliet* could have turned toward a comedic resolution. Even after that twist, had Shakespeare decided to deviate from his sources and have, say, Juliet wake up just in time for Romeo to see her alive and not kill himself, the play could have been a comedy. Conversely, had Claudio fallen dead of shock upon seeing what seemed to be Hero's ghost, *Much Ado about Nothing* could have ended in tragedy. Either might still have been a successful play. Both plays are still performed, but *The Tragedy of Romeo and Juliet* is clearly the more popular both in production and in education.

During Shakespeare's time, virtually everyone was familiar with the essential division of drama into comedies and tragedies. Plays at the Globe Theatre were advertised by way of pennants that flew high upon the theater walls, with a black flag promising a tragedy, white a comedy, and red an offering from the newly created genre of the history play. Without clear records of how often most plays were performed or how much box office revenue individual ones generated, we nonetheless have evidence of which plays stayed longest and most in repertory, with tragedies such as *Hamlet*, *Julius Caesar*, and *Romeo and Juliet* leading the list.

For some twenty-six years after Shakespeare's death, other playwrights continued mining the genre of tragedy, with plays by writers such as John Webster and John Ford growing ever more lurid and gruesome—and successful. Shakespeare's plays also remained popular. However, during the periods of the English Civil War and Interregnum (1642–60), all English theaters were closed by order of the ascendant Puritan forces, and of course playwriting ceased.

Beginning in 1660, newly restored King Charles II wanted theater to rise again, and he granted licenses to two playing companies, both of which began looking for material to perform. Due to the theater closures, no new plays had been produced for around eighteen years, so these companies turned to the inherited works of Renaissance playwrights such as Ben Jonson, and of course Shakespeare. However, despite admiring

Shakespeare's tragedies, writers and performers of the Restoration did not treat his works reverently. In fact, they deemed some of his tragedies too tragic, and freely adapted and reshaped Shakespeare's plays to fit what they saw as their more refined and sophisticated age. Nahum Tate adapted *Richard II*, altering first the title (it became *The Sicilian Usurper*) as well as character names. Tate also revised the text with the goal of making every scene "full of respect to Majesty and the dignity of courts." Tate's most famous revisioning of Shakespeare's works is his *King Lear*, which omits key characters including the Fool, as well as giving perhaps the bleakest of Shakespeare's tragedies a happy ending wherein Lear's beloved daughter Cordelia survives and marries Edgar. Tate's version of *King Lear* would be the only one presented and known in England—and later in the fledgling U.S.A.—for some 150 years.

The leading playwright of the Restoration, John Dryden (1631–1700), also adapted Shakespearean tragedy, with his 1677 play *All for Love*, or *A World Well Lost*, stemming from *Anthony and Cleopatra*. As did Tate, Dryden admired Shakespeare's tragedy but found the need to rework it. Dryden attempted to rein in the sprawling, epic *Antony and Cleopatra* to fit the classical "unities" of time and place outlined by Aristotle. Thus, rather than the fifteen-year span covered in Shakespeare's play, *All for Love* is compressed into one day; whereas *Antony and Cleopatra* spans settings from Rome through Egypt and features thirty-four characters, Dryden sets his entire tragedy in one location and uses a cast of only ten.

People of the Romantic era (loosely, the first half of the nineteenth century) loved Shakespeare, and the brooding Romantic temperament gravitated to the tragedies. The character of Hamlet epitomized the Romantic spirit of deep introspection and melancholia, and his story was easily the most popular Shakespearean play of the time.

Once modern educational systems were set into place—particularly in Anglophone countries—in the twentieth century, the perceived preeminence of tragedies became further entrenched, as those plays seem to have always been the ones most frequently taught to students. The new media of the twentieth century also reinforced the dominance of the tragedies; some of the earliest films made were silent adaptations of *Hamlet*, and subsequently more than fifty cinematic *Hamlet*s have been produced—far more versions than for any other play.

Overall, the placing of tragedies in the position of highest popularity and importance has continued in the centuries since these works were first written and performed—with something of an anomaly in the Restoration period, when too much tragedy was seen as unrefined, leading to adaptations (such as Tate's and Dryden's) to soften their rough edges. Throughout history, some have dissented from the idea of tragedy as the preeminent genre. Contemporary horror writer Stephen King said, "A tragedy is a tragedy, and at the bottom, all tragedies are stupid. Give me a choice and I'll take *A Midsummer Night's Dream* over *Hamlet* every time. Any fool with steady hands and a working set of lungs can build up a house of cards and then blow it down, but it takes a genius to make people laugh" (Stephen King). Though many of Shakespeare's comedies, histories, and romances are excellent and popular—and though tragedies bear no inherent superiority to the best plays of those genres—the common perception of tragedy as the most profound, weighty, and important type of play seems likely never to fade.

PRIMARY SOURCE DOCUMENT

SHAKESPEARE'S PLAYS BY GENRE

As emphasized throughout this chapter, generic classification is often inconsistent, imprecise, and to some extent subjective. Nonetheless, here is a listing that presents the most commonly agreed upon categorizations for Shakespeare's plays. Plays often classified as Romances are here noted with an R next to the title. Plays not found in the First Folio are noted with FF.

Comedies

The Tempest R
The Two Gentlemen of Verona
The Merry Wives of Windsor
Measure for Measure
The Comedy of Errors
Much Ado About Nothing
Love's Labour's Lost
A Midsummer Night's Dream
The Merchant of Venice
As You Like It
The Taming of the Shrew
All's Well That Ends Well
Twelfth Night
The Winter's Tale R
Pericles, Prince of Tyre R FF
The Two Noble Kinsmen R FF

Histories

King John
Richard II
Henry IV, Part 1
Henry IV, Part 2
Henry V
Henry VI, Part 1
Henry VI, Part 2
Henry VI, Part 3
Richard III
Henry VIII
Edward III^{FF}

Tragedies

Troilus and Cressida
Coriolanus
Titus Andronicus
Romeo and Juliet
Timon of Athens
Julius Caesar
Macbeth
Hamlet
King Lear
Othello
Antony and Cleopatra
Cymbeline

Further Readings

Barber, C. L. *Shakespeare's Festive Comedy*. Princeton: Princeton University Press, 1959.

Belsey, Catherine. *The Subject of Tragedy: Identity and Difference in Renaissance Drama*. London: Methuen, 1985.

Bevington, David M. *From Mankind to Marlowe: Growth of Structure in the Popular Drama of Tudor England*. Cambridge, MA: Harvard University Press, 1962.

Bowers, Fredson T. *Elizabethan Revenge Tragedy: 1587–1642*. Princeton: Princeton University Press, 1966.

Bradbrook, Muriel C. *The Growth and Structure of Elizabethan Comedy*. Berkeley and Los Angeles: University of California Press, 1956.

Bradbury, Malcolm, and David Palmer, eds. *Shakespearean Comedy*. London: Edward Arnold, 1972.

Braden, Gordon. *Renaissance Tragedy and the Senecan Tradition: Anger's Privilege*. New Haven, CT: Yale University Press, 1985.

Cartwright, Kent. *Shakespearean Tragedy and Its Double: The Rhythms of Audience Response*. University Park, PA: Pennsylvania State University Press, 1991.

Charlton, H. B. *The Senecan Tradition in Renaissance Tragedy*. Folcroft, PA: Folcroft Press, 1969.

Charney, Maurice. *Comedy High and Low: An Introduction to the Experience of Comedy*. New York: Oxford University Press, 1978.

Clare, Janet, and Roy T. Eriksen, eds. *Contexts of Renaissance Comedy*. Oslo: Novus Press, 1997.

Danson, Lawrence. *Shakespeare's Dramatic Genres*. Oxford: Oxford University Press, 2000.

Dollimore, Jonathan. *Radical Tragedy: Ideology and Power in the Drama of Shakespeare and His Contemporaries*. New York: Palgrave Macmillan, 2010.

Edwards, Philip. *Thomas Kyd and Early Elizabethan Tragedy*. London: Longmans, Green, 1966.

Eliot, T. S. "Shakespeare and the Stoicism of Seneca." *Selected Essays*. London: Faber & Faber, 1958.

Feldman, Sylvia D. *The Morality-Patterned Comedy of the Renaissance*. The Hague: Mouton, 1970.

French, Esther. "Which Shakespeare Plays Are Most Often Taught in High School English Classes?" *Folger Shakespeare Library: Shakespeare and Beyond*, August 30, 2016. https://shakespeareandbeyond.folger.edu/2016/08/30/shakespeare-plays-high-school-english-classes/

Fretz, Claude. "How Restoration Playwrights Reshaped Shakespeare's Plays to Fit Changing Political Norms and Theatrical Tastes." *Folger Shakespeare Library: Shakespeare and Beyond*. https://shakespeareandbeyond.folger.edu/2018/06/05/how-restoration-playwrights-reshaped-shakespeare-plays/

Gibbons, Brian. *Elizabethan and Jacobean Comedies*. Tonbridge, Kent: E. Benn, 1984.

Gibbons, Brian. *Elizabethan and Jacobean Tragedies*. Tonbridge, Kent: E. Benn, 1984.

Green, David C. *Plutarch Revisited: A Study of Shakespeare's Last Roman Tragedies and Their Source*. Salzburg: Universität Salzburg, 1979.

Griswold, Wendy. *Renaissance Revivals: City Comedy and Revenge Tragedy in the London Theater 1576–1980*. Chicago: University of Chicago Press, 1986.

Holderness, Graham, et al. *Shakespeare: The Play of History*. Basingstoke, Hampshire: Macmillan, 1988.

Leggatt, Alexander, ed. *The Cambridge Companion to Shakespearean Comedy*. Cambridge: Cambridge University Press, 2002.

Leggatt, Alexander. *Citizen Comedy in the Age of Shakespeare*. Toronto, Buffalo, NY: University of Toronto Press, 1973.

Lucas, F. L. *Seneca and Elizabethan Tragedy*. London: Forgotten Books, 2012.

McAlindon, T. *English Renaissance Tragedy*. Vancouver: University of British Columbia Press, 1986.

Miles, Geoffrey. *Shakespeare and the Constant Romans*. Oxford: Clarendon, 1996.

Nason, Arthur Huntington. "Shakespeare's Use of Comedy in Tragedy." *The Sewanee Review* 14, 1 (1906): 28–37. http://www.jstor.org/stable/27530731

Newman, Karen. *Shakespeare's Rhetoric of Comic Character: Dramatic Convention in Classical and Renaissance Comedy*. New York: Methuen, 1985.

Pearlman, E. *William Shakespeare, the History Plays*. New York: Twayne Publishers, 1992.

Poole, Adrian. *Tragedy: Shakespeare and the Greek Example*. Oxford and New York: Blackwell, 1987.

Pye, Christopher. *The Regal Phantasm: Shakespeare and the Politics of Spectacle*. London: Routledge, 1990.

Richman, David. *Laughter, Pain, and Wonder: Shakespeare's Comedies and the Audience in the Theater*. Newark: University of Delaware Press, 1990.

Salingar, Leo. *Shakespeare and the Traditions of Comedy*. Cambridge: Cambridge University Press, 1974.

Spencer, Hazelton, and Robert Ornstein, eds. *Elizabethan and Jacobean Tragedy: An Anthology*. Boston: Heath, 1973.

"Stephen King in His Own Words." *The Writer's Den*. https://davidhuntershaw.blogspot.com/2011/01/king-in-his-own-words-quotes-on-writing.html

Valency, Maurice Jacques. *Tragedy*. New York: New Amsterdam, 1991.

Velz, John W., ed. *Shakespeare's English Histories: A Quest for Form and Genre*. Tempe, Arizona: Medieval & Renaissance Texts & Studies, 1997.

Weld, John. *Meaning in Comedy: Studies in Elizabethan Romantic Comedy.* Albany: State University of New York Press, 1975.

Wilks, John S. *The Idea of Conscience in Renaissance Tragedy.* London: Routledge, 1990.

Young, David. *The Action to the Word: Structure and Style in Shakespearean Tragedy.* New Haven, CT: Yale University Press, 1990.

9

Shakespeare's Plays Are Elite and His Old English Is Incomprehensible for Contemporary Readers and Audiences

What People Think Happened

William Shakespeare created plays during the English Renaissance, a time when the average citizen of England could not read or write. People worked long hours in jobs that involved farming or other forms of difficult labor. Farmers earned enough to feed their families; people who worked for others might make four or five pounds per year, which, with food and drink typically also provided, was enough to live on. The Black Death was rampant, and average life expectancy was around thirty-five years. People lived harsh, difficult lives and lacked the time, energy, or money for leisure activities such as going to the theater.

Naturally, upper-class people had it better. Due to the unfair and arbitrary quirks of heredity, aristocrats had money, property, and time—they had no job other than to find ways to spend their money. Such wealthy people had the liberty to attend and to patronize the arts; they enjoyed poetry, dance, music, and the newly popular form of the theater. In fact, theater could not have grown and thrived as it did in Elizabethan England without the backing of the aristocracy.

Plays at theaters such as Shakespeare's Globe were performed in day-light, midafternoon, which gave the upper classes another incentive to attend: they liked to be seen by others, dressed in their finery. Even more did the aristocrats enjoy the indoor theaters, used by playing companies in winter, and illumined by candlelight. The setups of these venues, such as the Blackfriars where Shakespeare's company performed, had audience members surrounding three sides of the stage—and more, for the stages featured special places for wealthy and influential people who paid extra to sit: "gallant stools" right onstage and "lords' boxes" that stood above and behind the stage. Thus, simply by virtue of their social and economic standing, these aristocrats not only got to be seen by their peers in their VIP seating, but they could actually partake in the action, as actors frequently interacted with members of the audience—who would freely respond.

Shakespeare's plots also appealed to literate, upper-class citizens, deal-ing as they did so often with kings, queens, princes, dukes, and aristo-crats; at least twenty-five of the plays are set in foreign countries, which held great appeal for the aristocrats, many of whom had studied other languages and/or traveled abroad. Meanwhile, even the English language found in Shakespeare's plays displayed and demanded not mere literacy but a high level of linguistic skill. The Old English spoken by Shake-speare's characters is full of words such as "thee," "thou," "whither," and "wherefore," which tend to disorient the common contemporary reader or viewer. Not only is Shakespeare's vocabulary inscrutable, but his lines are also full of allusions to mythology and other texts only accessible to upper-class people. Typical lines from *Macbeth* read:

> Will all great Neptune's ocean wash this blood
> Clean from my hand? No; this my hand will rather
> The multitudinous seas incarnadine,
> Making the green one red. (II.ii.57–60)

Such words are so strange and complex that they would have confounded any lower-class person who managed to attend a performance in Shake-speare's 1606 London, let alone an eleventh grader—or a typical adult—in the twenty-first-century United States.

How the Story Became Popular

For this story, we will work backward from the present. The fact/fiction contains two related elements: first, that Shakespeare's plays—or, indeed, plays in general—constitute highbrow entertainment, and second, that Shakespeare's language is antiquated and incomprehensible for contemporary readers and audiences, especially those not highly educated. Both perceptions contain elements of fact and fiction, and both ideas arise perennially—that is, people's preferences in forms of entertainment, and people's affinity for certain modes of language, have always changed with time.

When we speak of entertainment, we refer to the human proclivity for storytelling, which has existed as long as history and which has constantly evolved. We know, for example, that ancient Greek epics such as the *Iliad* and the *Odyssey* were transmitted orally for centuries before being written and read. Beginning in the fifth century BCE, the great Athenian dramatists such as Aeschylus, Sophocles, and Euripides created the forms of public dramatic performance that still exist today. In Athens, up to 15,000 people from all levels of society would attend a single performance of a comedy or tragedy. Athenian dramatic performances were seen as such important and unifying civic events that the government paid for people too poor to buy their own admissions; thus, Western theater as it was first created and performed was far from limited to an elite few. Fast forwarding 2,000 years, theater became enormously popular in Renaissance England, with performances at theaters such as Shakespeare's Globe attracting up to 3,000 people per show, six days a week. As theater was thus appreciated by people from all levels of society in fifth century BCE Athens or in late sixteenth century CE England, the art form could not have been seen as highbrow or inaccessible, as it generally is today. It seems that only in the last century has the perception/reality arisen that theater is an upper-class pursuit, with the reasons being mostly economic. As film and television came into popularity in the early to midtwentieth century, those media developed into relatively affordable forms of entertainment; by contrast, theater became separated as a more expensive, elite art form.

In very recent decades, the costs of theatergoing have exploded, leaving even many drama practitioners displeased with the economics of their profession. In 2012, successful playwright Christopher Durang noted that when he came to New York City in 1975, he could see a show for $10, albeit standing room; in the 1980s, to see Durang's own hit comedy *Sister Mary Ignatius Explains It All for You* cost only $30 (Lambert 2012). However, by the 2000s, that formula had drastically changed, bringing major city theater ticket prices out of the range of the average consumer.

The average price for a Broadway show ticket is currently around $120. Big-budget, high-production-value musicals have driven much—but not all—of the cost increase. The musical *Hamilton*, which opened off Broadway in 2014 and moved the next year to Broadway, further changed the paradigm of what people will pay to see a show—and thus who can afford to do so; by 2016 the average price for a *Hamilton* ticket on Broadway surpassed $1,000, with some secondary ticket sales—meaning by outside vendors rather than through the already sold out box office—hitting $8,000 for one seat. In London—the other worldwide center for Anglophone theater—the average price for a theater ticket matches that for Broadway, at just over £100. Certainly prices are lower for smaller-market cities, but such figures nonetheless undeniably affirm the fact that, simply for economic reasons, the majority of people rarely or never find their way to the theater. By contrast, though the average U.S. movie ticket price has risen steadily over the years (in 1969 it was $1.42, equivalent to around $10 today, adjusting for inflation), it still comes in at $9 and places it within the reach of the average citizen.

Of course, in recent decades, television and personal devices such as laptops and mobile phones have offered more and more options for streaming entertainment, from concerts to films to plays and more. Such media remain within the reach of a far broader range of people than would ever think to attend a live play—thus reinforcing the image of theater as a rarified, highbrow mode of entertainment. Perhaps ironically, Shakespeare stands as something of an exception to the pricey nature of theater—especially during summers, when across the world, cities feature variations on free Shakespeare in the Park productions. At least thirty such festivals can be found around the United States, in cities such as Buffalo, Portland, Denver, Pittsburgh, Louisville, and Tallahassee. New York City alone has at least five such free, outdoor, summer Shakespeare productions, including the grandfather of them all: Shakespeare in the Park. Founded by Joseph Papp in 1954, Shakespeare plays in Central Park's Delacorte Theater each summer to around 80,000 people. Free summer Shakespeare can also be found across Canada, in New Zealand, Australia, continental Europe, and, of course, in the United Kingdom.

As for language, the success of free summer Shakespeare offerings may demonstrate that Shakespearean language is still accessible and entertaining for large numbers of people. However, that popularity cannot negate the undeniable fact that Shakespearean language challenges the comprehension of readers and viewers—though certainly the language generally makes more sense when one sees and hears it spoken by people engaging in relationships and actions, as opposed to one simply reading it.

We can trace complaints over Shakespeare's language even to his very well-educated friend and fellow playwright Ben Jonson. In his 1672 work *An Essay of Dramatic Poesy*, Restoration playwright John Dryden stated: "In reading some bombast speeches of Macbeth, which are not to be understood, [Jonson] used to say that it was horror; and I am much afraid that this is so" (Dryden). Jonson certainly had no trouble following Shakespearean language and matching it with equally elaborate writing of his own; Jonson may simply have failed to appreciate that Shakespeare sometimes uses deliberately convoluted language to portray the chaotic state of a character's mind, as he certainly did with Macbeth. As we have seen, in Dryden's own era, Shakespeare was commonly rewritten, not so much to increase comprehensibility but to tame what Restoration writers deemed as themes and plots too savage and unrefined for their mostly courtly, upper-class audiences (see chapter 8, "Shakespeare, His Colleagues, and His Audiences Saw Tragedies as More Important than Comedies").

Shakespeare's plays have long been edited to increase their accessibility, both for reading and for performance. The prologue to *Romeo and Juliet* speaks of the "two hours traffic of our stage," but in fact, if performed from full script with the typical pace of early twenty-first-century speech, the average play would take at least three hours, with *Hamlet* close to four—the length of the 1996 film version in which star/director Kenneth Branagh boldly decided not to cut any lines. Whether or not a script is cut, watching a stage or film performance of a Shakespeare play makes it far easier for most people to comprehend than through reading it. In the hands of talented actors and other stage practitioners, the script comes to life through costuming, inflection, action, and emotion.

In fact, many an English teacher has uttered words such as, "Shakespeare's plays weren't meant to be read—they were meant to be performed," to which many a student has retorted—or at least thought—"Then why are we reading it?" The kernel of truth in such exchanges points to the fact that, indeed, times have changed. In Shakespeare's time, playgoing was hugely popular, and reading was confined to the few; schools didn't have Shakespeare in the curriculum—instead, they read, recited, translated, and rewrote Ovid and Seneca. Nowadays books are abundant, and Shakespeare is a cornerstone of education in Anglophone countries, with many students struggling to comprehend what they perceive as "Old English," replete as it is with thees and thous, with subject-verb inversions and other unfamiliar features.

The suitability of Shakespearean language for young people was been debated at least since the Georgian era, when in 1807 brother and sister

Charles and Mary Lamb published *Tales of Shakespeare*, an illustrated children's book. The approach the Lambs took—emulated by myriad editions for young people in the succeeding centuries—tries to remove the actual or perceived obstacle of Shakespeare's language while preserving his stories ("tales"). Similarly, fear over the alleged impenetrability of Shakespeare's antiquated language has caused even large and successful contemporary Shakespeare productions to abandon the scripts Shakespeare created in favor of modernized versions. In 2015, the venerable Oregon Shakespeare Festival, founded in 1935 and based in Ashland, announced that it was commissioning contemporary authors to rewrite each of Shakespeare's plays for their future productions (Oregon Shakespeare is a year-round theater for pay, not one of the free summer festivals discussed above). The underlying assumption shared by the Lambs and the Oregon Shakespeare Festival—as well as by myriad other "translators" of Shakespeare over the years—is that Shakespeare's language constitutes an insurmountable impediment to people's comprehension and potential enjoyment of his works. This assumption is misguided in at least two ways.

First, assuming that such a "translation" approach aspires to foster a love for Shakespeare in audiences who would otherwise lack it, we have to ask: What makes Shakespeare Shakespeare? As we have seen in chapter 6 ("Shakespeare's Plays Were All Recycled and Not Original"), Shakespeare indeed bases much or all of most plays on various sources. The plots—what the Lambs and many adaptors since called the "tales"—are probably the least Shakespearean element of a Shakespearean play; thus, if we strip away or drastically reduce Shakespeare's language, do we succeed in making "Shakespeare" more accessible for readers or audiences? A second objection arises to the notion that "translating" or paraphrasing Shakespeare enhances comprehensibility. For many people, a great part of the artistry and appeal of Shakespearean drama lies in its poetry, the musicality of the words. One does not have to comprehend every word in order to follow the emotions, intentions, and actions of characters; the sounds and rhythms of Shakespeare's lines convey beauty and feeling even beyond their rational meanings—just as a poem may speak to a reader even as he or she wrestles with its meaning. Shakespeare's verse, and even his prose, contains imbedded, natural rhythms and inflections that cue us to the important words and syllables; when we remove those cues in order to simplify the language, we risk actually losing meaning.

Language is constantly evolving such that idioms and phrases that convey clear meanings fall into disuse and then, within a few years, may be forgotten or change meaning. We don't have to go back to Shakespeare's time to find words that become unfamiliar within a generation; for example, consider words such as bad, sick, and decadent. Each of those words currently carries—at least colloquially—a positive meaning. "Bad" was the first of those words to flip to mean the opposite of what it had always meant, coming into Black American slang by the 1960s and quickly catching on in the wider culture as suggestive of someone or something cool or formidable. "Sick" coming to mean "very good" came into usage in the 1980s. "Decadent" coming to mean "rich and yummy" rather than rotten and deadly seems gradually have slipped into usage through what might be called "forgotten irony"; as with the word "sinful," people began using "decadent" to mean "so delicious it must be bad for you," and today if one polled people under a certain age, few would know the true, negative meaning of the word.

Thus, we don't have to go back to Renaissance England to find words and expressions whose meanings are changeable, difficult, and elusive. The language of only a few years ago can rapidly become antiquated. Nonetheless, many students perceive Shakespeare's language to be "Old English"—just as they so perceive the language of Irving, Jefferson, Hawthorne, Twain, Faulkner, and even more recent authors. To overcome that perception requires teachers who themselves have a good grasp on Shakespearean language, which is not always the case.

PRIMARY SOURCE DOCUMENT

TALES FROM SHAKESPEARE (1807)

Brother and sister Charles and Mary Lamb published their Tales from Shakespeare *in 1807. The volume included illustrations and prose retellings of twenty plays; Charles handled the tragedies and Mary the comedies. The Lambs aspired to give children "a few hints and little foretastes of the great pleasure which awaits them in their elder years, when they come to the rich treasures from which these small and valueless coins are extracted; pretending to no other merit than as faint and imperfect stamps of Shakespeare's matchless image." The book has been reprinted numerous times, with several editions still in print today. The excerpt below comes from the Preface.*

The following Tales are meant to be submitted to the young reader as an introduction to the study of Shakespeare, for which purpose his words are used whenever it seemed possible to bring them in; and in whatever has been added to give them the regular form of a connected story, diligent care has been taken to select such words as might least interrupt the effect of the beautiful English tongue in which he wrote: therefore, words introduced into our language since his time have been as far as possible avoided.

In those Tales which have been taken from the Tragedies, the young readers will perceive, when they come to see the source from which these stories are derived, that Shakespeare's own words, with little alteration, recur very frequently in the narrative as well as in the dialogue; but in those made from the Comedies the writers found themselves scarcely ever able to turn his words into the narrative form: therefore it is feared that, in them, dialogue has been made use of too frequently for young people not accustomed to the dramatic form of writing. But this fault, if it be a fault, has been caused by an earnest wish to give as much of Shakespeare's own words as possible: and if the "He said" and "She said," the question and the reply, should sometimes seem tedious to their young ears, they must pardon it, because it was the only way in which could be given to them a few hints and little foretastes of the great pleasure which awaits them in their elder years, when they come to the rich treasures from which these small and valueless coins are extracted; pretending to no other merit than as faint and imperfect stamps of Shakespeare's matchless image. Faint and imperfect images they must be called, because the beauty of his language is too frequently destroyed by the necessity of changing many of his excellent words into words far less expressive of his true sense, to make it read something like prose; and even in some few places, where his blank verse is given unaltered, as hoping from its simple plainness to cheat the young readers into the belief that they are reading prose, yet still his language being transplanted from its own natural soil and wild poetic garden, it must want much of its native beauty. It has been wished to make these Tales easy reading for very young children. To the utmost of their ability the writers have constantly kept this in mind; but the subjects of most of them made this a very difficult task. It was no easy matter to give the histories of men and women in terms familiar to the apprehension of a very young mind. For young ladies, too, it has been the intention chiefly to write; because boys being generally permitted the use of their fathers' libraries at a much earlier age than girls are, they frequently have the best scenes of Shakespeare by heart, before their sisters are permitted to look into this manly book; and, therefore, instead of recommending these Tales to the perusal of young gentlemen who can read them so much better in the originals, their kind assistance is rather requested in explaining to their sisters such parts as are hardest for them to understand: and when they have helped them to get over the difficulties, then perhaps they will read to them (carefully selecting what is proper for a young sister's ear) some passage which has pleased them in one of these stories, in the very words of the scene from which it is taken; and it is hoped they will find that the beautiful extracts, the select passages, they may choose to give their sisters in this way will be much better relished and understood from their having some notion of the general story from one of these imperfect abridgments;—which if they be fortunately so done as to prove delightful to any of the young readers, it is hoped that no worse effect will result than to make them wish themselves a little older, that they may be allowed to read the Plays at full length (such a wish will be neither peevish nor irrational). When time and leave of judicious friends shall put them into their hands, they will discover in such of them as are here abridged (not to mention almost as many more, which are left untouched) many surprising events and turns of fortune, which for their infinite variety could not be contained in this little book, besides a world of sprightly and cheerful characters, both men and women, the humor of which it was feared would be lost if it were attempted to reduce the length of them. What these Tales shall have been to the *young* readers, that and much more it is the writers' wish that the true Plays of Shakespeare may prove to them in older years—enrichers of the fancy, strengtheners of virtue, a withdrawing from all selfish and mercenary thoughts, a lesson of all sweet and honorable thoughts and actions, to teach courtesy, benignity, generosity, humanity: for of examples, teaching these virtues, his pages are full.

Source: Charles and Mary Lamb. *Tales from Shakespeare* (New York: Thomas Y. Crowell, 1878).

What Really Happened

Aristocrats did indeed frequently populate and enjoy the theaters of Shakespeare's London, but so did everyone else. The novel phenomenon of public, secular theatrical performances became so popular that theaters would fill up to 3,000 people per show—six days a week, in the middle of the day. The vast majority of these people were middle to lower class, and the cheapest admissions cost a penny—for the "groundlings" who stood in the open area in front of the stage. Certainly, once indoor theaters also sprung up, they were more expensive, and thus featured a much higher class audience. For example, whereas it is commonly and correctly stated that Queen Elizabeth and King James both enjoyed the theater, we shouldn't picture them traipsing to the Globe with 3,000 citizens. Rather, they would either have viewed private performances at court or occasionally patronized one of the indoor theaters such as the Blackfriars.

So named because it was formerly a Dominican monastery, Blackfriars had been seized from the church by Henry VIII; when he proclaimed himself head of the newly formed Church of England, Henry banished all Catholic clergy and appropriated all their properties and other possessions. The Blackfriars first opened as a theater for a children's company around 1576. Twenty years later, it was purchased by James Burbage—father of Shakespeare's company fellow Richard Burbage, who was the leading actor for the Shakespeare's company, known first as the Lord Chamberlain's Men and then as the King's Men. When neighbors publicly objected to the notion of a theater company setting up shop (adult theatrical performances were, after all, still outlawed within London City limits), Blackfriars was allowed to remain open only for children's company use. In 1608, the King's Men took over and began performing there for the colder half of the year, evidently with no objections from the neighbors or city authorities.

We cannot underestimate the power and persistence of moral objections to theater. Such forces were strong throughout and beyond Shakespeare's career—when Puritans railed, wrote pamphlets, and sometimes achieved censorship over plays until they finally succeeded in altogether shutting down theater from 1642 to 1660. Even after the Restoration, theater did not regain its broad appeal across social classes. Though he personally loved and patronized the theater, King Charles II only granted licenses for two companies, who performed at court and in private, indoor theaters. Gone were the days of 3,000 audience members in Shakespeare's London, cutting across all social classes. Restoration audiences were aristocratic, and theater became indeed an upper-class art form—despite the fact that Restoration Drama was known for bawdiness, especially given the exciting new development of female players.

In the colonies and nascent United States of the eighteenth century, theater faced its own set of obstacles—mostly moral objections from Puritans who had left England to settle in the new world. The first theater was built in Williamsburg, Virginia as early as 1716, and producer/actor Lewis Hallam brought his theater company from England to the colonies in 1752, performing—among other fare—versions of *Hamlet*, *Othello*, *Richard III*, and *The Merchant of Venice*. However, Puritans and Quakers objected to dramatic performances, and colonies such as Massachusetts and Pennsylvania passed laws in the mid-18th century banning public plays. Thus, theater during this period was generally seen as anything but highbrow—rather, much as during Shakespeare's time, it had to fight against its reputation as a crude, low-class form of entertainment.

During the nineteenth century in the United States, theater grew with the nation, with companies springing up everywhere people lived. Shakespeare became the common denominator; even though he was English, the newly independent country adopted him as their own. People flocked to touring productions both by homegrown companies and to those featuring famous actors from Europe, such as English stars Charles Kean and William MacCready, and the famous French actress Sarah Bernhardt—known for her playing of Hamlet. Notoriously, John Wilkes Booth came from a famous Maryland acting family who loved Shakespeare. In 1864, the three Booth brothers (Edwin, Junius Brutus, and John Wilkes) starred in a special New York performance of *Julius Caesar* to raise funds to erect a statue of Shakespeare in Central Park—which still stands today. Ironically, the play deals with the assassination of a ruler perceived by some as a tyrant, the same motivation that—less than five months later—drove John Wilkes Booth to assassinate Abraham Lincoln in Ford's Theater in Washington, D.C., shouting "*sic semper tyrannus*" ("thus always to tyrants"). Also ironically, John Wilkes's brother Edwin was an ardent Unionist and supporter of Lincoln, who by a twist of fate saved the life of the president's son Robert on a train platform around 1864. Putting aside the horrendous associations with the murder of President Lincoln, the successful Booth project to erect the statue demonstrates the enduring popularity of Shakespeare as found in the nineteenth-century United States.

The twentieth century in the United States brought in the new media of radio, film, and television, all of which embraced Shakespeare in various forms and all of which helped change the dynamic of theatergoing. Some of the earliest films ever made involved Shakespeare's *Hamlet*. In 1900, Clement Maurice, the cameraman for the Lumiere brothers—who are among those credited with inventing the movies—directed French actress Sarah Bernhardt in a two-minute film of Hamlet's fencing scene with Laertes. That short work at the dawn of film actually featured sound, as Maurice recorded a soundtrack on phonograph to be played in conjunction with the action. The following decades featured at least eight silent versions of *Hamlet* produced in Italy, Germany, France, and England. As cinema grew through the silent and into the sound era, many films of various Shakespearean plays came into popularity and continue to be produced today.

As we have noted, moviegoing and television viewing have remained within economic reach of virtually anyone in society, whereas theater has come to be defined—both culturally and economically—as more of an elitist form. Several factors drive the higher cost of theater. One is the nature of the performance, which must be recreated night after night, week after week—including all associated workers for the cast, lighting, sound, costuming, props, and more. By contrast, films—though they can certainly be expensive to shoot—are able to be cheaply distributed and displayed several times a day, for as long as people buy tickets to see them. Even as ticket sales for movie theaters have fallen, other streaming means have arisen to allow people to view films anywhere, any time, at low cost.

With time, theater came to be seen as inherently highbrow, whereas television and film became the media for the masses. Shakespeare enters the mix as a cultural icon, with his perceived status as the greatest writer who ever lived—but one difficult to understand. Ironically, this perception has no doubt been exacerbated by the entry of Shakespeare into the high school curricula in England and the United States. Many students tend to chafe against books that they are forced to read, particularly in adolescence. Most children have little to no familiarity with Shakespeare until a full play is thrust upon them in ninth grade, and then their experience will largely depend upon their teacher's skill. If the students' initial encounter teaches them that Shakespeare is difficult, tedious, and/or irrelevant, they will likely never develop a different impression. Unfortunately, such negative experiences probably dominate for the majority of people. Thus, if later in life they have the opportunity to view a Shakespeare play—even, for example, a free summer performance—many would likely balk, stuck in the idea that "Shakespeare is only for the chosen few, and I am not one of them."

The encounter with Shakespeare in the educational setting brings us back to the second element of the fact/fiction: that William wrote in Old English too antiquated for modern comprehension. While one cannot deny that aspects of Shakespeare's language are obsolete, unfamiliar, and hard to fathom, that language change phenomenon (as noted in the previous section) occurs constantly and in much shorter time frame than the 400 or so years that separate the present from Shakespeare's writings. In the scheme of the history of the English language, Shakespeare by and large uses the same words and structures that we do in the early twenty-first century.

To be precise with terminology, Shakespeare wrote in an age known to linguists and historians as the Early Modern period. Linguists separate

English into three main periods. The beginnings of the English language are traced to the fifth century CE, when three Germanic tribes invaded the island of Britain. The Angles, the Saxons, and the Jutes came across the North Sea from areas that now would be Denmark and northern Germany. The natives of Britain spoke various Celtic dialects mixed with Latin—Britain had been invaded by Julius Caesar in 45 BCE and remained part of the Roman Empire until the conquest by the Germanic tribes. When the Angles, Saxons, and Jutes took over, Celtic speakers moved west and north into what would become Wales, Scotland, and Ireland. The words "England" and "English" derive from the homeland of the Angles (called "Angle-land" or "Engle-land"), whose language was called "Englisc." The other two tribes spoke similar languages, which became somewhat mixed and standardized in Britain/England as what we now know as Old English or Anglo-Saxon. And indeed, far more than is Shakespeare's Early Modern English, Old English is foreign to speakers of Modern English—for example, featuring letters no longer used, such as þ and ð. However, Old English provided the vocabulary basis for about half the words in Modern English, including "give," "father," "grow," "summer," and "life." The Old English period is generally dated from around 450 CE to 1100 CE.

Middle English flows from the 1066 conquest of England by William of Normandy. The Norman conquerors spoke a version of French, which remained the language of the ruling classes. For a time, the lower classes continued speaking their familiar English, and the upper classes spoke French; within a couple of centuries, the two languages had intermingled—or rather, we could say that Middle English absorbed thousands of the French-derived words we have in Modern English—many having to do with government, church, law, combat, and food—such as "governor," "beauty," "castle," "beef," and "liberty." Middle English appears more familiar to contemporary ears and eyes than does Old English, but it still defies comprehension for the average person.

Early Modern English is generally assigned as beginning in 1500. As with all such historical periods, the dating is rough and used for convenience rather than strict accuracy. In this case, the date follows shortly after Gutenberg's invention of the printing press around 1450 and William Caxton's establishment of the first press in England in 1476. Mass printing obviously brought into being many more books and also caused the (relative) standardization of spelling, grammar, and usage. However, the language of the Early Modern period was anything but static. It may be ironic that befuddled students complain of Shakespeare's "Old English," for one cannot easily think of a time in English language history when more creativity and innovation occurred. Many different currents contributed to the explosion of new vocabulary, and writers such as Shakespeare took advantage of the changing language to invent new words and phrases—many still used today. The number of words "created by Shakespeare" is highly debated, sometimes overstated, and difficult to specify. Through the years, many have claimed that Shakespeare invented thousands of new words, but such estimates are based on a word's first recorded use. That is, noting that the first printed use of a word appears in a Shakespeare text does not equate to his having "invented" the word. Nonetheless, Shakespeare did indeed wonderfully create words and phrases. He did not pull new words out of the air, but rather often morphed existing words into new forms and uses. For example, he would form a new compound out of two words, as with "blood-sucking" or "madwoman." Shakespeare frequently added prefixes and suffixes to existing root words, as with taking "assassin" and creating the first use of "assassination," making "formal" into "informal," "audible" into "inaudible," and "immediate" into "immediacy." He changed nouns into verbs and vice versa, made verbs into adjectives and vice versa, freely created adverbs from adjectives, and so forth. For example, the word "split" existed, but Shakespeare first used the adjective "splitting." He took the common adjective "secure" and first used it as a verb and employed the adjective "tardy" as the noun "tardiness." Under Shakespeare's pen, "gloom" first became "gloomy," "scuffle" first became a noun, and, adapting the Spanish word "aligarto," Shakespeare gave us the first "alligator." Perhaps even more notably than his creation of new words, Shakespeare coined hundreds of new phrases, many still in common use today—such as "the be-all and the end-all," "heart of gold," "too much of a good thing," to have "eaten me out of house and home," and to come "full circle." Even those vexing pronouns such as "thee," "thou," "thy," and "thine" were used creatively by Shakespeare; they represented older forms that were rapidly going out of favor in the Renaissance. Shakespeare could very well simply have used the newer "you" and "yours" but chose to employ both forms as a way of distinguishing means of address—for example, "you" is generally used between people of equal status and/or neither too close or too distant, whereas the "th" forms such as "thou" are used to indicate either greater closeness or greater distance, socially or interpersonally. For example, upper classes speaking to lower classes usually use "thou," as do lovers such as Romeo and Juliet.

Early Modern English is generally dated from 1500–1800, giving way to Late Modern English or simply Modern English from 1800 on. The beginning of the Modern English period approximately coincides with the advent of the Industrial Revolution and the expansion of the British Empire, both of which have brought into English thousands of new words from new technologies and from interaction with myriad faraway cultures and languages.

Ultimately, without denying the challenges presented by portions of Shakespeare's texts, his language is essentially our own, and his purported difficulty is often overrated. Various companies have performed Shakespeare for highly diverse and nonelite audiences throughout the years, including children, homeless people, and people in prison. New York's Public Theater Mobile Unit presents free performances of Shakespeare in prisons, homeless shelters, and community centers throughout New York's five boroughs—and beyond, with their touring company. Not only are such programs entertaining and accessible for decidedly non-highbrow audiences, but they have been shown to produce benefits in people's lives. For example, the twenty-five-year-old "Shakespeare Behind Bars" program—which operates in thirteen prisons in Kentucky and Michigan—maintains core goals that the audience "relate the universal human themes contained in Shakespeare's works to themselves including their past experiences and choices, their present situation, and their future possibility . . . relate the universal themes of Shakespeare to the lives of other human beings and to society at-large . . . [and] return to society as a contributing member" (Shakespeare Behind Bars). The program can point to measurable success in achieving those goals, citing a national recidivism rate of 76.6 percent compared with a 6 percent rate for inmates who have participated in Shakespeare Behind Bars. Dozens of such programs flourish across the United States, as well as in nations including Australia, Canada, England, Italy, Scotland, and Wales.

Another population typically presumed too unsophisticated for Shakespeare is children; as we have seen, Charles and Mary Lamb paved the way for the philosophy of dumbing down Shakespeare for young children by rewriting his words and preserving his "tales." However, across the country and world there exist myriad other ways children can experience Shakespeare—from abridged film versions such as the BBC/Time Life series "Shakespeare: The Animated Tales" to thousands of print versions, many of which incorporate mostly Shakespearean language. Also, many live opportunities around the globe allow children to engage with Shakespeare in creative and fun ways, such as the Pittsburgh Public Theater's annual Shakespeare Monologue and Scene Competition, which allows around 1,000 children in grades four through twelve to receive free coaching and then to present their pieces in front of audiences and judges. The Pittsburgh Public and myriad other theater companies also conduct versions of summer Shakespeare camps or institutes where children learn to play with—rather than be intimidated by—Shakespeare.

Examples such as prison projects and various children's experiences demonstrate that Shakespearean plays are in no way inherently appropriate only for upper-class or highly sophisticated audiences, and neither is his language too antiquated as to be accessible. Examining perhaps the most famous line in the history of literature, "To be or not to be: that is the question," one finds that every word but one contains a single syllable. When Shakespeare wished to express deep thoughts simply, he clearly did so. Readers and viewers of Shakespeare are advised not to fret over understanding or not understanding every single word and phrase but rather to follow characters' desires, interactions, and intentions in a given scene. Doing so will usually allow the overall sense of the action and story to be clear. With time and exposure, one may also come to appreciate the beauty—and the sense—of Shakespeare's not-so-Old English.

PRIMARY SOURCE DOCUMENTS

These three colorful, contemporary accounts describe Renaissance London theater audiences.

FYNES MORRISON, *ITINERARY* (1617)

The City of London alone hath four or five companies of players with their peculiar theaters capable of many thousands, wherein they all play every day in the week but Sunday, with most strange concourse of people, besides many strange toys and fancies exposed by signs to be seen in private houses, to which . . . the people flock in great numbers . . . as there be, in my opinion, more plays in London than in all parts of the world I have seen, so do these players . . . excel all others in the world.

Source: Fynes Moryson. *An Itinerary Written by Fynes Moryson Gent* (London: Printed by John Beale, 1617).

THOMAS NASHE, *PIERCE PENNILESS* (1592)

The afternoon being the idlest time of the day, wherein men that are their own masters (as gentlemen of the Court, the Inns of the Court, and the number of captains and soldiers about London) do wholly bestow themselves upon pleasure, and that pleasure they divide (how virtuously it skills not) either upon gaming, following of harlots, drinking, or seeing a play.

Source: Thomas Nashe. *Pierce Penniless, His Supplication to the Divell* (London: 1592).

THOMAS DEKKER, *THE GULL'S HORNBOOK* (1609)

Though himself a playwright, Thomas Dekker clearly grew annoyed that even the smaller, more expensive indoor theaters were attracting the lower classes alongside the aristocrats. Dekker wrote specifically and harshly about the Blackfriars Theater and its diverse spectators.

The place [Blackfriars] is so free in entertainment, allowing a stool as well to the farmer's son as to your Templar, that your stinkard has the self-same liberty to be there in his tobacco-fumes, which your sweet courtier hath; and that your carter and tinker claim as strong a voice in their suffrage, and sit to give judgement on the play's life and death as well as the proudest Momus [*Greek mythological deity of satire, used by dramatists in Athens and in Renaissance England to mock figures of power*] among the tribe of critics.

Source: Thomas Dekker. *The Gull's Handook.* R. B. McKerrow, editor. (London: Alexander Moring Ltd., 1905).

THE LORD'S PRAYER IN OLD ENGLISH, MIDDLE ENGLISH, EARLY MODERN ENGLISH, AND MODERN ENGLISH

Old English
Matthew 6.9 (WSCp, 11th c.)
Fæder ure þu þe eart on heofonum; Si þin nama gehalgod to becume þin rice gewurþe ðin willa on eorðan swa swa on heofonum. urne gedæghwamlican hlaf syle us todæg and forgyf us ure gyltas swa swa we forgyfað

urum gyltendum and ne gelæd þu us on costnunge ac alys us of yfele
soþlice.

Source: Corpus Christi College MS 140.

Lord's Prayer I
[. . .]g fæder, þu þe on heofonum eardast,
geweorðad wuldres dreame. Sy þinum weorcum halgad
noma niþþa bearnum; þu eart nergend wera.
Cyme þin rice wide, ond þin rædfæst willa
aræred under rodores hrofe, eac þon on rumre foldan.
Syle us to dæge domfæstne blæd,
hlaf userne, helpend wera,
8 þone singalan, soðfæst meotod.
Ne læt usic costunga cnyssan to swiðe,
ac þu us freodom gief, folca waldend,
from yfla gewham, a to widan feore.

Source: George Philip Krapp and Elliott van Kirk Dobbie. *The Exeter Book* (New
York: Columbia University Press, 1936).

Middle English
Matthew 6.9
Oure fadir that art in heuenes, halewid be thi name; thi kyndoom come
to; be thi wille don in erthe as in heuene: gyue to us this dai oure breed
ouer othir substaunce; and forgyue to us oure dettis, as we forgyuen to
oure gettouris; and lede us not in to temptacioun, but delyuere us fro yuel.

Source: *Wycliffe's Bible*, 1395. Available online at https://www.studylight.org/desk/?t1
=en_wyc&q1=Matthew%206

Early Modern English
Book of Common Prayer (1559)
Our Father which art in heaven, hallowed be thy name. Thy kingdom
come. Thy will be done in earth as it is in heaven. Give us this day our
daily bread. And forgive us our trespasses, as we forgive them that trespass
against us. And lead us not into temptation. But deliver us from evil.
Amen.

Source: Rev. William Keatinge Clay. *Liturgical Services: Liturgies and Occasional Forms
of Prayer Set Forth in the Reign of Queen Elizabeth* (Cambridge: Cambridge University
Press, 1847), 55.

The King James Bible (1611)

Our father which art in heauen, hallowed be thy name. Thy kingdome come. Thy will be done, in earth, as it is in heauen.Giue us this day our daily bread. And forgiue us our debts, as we forgiue our debters. And lead us not into temptation, but deliuer us from euill: For thine is the kingdome, and the power, and the glory, for euer, Amen.

Source: Available online at https://www.kingjamesbibleonline.org/1611_Matthew -Chapter-6/#9

Late Modern English

Book of Common Prayer (1928)

Our Father, who art in heaven, Hallowed be thy Name. Thy kingdom come. Thy will be done, On earth as it is in heaven. Give us this day our daily bread. And forgive us our trespasses, As we forgive those who trespass against us. And lead us not into temptation, But deliver us from evil. For thine is the kingdom, and the power, and the glory, for ever and ever. Amen.

Source: Available online at http://justus.anglican.org/resources/bcp/1928/Litany .htm

The New Testament in Modern English

Our Father in heaven,
hallowed be your name,
your kingdom come,
your will be done,
on earth as it is in heaven.
Give us today our daily bread.
And forgive us our debts,
as we also have forgiven our debtors.
And lead us not into temptation,
but deliver us from the evil one.

Source: *Holy Bible*, New International Version®, NIV® Copyright ©1973, 1978, 1984, 2011 by Biblica, Inc.® Used by permission. All rights reserved worldwide.

Further Readings

"Annual Average U.S. Ticket Price." *National Association of Theatre Owners*. https://www.natoonline.org/data/ticket-price/

"Average Paid Admission at Broadway Shows in New York from 2007 to 2019, by Category (in U.S. dollars)." *Statista.com*. https://www.statista.com/statistics/198306/average-paid-admission-at-broadway-shows-since-2006/

Berry, Ralph. *Shakespeare and the Awareness of the Audience*. London: Macmillan, 1984.

Blake, Norman F. *A Grammar of Shakespeare's Language*. New York: Palgrave, 2002.

Cook, Ann Jennalie. *The Privileged Playgoers of Shakespeare's London, 1576–1642*. Princeton: Princeton University Press, 1981.

Dawson, Anthony B., and Paul Yachnin. *The Culture of Playgoing in Shakespeare's England: A Collaborative Debate*. Cambridge: Cambridge University Press, 2001.

Dessen, Alan C. *Elizabethan Drama and the Viewer's Eye*. Chapel Hill: University of North Carolina Press, 1977.

Dryden, John. "An Essay of Dramatic Poesy." https://www.poetryfoundation.org/articles/69377/an-essay-of-dramatic-poesy

Dutton, Richard. *Mastering the Revels*. London: Macmillan, 1991.

Furness, Hannah. "Shakespeare Read in Elizabethan Accent Reveals 'Puns, Jokes and Rhymes.'" *The Telegraph*, October 11, 2013. https://www.telegraph.co.uk/culture/theatre/william-shakespeare/10372964/Shakespeare-read-in-Elizabethan-accent-reveals-puns-jokes-and-rhymes.html

Gurr, Andrew. *Playgoing in Shakespeare's London*. Cambridge: Cambridge University Press, 1996.

Harbage, Alfred. *As They Liked It*. New York: Macmillan, 1947.

Harbage, Alfred. *Shakespeare's Audience*. New York: Columbia University Press, 1941.

Homan, Sidney. *Shakespeare's Theater of Presence: Language, Spectacle, and the Audience*. Cranbury, NJ: Associated University Presses, 1986.

Howard, Jean E. *Shakespeare's Art of Orchestration: Stage Technique and Audience Response*. Urbana: University of Illinois Press, 1984.

Kermode, Frank. *Shakespeare's Language*. New York: Farrar, Straus and Giroux, 2001.

Kökeritz, Helge. *Shakespeare's Pronunciation*. New Haven, CT: Yale University Press, 1953.

Lamb, Charles, and Mary Lamb. *Tales from Shakespeare*. Boston: Digireads.com Publishing, 2018.

Lambert, Craig. "The Future of Theater: In a Digital Era, Is the Play Still the Thing?" *Harvard Magazine*, January–February 2012. https://harvardmagazine.com/2012/01/the-future-of-theater

Levin, Richard. "Women in the Renaissance Theater Audience." *Shakespeare Quarterly* 40, 2 (1989): 165–74.

Onions, C. T., and Robert D. Eagleson. *A Shakespeare Glossary*. Oxford: Clarendon Press, 1986.

Palfrey, Simon. *Late Shakespeare: A New World of Words*. Oxford: Clarendon Press, 1997.

Partridge, Eric. *Shakespeare's Bawdy*. New York: Routledge, 2001.

Richman, David. *Laughter, Pain, and Wonder: Shakespeare's Comedies and the Audience in the Theater*. Newark: University of Delaware Press, 1990.

Rubinstein, Frankie. *A Dictionary of Shakespeare's Sexual Puns and Their Significance*. Houndmills, Basingstoke, Hampshire: Macmillan, 1989.

Shakespeare Behind Bars. https://www.shakespearebehindbars.org/

"Shakespeare in Prisons Network." Shakespeare at Notre Dame. https://shakespeare.nd.edu/spn/

Shapiro, James. "Shakespeare in Modern English." *New York Times*, October 7, 2015. https://www.nytimes.com/2015/10/07/opinion/shakespeare-in-modern-english.html

Weimann, Robert. *Shakespeare and the Popular Tradition in the Theater*. Ed. Robert Schwartz. Baltimore, MD: Johns Hopkins Press, 1978.

West, Gilian. *A Dictionary of Shakespeare's Semantic Wordplay*. Lewiston, NY: Edwin Mellen Press, 1998.

Whitney, Charles. "'Usually in the Werking Daies': Playgoing Journeymen, Apprentices, and Servants in Guild Records, 1582–92." *Shakespeare Quarterly* 50, 4 (1999): 433–58.

Williams, Gordon. *A Dictionary of Sexual Language and Imagery in Shakespearean and Stuart Literature*. Atlantic Highlands, NJ: Athlone Press, 1994.

Williams, Marcia. *More Tales from Shakespeare*. Somerville, MA: Candlewick Press, 2005.

Williams, Marcia. *Tales from Shakespeare*. Somerville, MA: Candlewick Press, 2004.

10

To Give Audiences the Most Authentic Experience Possible, Shakespeare's Plays Should Be Produced with Renaissance Costumes and Staging

What People Think Happened

Shakespeare lived and wrote during the Elizabethan era, and the staging of his plays reflected the tastes of the time with regard to dress, music, and other stage elements such as props. Contemporary productions that attempt to "modernize" or place the action in different times and places than Shakespeare intended fail to do justice to his works. In fact, by attempting to graft a "concept" onto a play—for example, by setting it in the present and/or in a specific country different from the original— one detracts from the meaning and impact of Shakespeare's masterpieces. People in Shakespeare's England talked and dressed in specific ways that he reflected in creating his characters and scenes, and those modes should be preserved in order to best convey Shakespeare's intentions. Costumes other than Renaissance garb simply distract from Shakespeare's plots and characters. Contemporary companies waste much money and energy trying to reset the plays in time periods such as World War II or the future, and they could create more authentic productions by using Renaissance costuming.

Throughout the centuries since Shakespeare's death, productions of his plays adhered to the tradition of using Renaissance staging and costuming traditions, and certainly nobody in the nineteenth or eighteenth centuries would have dreamt of—for example—setting *King Lear* in a circus or *The Taming of the Shrew* in the wild West. The furor for inventing Shakespeare with all manner of times, places, costumes, and concepts only began in the twentieth century and stems from the Modernist obsession to—as poet Ezra Pound said—"make it new" (Pound 1971). That same artistic impulse for novelty produced some powerful art but also gave us much experimentation for the sake of provocation. For example, in 1917 Marcel Duchamp mounted an ordinary urinal for a New York exhibition of the Society of Independent Artists, titling it "Fountain"—and was hailed as an innovator and great artist. By the middle of the century, as Modernism passed into post-Modernism, painter Jackson Pollack created huge paintings that still sell for millions by standing over canvases and randomly splattering them with paint. Such works represent nothing, reflect no image of anything in nature. They are self-indulgent demonstrations that became famous because the people and art of the twentieth century and beyond lost their sense of meaning and aesthetic beauty. At their essence, such works are nihilistic. In the absence of expressing any beauty or meaning in art, the artist takes or makes something ugly, fractured, and meaningless and declares it beautiful and/or profound; the critics and the public follow.

The same principle of absent and manufactured meaning explains the Modernist and post-Modernist craze for reimagining, resetting, and refashioning Shakespeare. Early in the twentieth century, like other artists, theater practitioners began imposing their own meanings on the canvases of Shakespeare's plays. The horrors and destruction of the century's two world wars further eroded people's sense of beauty and meaning, and players of Shakespeare felt the need to push the envelope by producing stranger and more abstract versions of the plays. Many such theater practitioners increasingly came to believe that Shakespeare was no longer relevant to our tumultuous times of genocide, dictatorships, and weapons of mass destruction, and they felt the need to produce the relevance themselves through ever more audacious "concepts."

The craze of modernizing Shakespeare's plays has not abated, but it is never too late to return to the traditional practice of trusting Shakespeare's plays enough to produce and perform them as they were meant to be: with their original costuming and staging.

How the Story Became Popular

To get to the root of the myth that Shakespeare should only be produced with Renaissance staging and costuming, we must explore what terms such as "original" and "traditional" actually imply. For example, if we take this concept to its logical conclusion, we would have to advocate for women to be banished from Shakespearean stages, for we know that all roles in Shakespeare's time were played by men or boys. And in fact, a few companies in recent years have experimented with that practice. In 2002, Tim Carroll directed an all-male casting of *Twelfth Night* for Shakespeare's Globe in London. The production, specifically designed to coincide with the 400th anniversary of the first known performance of *Twelfth Night*, starred the Globe's then-artistic director Mark Rylance as Olivia. The Globe, which uses "original practices" (including original pronunciation, discussed in "What Really Happened" below) only for some of its productions, upped the authenticity ante for *Twelfth Night*; rather than perform at the Globe—the recreation of Shakespeare's great outdoor theater, opened in 1997 and located on the south bank of the Thames— Rylance and company crossed the river to perform at the site of the only recorded performance of *Twelfth Night* in Shakespeare's time: the Middle Temple. Then as now, the Middle Temple was one of London's four Inns of Court, the equivalent of an American law school. A diary entry by a clerk named John Manningham records what was likely the first performance of *Twelfth Night*, which took place in 1602 in the huge dining hall at the Middle Temple. Thus, the Globe Theatre production attempted to drive to the heart of original playing conditions, including costumes, makeup, casting, and even location. The play's run was well received by critics and audiences and spawned a 2012 film version, also directed by Carroll and featuring largely the same cast. Among this production's efforts to emulate original practices, the costuming team painstakingly researched and created exquisite replicas of Elizabethan original garb.

As much as any other Shakespeare play, *Twelfth Night* requires specific wardrobe cues to work. The play features characters defined by their dress; for example, Feste would have worn the motley uniform signifying his role as a jester or "wise fool." Later in the play, Feste dons the garb and puts on the voice of the priest Sir Topas in order to harass the imprisoned Malvolio. Malvolio also changes costumes throughout the play, going from his stern and puritanical steward's uniform to the ridiculous and hilarious yellow stockings and cross gartering that demonstrate his pathetic lovesickness for Olivia; after his release from prison at the play's end, he typically wears some tattered remnants of his former outfit. Olivia's character is also defined by costume, as through the early part of the play she appears in black dress of mourning for her lost brother—a sartorial device she actually uses to deter unwanted suitors; she utilizes her veil as a sort of prop to first conceal and then reveal herself to Viola-Cesario, who herself begins the play by donning male clothing so as to conceal her female identity in the strange land of Illyria. Viola's reunion with her presumed drowned twin brother Sebastian ostensibly shocks all people on and off stage by their astonishing resemblance ("An apple, cleft in two, is not more twin / Than these two creatures," V.i.2423–2424)—which, during Shakespeare's time, would have been suggested not so much by physical similarity between the actors but rather by their precisely matching costumes. And the happy ending of the play, including the wedding of Orsino and Viola, is deferred through reference to the need for appropriate apparel; Orsino, having only just learned that Viola—whom he has known throughout the play only as the male Cesario—is a woman and thus eligible for marriage, proclaims, "Cesario, come: / For so you shall be, while you are a man; / But when in other habits you are seen, / Orsino's mistress, and his fancy's queen" (V.i.2598–2601).

The importance of particular forms of dress was reflected in *Twelfth Night* and in all of Shakespeare's plays, but dress was equally significant offstage. Not only did the people of Renaissance England exhibit the specific fashion tastes of the time, but their means of dress, right down to colors and fabric, were enshrined in law. It may seem bizarre to those in twenty-first-century Western cultures to imagine laws telling people what they can and cannot wear. Why did such "sumptuary laws" exist in England in Shakespeare's time and well before? The term *sumptuary* comes from the Latin words *sumptus*, meaning expense, and *sumere*, meaning to take or spend, and is related to contemporary words such as *sumptuous* and *consumption*. Such laws date from Roman times and before, and they can deal not only with clothing but also with other potential excesses of consumption, such as food and alcohol. Most commonly in England, they referred to clothing—specifically, the perceived dangers of someone dressing above his or her means or station in life. For example, certain young men became known as "roaring boys"—Renaissance versions of street hoodlums who derived some of their arrogance from dressing like higher-class people.

Sumptuary laws were largely targeted at young gentlemen and nobles who might tend to flaunt their wealth by wearing the finest clothing, of the finest fabrics. Many such people spent above their means and could run through all their inherited wealth—leaving them in the socially undesirable state of impoverished aristocrats. Sometimes such noblemen gravitated toward imported fabrics and garments, and the sumptuary laws aimed to boost the English economy by forbidding such purchases in favor of locally produced goods. The government also wanted to maintain the rigid class system such that distinctions remained clear and unblurred by lower-class people dressing and posing as aristocrats. Economic opportunities during the Renaissance bred a new, mostly merchant middle class; in some cases, merchants prospered so much that their wealth could rival that of aristocrats, and the ruling class could not allow them to dress like their betters.

The first English sumptuary laws came into being in the late 1200s, and different acts were passed at various points in the fourteenth and fifteenth centuries. Under Henry VIII, laws were further refined to include women's as well as men's apparel. Shortly after Elizabeth took the throne in 1558, she issued sumptuary proclamations confirming and expanding on those of her father. In 1559, her order included new mechanisms for monitoring and enforcing the sumptuary laws, such as suggesting that each London city parish appoint at least two "watchers" to enforce the ordinances. Additional "Statutes of Apparel" followed, with the most extensive rules coming from the queen in 1574. This proclamation— reprinted in full at the end of this section—delineates in extreme detail the precise fabrics, styles, and colors that could and could not be worn by certain people and classes. For example, purple or gold silk cloth could generally only be worn by the queen. Dukes and marquises were allowed to wear purple doublets, jerkins, and stockings. Clothes containing or embroidered with gold or silver were to be worn only by the upper class; however, even upper-class people were forbidden to spend more than £100 per year on clothing—a huge sum for the time. We have no records of the government actually auditing a gentleman's clothing expenditures, but the laws were nonetheless on the books to discourage ostentatious displays of finery.

Records do not indicate that Statutes of Apparel were harshly enforced; punishments typically consisted of fines, though a 1562 royal proclamation allowed for imprisonment for up to three months for people below the rank of knight caught wearing silk ribbons on hats and other garments. Other apparel statutes prohibited cross-dressing, a common practice onstage and one of the reasons the theater was perennially viewed as a salacious and immoral environment. Offstage, cross-dressing was rare, but ladies might find practical reasons for doing so. For example, traveling alone as a woman was dangerous, and some women might dress like men as a means of protection against attack and potential violation.

At least one woman flouted the Renaissance English strictures against cross-dressing: the notorious Londoner Mary Frith, better known by her criminal name, Moll (or Mal) Cutpurse. "Moll" was a diminutive for "Mary" but had also come to mean a disreputable woman or a prostitute. "Cutpurse" points to one of Mary's occupations—on the crowded streets, she would deftly cut the strings that attached a purse (usually a man's) to the belt and make off with it—for which she was several times arrested and punished by burning of her hand. We must note that although Frith was a real person, it is difficult to separate fact from fiction, as her exploits became so colorful and legendary. In fact, two plays were produced about Moll, one lost and the other by Thomas Dekker and Thomas Middleton (the latter being Shakespeare's friend, collaborator, and successor). The play puns off the term for the young male hooligans—"roaring boys"— and is called *The Roaring Girl*. From her childhood, Moll clearly broke with gender conventions. *The Newgate Calendar*, an eighteenth-century encyclopedia of rogues and criminals throughout English history, describes Mary: "She was above all breeding and instruction. She was a very tomrig or hoyden [terms for wild, rude girls or tomboys], and delighted only in boys' play and pastime, not minding or companying with the girls. . . . She would fight with boys, and courageously beat them . . ." (*The Life and Death of Mrs. Mary Frith*). Moll's parents died when she was young, and according to legend, she got into so much trouble that her minister uncle tricked her onto a ship bound for New England; when Moll figured out the plan, she jumped overboard before the ship could sail and swam to shore—to begin her life on the streets.

As she grew to womanhood, Moll became notorious and prosperous through various criminal activities. She acted as a procurer (pimp) for both genders, a fortune-teller, and a fence for stolen goods. Later she resorted to robbing coaches along highways, for which she was eventually imprisoned. Later in life she was sent to Bethlehem, the famed London asylum for persons with mental illness. Throughout her life, Moll dressed as a man, often accompanied by one or more of her huge dogs and smoking a long pipe. Though Mary eventually wed a young man, many believed the marriage was a sham to provide her cover; she was often accused of being a hermaphrodite, an allegation apparently put to rest by medical examination upon her death.

Not only did Mary Frith consistently flout the laws against cross-dressing—though she was arrested for it at least once—she also managed to defy the prohibitions against women appearing onstage. She did a sort of one-woman cabaret show in 1611—dressed in her usual man's attire—performing no doubt bawdy songs and stories and playing the lute. Frith's life demonstrates some of the complex dynamics regarding what constituted traditional and acceptable English Renaissance dress on and off stage.

PRIMARY SOURCE DOCUMENTS

THE NEWGATE CALENDAR (SEVENTEENTH AND EIGHTEENTH CENTURIES)

The Newgate Calendar, *subtitled the* Malefactors' Bloody Register, *began simply as a schedule of which criminals were executed when, but publishers saw an opportunity to capitalize on public interest in notorious scoundrels from history. The biographies of the malefactors were designed as cautionary tales to discourage immorality. The entry on Moll Cutpurse concludes with a poem by John Milton, a contemporary of hers. This is far from* Paradise Lost, *but is rather a humorous, whimsical epitaph; the great poet seems to have been as fascinated with Moll's strange and unique life as were most people.*

MARY FRITH OTHERWISE MOLL CUTPURSE

A Famous Master-Thief and an Ugly, Who Dressed like a Man, and Died in 1663

MARY FRITH, otherwise called Moll Cutpurse, from her original profession of cutting purses, was born in Barbican in Aldersgate Street, in the year 1589. Her father was a shoemaker; and though no remarkable thing happened at her nativity, such as the flattering soothsayers pretend in eclipses, and other the like motions above, or tides, and whales, and great fires . . . yet . . . in her time she was superior in the mystery of diving in purses and pockets, and was very well read and skilled too in the affairs of the placket among the great ones.

Both the parents (as having no other child living) were very tender of this daughter, but especially the mother . . . most affectionate she was to her in her infancy, most careful of her in her youth, manifested especially in her education, which was the most strictly and diligently attended, by reason of her boisterous and masculine spirit, which then showed itself, and soon after became predominant. She was above all breeding and

instruction. She was a very tomrig or hoyden, and delighted only in boys'
play and pastime, not minding or companying with the girls . . . she was
not so to be tamed, or taken off from her rude inclinations. She could not
endure that sedentary life of sewing or stitching; a sampler was as grievous
to her as a winding sheet; and on her needle, bodkin and thimble she
could not think quietly, wishing them changed into sword and dagger for
a bout at cudgels. Her headgear and handkerchief (or what the fashion of
those times was for girls to be dressed in) were alike tedious to her, she
wearing them as handsomely as a dog would a doublet. . . . She would
fight with boys, and courageously beat them; run, jump, leap or hop with
any of her contrary sex, or recreate herself with any other play whatsoever.
She had an uncle, brother to her father, who was a minister, and of him
she stood in some awe, but not so much as to restrain her in these courses;
so that seeing he could not effectually remedy that inveterating evil in her
manners, he trepanned her on board a merchant ship lying at Gravesend,
and bound for New England, whither he designed to have sent her. But
having learned to swim, she one night jumped overboard and swam to
shore, and after that escape would never go near her uncle again. . . . She
was now a lusty and sturdy wench, and fit to put out to service . . . but as
she was a great libertine, she lived too much in common to be enclosed
in the limits of a private domestic life. . . . She would go to the ale house
when she had made shift to get a little stock, spend her penny, come into
anyone's company, and club till she had none left; and then she was fit
for any enterprise. Moreover, she had a natural abhorrence to tending
of children, to whom she ever had an averseness in her mind, equal to
the sterility and barrenness in her womb, never (to our best information)
being made a mother.

She generally went dressed in man's apparel. No doubt but Moll's converse with herself informed her of her defects, and that she was not made
for the pleasure or delight of man; and therefore, since she could not be
honoured with him, she would be honoured by him, in that garb and
manner of raiment which he wore. This she took to from her first entrance
into a competency of age, and to her dying day she would not leave it off.

Though she was so ugly in any dress as never to be wooed nor solicited
by any man, yet she never had the green sickness, that epidemical disease of maidens after they have once passed their puberty; she never ate
lime, coals, oatmeal, tobacco pipes, cinders, or such like trash; no sighs,
dejected looks, or melancholy clouded her vigorous spirits, or repressed
her joviality; she was troubled with none of those longings which poor
maidens are subject to. She had the power and strength to command
her own pleasure of any person who had reasonable ability of body; and

therefore she needed not to whine for it, as she was able to beat a fellow to compliance, without the unnecessary trouble of entreaties.

Now Moll . . . got acquainted with some fortune tellers of the town, from whom, learning some smatch and relish of that cheat, by their insignificant schemes, and calculating of figures, she got a tolerably good livelihood. But her income being not equivalent to her expenses, she entered herself into the Society of Divers, otherwise called file clyers, cutpurses or pickpockets; which people are a kind of land pirates. . . . In this unlawful way she got a vast deal of money; but having been very often in Old Bridewell, the Compters and Newgate for her irregular practices, and burnt in the hand four times, she left off this petty sort of theft, and went on the highway, committing many great robberies, but all of them on the Roundheads, or rebels, that fomented the Civil War against King Charles I; against which villains she had . . . great antipathy. . . .

A long time had Moll Cutpurse robbed on the road; but at last, robbing General Fairfax of two hundred and fifty jacobuses on Hounslow Heath, shooting him through the arm for opposing her, and killing two horses on which a couple of his servants rode, a close pursuit was made after her by some Parliamentarian officers quartering in the town of Hounslow, to whom Fairfax had told his misfortune. Her horse failed her at Turnham Green, where they apprehended her, and carried her to Newgate. After this she was condemned, but procured her pardon by giving her adversary two thousand pounds. . . .

In her time tobacco being grown a great mode, she was mightily taken with the pastime of smoking, because of its singularity, and that no woman ever smoked before her, though a great many of her sex since have followed her example.

Moll being quite scared from thieving herself, she turned fence—that is to say, a buyer of stolen goods; by which occupation she got a great deal of money. In her house she set up a kind of brokery, or a distinct factory for jewels, rings and watches which had been pinched or stolen any manner of way, at never so great distance, from any person. It might properly enough be called the Insurance Office for such merchandise, for the losers were sure, upon composition, to recover their goods again, and the pirates were sure to have a good ransom, and she so much in the gross for brokage, without any more danger, the hue and cry being always directed to her for the discovery of the goods, not the takers. . . .

Moll was always accounted by her neighbours to be an hermaphrodite, but at her death was found otherwise. She had not lived long in Fleet Street before she became acquainted with a new sort of thieves, called heavers, whose employment was stealing shop books from drapers and mercers, or other rich traders; which bringing to her, she, for some considerable profit for herself, got them a *quantum meruit* [reward] for restoring them again to the losers. While she thus reigned free from the danger of the common law, an apparitor, set on by an adversary of hers, cited her to appear in the Court of Arches, where was an accusation exhibited against her for wearing indecent and manly apparel. She . . . was there sentenced to stand and do penance in a white sheet at St Paul's Cross during morning sermon on a Sunday. They might as soon have shamed a black dog as Moll with any kind of such punishment; for a halfpenny she would have travelled through all the market towns in England with her penitential habit, and been as proud of it as that citizen who rode to his friends in the country in his livery gown and hood. . . .

However, this penance did not reclaim her, for she still went in men's apparel, very decently dressed; nor were the ornaments of her house less curious and pleasing in pictures than in the delight of looking glasses; so that she could see her sweet self all over in any part of her rooms.

[. . .] To get money, Moll would not stick out to bawd for either men or women; insomuch that her house became a double temple for Priapus and Venus, frequented by votaries of both sorts. Those who were generous to her labour, their desires were favourably accommodated with expedition; whilst she lingered with others, laying before them the difficult but certain attainment of their wishes, which served as a spur to the dullness of their purses. . . .

After seventy four years of age, Moll being grown crazy in her body, and discontented in mind, she yielded to the next distemper that approached her, which was the dropsy; a disease which had such strange and terrible symptoms that she thought she was possessed, and that the devil had got within her doublet. Her belly, from a withered, dried, wrinkled piece of skin, was grown to the tightest, roundest globe of flesh that ever any beauteous young lady strutted with . . . her legs represented a couple of mill posts. . . .

It may well be expected that, considering what a deal of money she got by her wicked practices, she might make a will; but yet, of five thousand pounds which she had once by her in gold, she had not above one hundred pounds left her latterly which she thought too little to give to the charitable uses of building hospitals and almshouses. . . . In short, she made no will at all, because she had had it so long before to no better purpose; and that if she had had her desert, she should have had an executioner instead of an executor.

Out of the one hundred pounds which she had by her, she disposed of thirty pounds to her three maids which she kept, and charged them to occupy it the best way they could . . . and would be able to keep them in repair, and promote them to weavers, shoemakers and tailors. The rest of her personal estate, in money, movables and household goods, she bequeathed to her kinsman Frith, a master of a ship . . . whom she advised not to make any ventures therewith, but stay at home and be drunk, rather than go to sea and be drowned with them.

[. . . S]he desired to be buried with her breech upwards, that she might be as preposterous in her death as she had been all along in her infamous life. When she was dead she was interred in St. Bridget's churchyard, having a fair marble stone put over her grave; on which was cut the following epitaph, composed by the ingenious Mr. Milton, but destroyed in the great conflagration of London:

Here lies, under this same marble,
Dust, for Time's last sieve to garble;
Dust, to perplex a Sadducee,
Whether it rise a He or She,
Or two in one, a single pair,
Nature's sport, and now her care.
For how she'll clothe it at last day,
Unless she sighs it all away;
Or where she'll place it, none can tell:
Some middle place 'twixt Heaven and Hell
And well 'tis Purgatory's found,
Else she must hide her under ground.
These reliques do deserve the doom,
Of that cheat Mahomet's fine tomb
For no communion she had,
Nor sorted with the good or bad;
That when the world shall be calcin'd,
And the mix'd mass of human kind
Shall sep'rate by that melting fire,
She'll stand alone, and none come nigh her.
Reader, here she lies till then,
When, truly, you'll see her again.

Source: *The Life and Death of Mrs. Mary Frith: Commonly Called Mal Cutpurse* (London: W. Gilbertson, 1662).

ENFORCING STATUTES OF APPAREL. GREENWICH, 15 JUNE 1574, 16 ELIZABETH I

Following on laws that had been on the books since the 1460s—and which had been expanded by her father Henry VIII—in 1574 Queen Elizabeth proclaimed the most stringent and detailed sumptuary laws yet. The statutes of apparel had two main goals: to curb excessive and frivolous spending on (often imported) fabric and clothing—money the queen felt could better be spent or saved; and to reinforce social conformity and the rigid class system on which English society—though evolving—was still based.

The excess of apparel and the superfluity of unnecessary foreign wares thereto belonging now of late years is grown by sufferance to such an extremity that the manifest decay of the whole realm generally is like to follow (by bringing into the realm such superfluities of silks, cloths of gold, silver, and other most vain devices of so great cost for the quantity thereof as of necessity the moneys and treasure of the realm is and must be yearly conveyed out of the same to answer the said excess) but also particularly the wasting and undoing of a great number of young gentlemen, otherwise serviceable, and others seeking by show of apparel to be esteemed as gentlemen, who, allured by the vain show of those things, do not only consume themselves, their goods, and lands which their parents left unto them, but also run into such debts and shifts as they cannot live out of danger of laws without attempting unlawful acts, whereby they are not any ways serviceable to their country as otherwise they might be:

Which great abuses, tending both to so manifest a decay of the wealth of the realm and to the ruin of a multitude of serviceable young men and gentlemen and of many good families, the Queen's majesty hath of her own princely wisdom so considered as she hath of late with great charge to her council commanded the same to be presently and speedily remedied both in her own court and in all other places of her realm, according to the sundry good laws heretofore provided.

For reformation whereof, although her highness might take great advantage and profit by execution of the said laws and statutes, yet of her princely clemency her majesty is content at this time to give warning to her loving subjects to reform themselves, and not to extend forthwith the rigor of her laws for the offences heretofore past, so as they shall now reform themselves according to such orders as at this present, jointly with this proclamation, are set forth, whereby the statute of the 24th year of her majesty's most noble father King Henry VIII and the statute made in the second year of her late dear sister Queen Mary are in some part moderated according to this time.

Wherefore her majesty willeth and straightly commandeth all manner of persons in all places within 12 days after the publication of this present proclamation to reform their apparel according to the tenor of certain articles and clauses taken out of the said statutes and with some moderations annexed to this proclamation, upon pain of her highness's indignation, and punishment for their contempts, and such other pains as in the said several statutes be expressed.

For the execution of which orders her majesty first giveth special charge to all such as do bear office within her most honorable house to look unto it, each person in his degree and office, that the said articles and orders be duly observed, and the contrary reformed in her majesty's court by all them who are under their office, thereby to give example to the rest of the realm; and further generally to all noblemen, of what estate or degree soever they be, and all and every person of her privy council, to all archbishops and bishops, and to the rest of the clergy according to their degrees, that they do see the same speedily and duly executed in their private households and families; and to all mayors and other head officers of cities, towns, and corporations, to the chancellors of the universities, to governors of colleges, to the ancients and benchers in every one of the Inns of Court and Chancery, and generally to all that hath any superiority or government over and upon any multitude, and each man in his own household for their children and servants, that they likewise do cause the said orders to be kept by all lawful means that they can.

And to the intent the same might be better kept generally throughout all the realm, her majesty giveth also special charge to all justices of the peace to inquire of the defaults and breaking of those orders in their quarter sessions, and to see them redressed in all open assemblies by all wise, godly, and lawful means; and also to all Justices of Assizes in their circuits to cause inquiry and due presentment to be made at their next assizes how these orders be kept; and so orderly, twice a year at every assize after each other circuits done, to certify in writing to her highness's Privy Council under their hands, with as convenient speed as they may, what hath been found and done as well by the justices of the peace in their quarter sessions, of whom they shall take their certificate for each quarter session, as also at the assizes, for the observing of the said orders and reformation of the abuses.

A brief content of certain clauses of the statute of King Henry VIII and Queen Mary, with some moderation thereof, to be observed according to her majesty's proclamation above mentioned.

None shall wear in his apparel:

Any silk of the color of purple, cloth of gold tissued, nor fur of sables, but only the King, Queen, King's mother, children, brethren, and sisters, uncles and aunts; and except dukes, marquises, and earls, who may wear the same in doublets, jerkins, linings of cloaks, gowns, and hose; and those of the Garter, purple in mantles only.

Cloth of gold, silver, tinseled satin, silk, or cloth mixed or embroidered with any gold or silver: except all degrees above viscounts, and viscounts, barons, and other persons of like degree, in doublets, jerkins, linings of cloaks, gowns, and hose.

Woolen cloth made out of the realm, but in caps only; velvet, crimson, or scarlet; furs, black genets, lucernes [lynx fur]; embroidery or tailor's work having gold or silver or pearl therein: except dukes, marquises, earls, and their children, viscounts, barons, and knights being companions of the Garter, or any person being of the Privy Council.

Velvet in gowns, coats, or other uttermost garments; fur of leopards; embroidery with any silk: except men of the degrees above mentioned, barons' sons, knights and gentlemen in ordinary office attendant upon her majesty's person, and such as have been employed in embassages to foreign princes.

Caps, hats, hatbands, capbands, garters, or boothose trimmed with gold or silver or pearl; silk netherstocks; enameled chains, buttons, aglets: except men of the degrees above mentioned, the gentlemen attending upon the Queen's person in her highness's Privy chamber or in the office of cupbearer, carver, sewer [server], esquire for the body, gentlemen ushers, or esquires of the stable.

Satin, damask, silk, camlet, or taffeta in gown, coat, hose, or uppermost garments; fur whereof the kind groweth not in the Queen's dominions, except foins [marten fur], grey genets [civet cat fur], and budge [African or Spanish lambskin]: except the degrees and persons above mentioned, and men that may dispend £100 by the year, and so valued in the subsidy book.

Hat, bonnet, girdle, scabbards of swords, daggers, etc.; shoes and pantofles [slip on overshoes] of velvet: except the degrees and persons above names and the son and heir apparent of a knight.

Silk other than satin, damask, taffeta, camlet, in doublets; and sarcanet, camlet, or taffeta in facing of gowns and cloaks, and in coats, jackets, jerkins, coifs, purses being not of the color scarlet, crimson, or blue; fur of foins, grey genets, or other as the like groweth not in the Queen's dominions: except men of the degrees and persons above mentioned, son of a knight, or son and heir apparent of a man of 300 marks land by the year, so valued in the subsidy books, and men that may dispend £40 by the year, so valued *ut supra* [as above].

None shall wear spurs, swords, rapiers, daggers, skeans, woodknives, or hangers, buckles or girdles, gilt, silvered or damasked: except knights and barons' sons, and others of higher degree or place, and gentlemen in ordinary office attendant upon the Queen's majesty's person; which gentlemen so attendant may wear all the [preceding] saving gilt, silvered, or damasked spurs.

None shall wear in their trappings or harness of their horse any studs, buckles, or other garniture gilt, silvered, or damasked; nor stirrups gilt, silvered, or damasked; nor any velvet in saddles or horse trappers: except the persons next before mentioned and others of higher degree, and gentlemen in ordinary, *ut supra*.

Note that the Lord Chancellor, Treasurer, President of the council, Privy Seal, may wear any velvet, satin, or other silks except purple, and furs black except black genets.

These may wear as they have heretofore used, *viz.* any of the King's council, justices of either bench, Barons of the Exchequer, Master of the Rolls, sergeants at law, Masters of the Chancery, of the Queen's council, apprentices of law, physicians of the King, queen, and Prince, mayors and other head officers of any towns corporate, Barons of the Five Ports, except velvet, damask, [or] satin of the color crimson, violet, purple, blue.

Note that her majesty's meaning is not, by this order, to forbid in any person the wearing of silk buttons, the facing of coats, cloaks, hats and caps, for comeliness only, with taffeta, velvet, or other silk, as is commonly used.

Note also that the meaning of this order is not to prohibit a servant from wearing any cognizance of his master, or henchmen, heralds, pursuivants at arms; runners at jousts, tourneys, or such martial feats, and such as wear apparel given them by the Queen, and such as shall have license from the Queen for the same.

Women's apparel

None shall wear

Any cloth of gold, tissue, nor fur of sables: except duchesses, marquises, and countesses in their gowns, kirtles [girdles], partlets, and sleeves; cloth of gold, silver, tinseled satin, silk, or cloth mixed or embroidered with gold or silver or pearl, saving silk mixed with gold or silver in linings of cowls, partlets, and sleeves: except all degrees above viscountesses, and viscountesses, baronesses, and other personages of like degrees in their kirtles and sleeves.

Velvet (crimson, carnation); furs (black genets, lucerns); embroidery or passment lace of gold or silver: except all degrees above mentioned, the wives of knights of the Garter and of the Privy Council, the ladies and gentlewomen of the privy chamber and bedchamber, and maids of honor.

None shall wear any velvet in gowns, furs of leopards, embroidery of silk: except the degrees and persons above mentioned, the wives of barons' sons, or of knights.

Cowls, sleeves, partlets, and linings, trimmed with spangles or pearls of gold, silver, or pearl; cowls of gold or silver, or of silk mixed with gold or silver: except the degrees and persons above mentioned; and trimmed with pearl, none under the degree of baroness or like degrees.

Enameled chains, buttons, aglets, and borders: except the degrees before mentioned.

Satin, damask, or tufted taffeta in gowns, kirtles, or velvet in kirtles; fur whereof the kind groweth not within the Queen's dominions, except foins, grey genets, bodge, and wolf: except the degrees and persons above mentioned, or the wives of those that may dispend £100 by the year and so valued in the subsidy book.

Gowns of silk grosgrain, doubled sarcenet, camlet, or taffeta, or kirtles of satin or damask: except the degrees and persons above mentioned, and the wives of the sons and heirs of knights, and the daughters of knights, and of such as may dispend 300 marks by the year so valued *ut supra*, and the wives of those that may dispend £40 by the year.

Gentlewomen attendant upon duchesses, marquises, countesses may wear, in their liveries given them by their mistresses, as the wives of those that may dispend £100 by the year and are so valued *ut supra*.

None shall wear any velvet, tufted taffeta, satin, or any gold or silver in their petticoats: except wives of barons, knights of the order, or councilors' ladies, and gentlewomen of the privy chamber and bed chamber, and the maids of honor.

Damask, taffeta, or other silk in their petticoats: except knights' daughters and such as be matched with them in the former article, who shall not wear a guard of any silk upon their petticoats.

Velvet, tufted taffeta, satin, nor any gold or silver in any cloak or safeguard: except the wives of barons, knights of the order, or councilor's ladies and gentlewomen of the privy chamber and bedchamber, and maids of honor, and the degrees above them.

Damask, taffeta, or other silk in any cloak or safeguard: except knights' wives, and the degrees and persons above mentioned.

No persons under the degrees above specified shall wear any guard or welt [trim or braid] of silk upon any petticoat, cloak, or safeguard.

Source: Elizabeth I. "Statute Issued at Greenwich, 15 June 1574." *Elizabethan Sumptuary Statutes*, July 14, 2001. http://elizabethan.org/sumptuary/

What Really Happened

There is no long tradition of doing Shakespearean plays in Renaissance costuming; in fact, beginning with the Restoration (1660), each age-seems to have produced Shakespeare in the dress of its own time—until the Victorian era, when practitioners such as Charles Kean and William MacCready began staging plays with a keen focus on historical detail, from acting style to sets to original costuming. In 1895, actor/producer William Poel founded the Elizabethan Stage Society, dedicated to producing Shakespeare's works with minimal scenery (as would have been the case for Shakespeare), period costuming, and a focus on the beauty of the language, in contrast with earlier Victorian productions that had featured huge spectacle. Thus, when people today suggest that companies should strive for the purity of doing Shakespeare traditionally, that tradition of Renaissance staging and costuming actually only dates to the late 1800s. Then, with the turn into the twentieth century, the pendulum swung toward an "anything goes" approach to Shakespeare productions, as directors and producers saw the green light to reimagine the plays in myriad ways.

Before examining some of the more recent resettings of Shakespearean plays, we should more closely question what we mean by "traditional costumes and settings," the concept lying at the heart of the fact/fiction of creating a more "authentic" Shakespeare experience. We have explored Elizabethan sumptuary laws that dictated dress among the citizenry of Shakespeare's time. One might view the Renaissance English theater as an island of immunity from such laws. Here, an actor of the lower class (as most were) could be a king or queen—and dress like one. In fact, a theater company's most valuable possessions were its costumes. Often, wealthy people who died would bequeath their wardrobes to a servant, who—though not allowed to wear the fine clothing him- or herself—could then sell it to a theater company for good money.

Many of the costumes and props were owned by theater companies, but some were then sold to individual actors at great expense. Whoever owned the costumes, they were lavish, and they served more than ornamental purposes in plays. During this era, sets and backdrops were minimal—especially at the larger, outdoor theaters. Thus, costumes and simple props served to convey to audiences essential information such as setting, occupation, gender, and social status. For instance, in *King Lear*, the king's self-deposition is marked by his change in costumes. At the play's outset, no costume needs be designated; King Lear is dressed royally, "every inch a king." By Act III, Lear is banished into the stormy wilderness, where he meets the deranged and half-naked "Poor Tom." The son and heir of a duke, Edgar has changed his identity to Poor Tom by his own costume change, as he goes into hiding by dressing himself in rags and playing at insanity. Lear, himself wearing a "crown" of wild flowers and actually going mad, decides to emulate Poor Tom by getting naked, perceiving that clothing is a disguise that prevents a person from being authentically human:

> Is man no more than this? Consider him well. Thou ow'st the worm no silk, the beast no hide, the sheep no wool, the cat no perfume. Ha! Here's three of us are sophisticated! Thou art the thing itself; unaccommodated man is no more but such a poor, bare, forked animal as thou art. Off, off, you lendings! Come, unbutton here. (III.iv.1897–1903)

Lear and Edgar both indicate their chaotic states of mind through costume changes, and costuming also helps the audience visualize the setting (outdoors, storming, and cold) in this and other scenes.

Later, when Lear is reunited with his loyal daughter Cordelia, his recovery of sanity and symbolic rebirth are signified by another costume change, as a servant tells Cordelia that they have "put fresh garments on him" (IV.iv.2935), and Lear notes that he can't remember how he came by his present clothing. The costuming of other characters in this play (and others) similarly conveys important information as to status or change of situation, as when Lear's loyal follower Kent disguises himself so he can continue to serve the king, who has unjustly banished him. We also have strong evidence that many roles were doubled in *King Lear* and other plays of Shakespeare, with a change of costume often standing as the only indicator of the actor's change of role.

In fact, Shakespeare and his company seem to have made little effort at period authenticity; the costuming and staging directions in his plays contain numerous anachronisms and other inaccuracies about which Shakespeare and company clearly did not care. We can see such elements most clearly in the plays set in ancient Rome, which Shakespeare casually morphed with his own era. Famously, *Julius Caesar* features a clock bell tolling while the conspirators Brutus and Cassius plot Caesar's assassination; of course, the Romans used sundials and stars to tell the time, with the mechanical clock long from invention. Costumes designated in *Julius Caesar* are very Elizabethan, including references to non-Roman garb such as hats and cloaks, nightgowns, doublets, and kerchiefs. Queen Cleopatra plays billiards, which would not be invented until at least a millennium after her death. Non-Roman plays also feature anachronisms; for example, Prince Hamlet returns to Denmark from his studies at the University at Wittenberg—which was founded in 1502 (Shakespeare's play being written around 1600 but set much earlier). The Hamlet story derives from sources written in the twelfth and thirteenth centuries, looking back on events from even earlier. Thus, period accuracy and authenticity seems to have been of little concern to Shakespeare and company.

The only existing image of a production from Shakespeare's time is a sketch of a scene from *Titus Andronicus* signed by Henry Peacham. The famous image is dated 1595, and it includes forty lines from the play. As this drawing is purely informal, we can question its accuracy and even its authenticity. However, if we consider it as a real and rare artifact, it provides information and raises questions. First, we see the character Aaron the Moor, one of Shakespeare's most villainous villains, who in the Peacham drawing is very black indeed. This portrayal raises questions, as we have no records of any African people performing on the English Renaissance stage. Was this actually a black man? A white actor with very black makeup for face, neck, chest, and hands? Perhaps it was simply a white actor and Peacham—knowing the character to be a "moor" from references throughout the play—supplied the coloration from his imagination. The costumes seen in the sketch seem to confirm that Shakespeare's company was none too concerned with consistency or "authenticity." The seven characters depicted wear mostly Elizabethan garb. Titus's sons wear quasi-military uniforms that do not match each other. Titus is the only one in Roman-ish garb, wearing a leaf garland and toga. Aaron and Tamora's sons wear Elizabethan dress, and Queen Tamora wears a royal-looking Elizabethan gown and crown—far from her characterization in the play as a Goth warrior-queen.

Given the Peacham sketch of the *Titus Andronicus* production plus other records of costume inventories, we might say that the concept of the pure, authentic costuming and staging of a Shakespeare play—much like the "dream of the master text" (see chapter 7, "Shakespeare Was a Solitary Genius Whose Talents Cannot Be Explained")—is a chimera. Shakespeare's companies made good use of the available props and clothing, some of which were strikingly authentic in depicting a character's social status, location, and position, and others—not so much. One might ask: If Shakespeare's work truly is "not of an age, but for all time"—as Ben Jonson proclaimed—then why attempt to freeze him in time by striving for textual or costuming purity that is impossible to know or attain? If Shakespeare's company put on plays set in ancient Rome using dress contemporary to their own time, then why should twenty-first-century productions not feel free to use Renaissance, or Roman, or modern dress as they see fit? Similarly, American teachers and students occasionally see fit to do Shakespeare in a British accent, as if that makes it more "authentic." In fact, Renaissance English pronunciation would have been quite different from a contemporary English accent and closer to some forms of southern American or Canadian dialect.

This is not to say that all attempts to mimic aspects of Shakespeare's original production conditions are useless or ill-fated. Several companies utilize original stage practices with great success. For example, the American Shakespeare Center (ASC) in Staunton, Virginia, has performed since 2001 in the Blackfriars Playhouse, the world's only replica of Shakespeare's indoor theater. The ASC motto is "we do it with the lights on," pointing to their practice of emulating original performance conditions. That is, there is "universal lighting" onstage and in the house, such that everyone in the audience and onstage can clearly see everyone else. The ASC also features onstage "gallant stools" seating for a few patrons, as the original Blackfriars would have. With people sitting onstage, the lights fully on—electric chandeliers rather than the candles that would have illuminated the original theater—and seating around three-fourths of the stage, every performance at the Blackfriars Playhouse allows for the dynamic interaction that Shakespeare's performances surely featured: there is no "fourth wall." Performers interact with audience members; audience members can clearly see each other from a variety of angles, and the experience of seeing a play is quite different—most would say far more enjoyable—than that of sitting in the dark, separated from the performers on a proscenium stage. However, whereas the ASC works with original staging practices, they freely produce Shakespearean plays in various time settings with costuming varying from Renaissance to contemporary.

Another emulation of original performance conditions that has been successfully utilized is called "original pronunciation" (OP). Beginning in 2004, Shakespeare's Globe Theatre in London has produced several plays based on how the words actually were pronounced in Shakespeare's time, and a few other companies have also experimented with OP. Working with the Globe, linguist David Crystal and his actor son Ben have led the OP charge, and they find that using OP allows certain puns and rhymes to come out that do not work with contemporary pronunciation. Original pronunciation productions garner mixed reviews and constitute more an interesting experiment than a movement to change the way people perform Shakespeare. But attempts to emulate OP or original staging and lighting conditions are more feasible and fruitful than is a quest for "authentic" costuming or period setting.

Over the last century or more, productions have adapted Shakespeare in thousands of ways, some more successful than others. Even without considering film adaptations of Shakespeare—which have set *Macbeth* in a fast food joint (*Scotland, PA*, 2001) and in samurai Japan (*Throne of Blood*, 1957), *The Tempest* on another planet (*Forbidden Planet*, 1956), *Hamlet* in the twenty-first-century New York "Denmark Corporation" (*Hamlet 2000*)—beginning in the twentieth century, theater producers and directors began feeling free to reset Shakespeare's plays as exotically as possible.

A 1911–12 Moscow production of *Hamlet* dramatically broke this ground. English director/set designer Edward Gordon Craig collaborated with Konstantin Stanislavski, Artistic Director of the Moscow Art Theatre and creator of the system of "method acting." Craig's sets utilized huge pieces of colored canvas stretched on hinged wooden frames. The effect mirrored the cutting edge Modernist artistic technique of cubism—as pioneered by Pablo Picasso and Georges Braque—and brought to the production of *Hamlet* an abstract flavor never before applied to Shakespeare.

The 1920s brought perhaps the first full-blown "modern dress" productions of Shakespeare, with the Birmingham Repertory Theatre doing innovative costumings of *Cymbeline* and *Hamlet*. Since then, producers and directors have staged Shakespeare with all manner of settings, costuming, sets, and castings that have experimented with gender and race. One of the most famous productions in history was Orson Welles's 1936 "voodoo *Macbeth*," done in Harlem with an all-black cast. Welles set the play in nineteenth-century Haiti, with the weird sisters/witches depicted as African voodoo priestesses who control Macbeth. Funded by the Federal

Theater Project, the production became a huge success, running in Harlem, on Broadway, and eventually on tour. The following year, Welles set a *Julius Caesar* in Nazi Germany—long before World War II broke out. In 1997, Washington, DC's, Shakespeare Theater produced *Othello*, reversing traditional (and textual) casting by having Patrick Stewart play the title character (called "the moor") and the remainder of the cast played by African-Americans. In the 2000s, Rick Miller created and performed *MacHomer*, a one-man version of *The Simpsons* performing *Macbeth*.

2016 brought perhaps the ultimate costuming experimentation Shakespeare production. Whereas throughout the last century, various productions—stage and screen—of Shakespeare plays have featured some nudity, the company "Torn Out Theater" put on a free, all-female, nude production of *The Tempest* in New York's Central Park and Prospect Park. The play's consulting director noted their rationale : "[W]e want the audience to see it through fresh eyes, as 'something rich and strange,' the way an audience four hundred years ago would have." One is tempted to say that this production of *The Tempest* takes experimentation with nontraditional Shakespeare costuming and staging as far as it could go, but who knows? As we have seen, the concept of what actually would constitute authentic or traditional stagings of Shakespeare is complex, and the notion that Shakespeare should only be done in Renaissance garb stands as a small minority view. Nonetheless, it seems clear that throughout the last century or so, in efforts to place their own stamp on Shakespeare, many productions have strayed far from what Shakespeare actually gives us with his texts. The truest traditions—worthy of being maintained in whatever the production—are the essential depth, beauty, and rich humanity at the core of Shakespeare's works.

Further Readings

Adams, John Cranford. *The Globe Playhouse: Its Design and Equipment.* New York: Barnes and Noble, 1942.

Arnold, Janet. *Patterns of Fashion: The Cut and Construction of Clothes for Men and Women, 1560–1620.* London: Macmillan, 1985.

Astington, John H., ed. *The Development of Shakespeare's Theater.* New York: AMS Press, 1992.

Bate, Jonathan, and Russell Jackson. *Shakespeare: An Illustrated Stage History.* Oxford: Oxford University Press, 1996.

Beckerman, Bernard. *Shakespeare at the Globe, 1599–1609.* London: Collier-Macmillan, 1962.

Berry, Herbert. *Shakespeare's Playhouses*. New York: AMS, 1987.

Biggs, Murray, et al., eds. *The Arts of Performance in Elizabethan and Early Stuart Drama: Essays for G. K. Hunter*. Edinburgh: Edinburgh University Press, 1991.

Campbell, Lily B. *Scenes and Machines on the English Stage During the Renaissance*. New York: Barnes and Noble, 1960.

Cressy, David. "Gender Trouble and Cross-Dressing in Early Modern England." *Journal of British Studies* 35, 4 (October 1996): 438–65.

Crystal, David. *Think on My Words: Exploring Shakespeare's Language*. Cambridge: Cambridge University Press, 2008.

Cunnington, C. Willet, and Phillis Cunnington. *Handbook of English Costume in the Sixteenth Century*. Boston: Plays, Inc., 1970.

Davies, Robertson. *Shakespeare's Boy Actors*. New York: Russell & Russell, 1964.

Day, Barry. *This Wooden 'O,' Shakespeare's Globe Reborn, the Official Story*. London: Oberon Books, 1996.

Dessen, Alan C. *Elizabethan Stage Conventions and Modern Interpreters*. Cambridge: Cambridge University Press, 1984.

Dobson, Michael, ed. *Performing Shakespeare's Tragedies Today: The Actor's Perspective*. Cambridge: Cambridge University Press, 2006.

Elizabeth I. "Enforcing Statutes of Apparel, Greenwich, 15 June 1574." *Elizabethan Sumptuary Statutes*, July 14, 2001. http://elizabethan.org /sumptuary/who-wears-what.html

Foakes, R. A. *Illustrations of the English Stage 1580–1642*. Stanford: Stanford University Press, 1985.

Graves, R. E. *Lighting the Shakespearean Stage, 1567–1642*. Carbondale: Southern Illinois University Press, 1999.

Gurr, Andrew. *The Shakespearean Playing Companies*. Oxford: Oxford University Press, 1996.

Gurr, Andrew. *Staging in Shakespeare's Theatres*. Oxford: Oxford University Press, 2000.

Hattaway, Michael. *Elizabethan Popular Theatre: Plays in Performance*. London: Routledge & Kegan Paul, 1982.

Hayles, Nancy K. "Sexual Disguise in *As You Like It* and *Twelfth Night*." *Shakespeare Survey* 32 (1979): 63–72.

Hodges, C. Walter. *Enter the Whole Army: A Pictorial Study of Shakespearean Staging 1576–1616*. Cambridge: Cambridge University Press, 1999.

Hodges, C. Walter. *The Globe Restored*. London: Ernest Benn, 1953.

Hodges, C. Walter. *Shakespeare's Second Globe: The Missing Monument*. Oxford: Oxford University Press, 1973.

Hodges, C. Walter, Samuel Schoenbaum, and Leonard Leone. *The Third Globe: Symposium for the Reconstruction of the Globe Playhouse, Wayne State University, 1979*. Detroit: Wayne State University Press, 1981.

Hooper, Wilfrid. "The Tudor Sumptuary Laws." *English Historical Review* 30, 119 (July 1915): 433–449.

Hotson, Leslie. *Shakespeare's Wooden O*. London: Rupert Hart-Davis, 1959.

Howard, Jean E. *Shakespeare's Art of Orchestration: Stage Technique and Audience Response*. Urbana: University of Illinois Press, 1984.

Hyland, Peter. "Shakespeare's Heroines: Disguise in the Romantic Comedies." *Ariel* 9 (1978): 23–39.

Joseph, B. L. *Elizabethan Acting*. Oxford: Oxford University Press, 1964.

Kiernan, Pauline. *Staging Shakespeare at the New Globe*. Basingstoke: Macmillan Press, 1999.

King, T. J. *Shakespearean Staging 1599–1642*. Cambridge: Harvard University Press, 1971.

King, Thomas J. *Casting Shakespeare's Plays: London Actors and Their Roles 1590–1642*. Cambridge: Cambridge University Press, 1992.

Knutson, Roslyn Lander. *The Repertory of Shakespeare's Company, 1594–1613*. Fayetteville: University of Arkansas Press, 1991.

Langley, Andrew. *Shakespeare's Theatre*. Oxford: Oxford University Press, 1999.

Leed, Drea. "Overview of an Elizabethan Outfit." Elizabethan Costume Page, 2008. http://www.elizabethancostume.net/overview.html

The Life and Death of Mrs. Mary Frith: Commonly Called Mal Cutpurse. https://web.archive.org/web/20150224050017/http://www.crime culture.com/earlyunderworlds/Contents/Cutpurse.html

Linthicum, Marie C. *Costume in the Drama of Shakespeare and His Contemporaries*. London: Oxford University Press, 1936.

Mann, David. *The Elizabethan Player: Contemporary Stage Representation*. London: Routledge, 1991.

Menzer, Paul, ed. *Inside Shakespeare: Essays on the Blackfriars Stage*. Selinsgrove, PA: Susquehanna University Press, 2006.

Mulryne, J. R., and Margaret Shewring, eds. *Shakespeare's Globe Rebuilt*. New York: Cambridge University Press, 1997.

Newton, Stella Mary. *Renaissance Theatre Costume and the Sense of the Historic Past*. London: Rapp & Whiting, 1975.

Orrell, John. *The Human Stage: English Theatre Design, 1567–1640*. Cambridge: Cambridge University Press, 1988.

Orrell, John. *The Quest for Shakespeare's Globe*. Cambridge: Cambridge University Press, 1983.

Parsons, Keith, and Pamela Mason, eds. *Shakespeare in Performance*. London: Salamander Books Ltd., 1995.

Pound, Ezra. *Make It New*. St. Clair Shores, MI: Scholarly Press, 1971.

Salgado, Gamini. *Eyewitnesses of Shakespeare: First Hand Accounts of Performances 1590–1890*. London: Sussex University Press, 1975.

Secara, Maggie. "Elizabethan Sumptuary Statutes." Elizabethan.Org. http://elizabethan.org/sumptuary/index.html

Shurgot, Michael W. *Stages of Play: Shakespeare's Theatrical Energies in Elizabethan Performance*. Newark: University of Delaware Press, 1998.

Stern, Tiffany. *Documents of Performance in Early Modern England*. Cambridge: Cambridge University Press, 2009.

Taylor, Gary. *Reinventing Shakespeare: A Cultural History from the Restoration to the Present*. London: Vintage, 1991.

Wilson, Jean. *The Archaeology of Shakespeare: The Material Legacy of Shakespeare's Theatre*. Gloucestershire: Alan Sutton Publishing, 1995.

Bibliography

Baker, Oliver. *In Shakespeare's Warwickshire and the Unknown Years.* London: S. Marshall, 1937.

Barroll, J. Leeds. *Politics, Plague, and Shakespeare's Theater: The Stuart Years.* Ithaca, NY: Cornell University Press, 1991.

Bate, Jonathan. *Soul of the Age: The Life, Mind and World of William Shakespeare.* London: Penguin, 2008.

Beckwith, Sarah. *Shakespeare and the Grammar of Forgiveness.* Ithaca, NY: Cornell University Press, 2011.

Bentley, Gerald E. *The Profession of Dramatist in Shakespeare's Time, 1590–1642.* Princeton, NJ: Princeton University Press, 1971.

Bentley, Gerald E. *The Profession of Player in Shakespeare's Time, 1590–1642.* Princeton, NJ: Princeton University Press, 1984.

Bloom, Harold. *Shakespeare: The Invention of the Human.* New York: Riverhead Books, 1998.

Bradbrook, M. C. *The Rise of the Common Player: A Study of Actor and Society in Shakespeare's England.* London: Chatto and Windus, 1962.

Burgess, Anthony. *Nothing Like the Sun: A Story of Shakespeare's Love-Life.* London: Heinemann, 1964.

Burgess, Anthony. *Shakespeare.* London: Jonathan Cape, 1970.

Callaghan, Dympna. *Shakespeare without Women: Representing Gender and Race on the Renaissance Stage.* London and New York: Routledge, 2000.

Chute, Marchette. *Shakespeare of London.* New York: E. P. Dutton, 1949.

Cohen, Derek. *Shakespeare's Culture of Violence.* London: Macmillan, 1993.

Cooper, Tarnya. *Searching for Shakespeare*. New Haven: Yale University Press, 2006.

de Grazia, Margreta, and Stanley Wells, eds. *The Cambridge Companion to Shakespeare*. Cambridge: Cambridge University Press, 2001.

Dillon, Janette. *Language and Stage in Medieval and Renaissance England*. Cambridge: Cambridge University Press, 1998.

Dillon, Janette. *Theatre, Court and City, 1595–1610: Drama and Social Space in London*. Cambridge and New York: Cambridge University Press, 2000.

Doran, Madeleine. *Shakespeare's Dramatic Language*. Madison: University of Wisconsin Press, 1976.

Duncan-Jones, Katherine. *Shakespeare: Upstart Crow to Sweet Swan, 1592–1623*. London: A. & C. Black, 2011.

Fraser, Russell A. *Young Shakespeare*. New York: Columbia University Press, 1988.

Frye, Roland Mushat. *Shakespeare's Life and Times: A Pictorial Record*. Princeton, NJ: Princeton University Press, 1967.

Gair, W. Reavley. *The Children of Paul's: The Story of a Theatre Company, 1553–1608*. Cambridge: Cambridge University Press, 1982.

Gibson, Joy Leslie. *Squeaking Cleopatras: The Elizabethan Boy Player*. Stroud, Gloucestershire: Sutton, 2000.

Grebanier, Bernard D. N. *Then Came Each Actor: Shakespearean Actors, Great and Otherwise, Including Players and Princes, Rogues, Vagabonds and Actors Motley, from Will Kempe to Olivier and Gielgud and After*. New York: McKay, 1975.

Greenblatt, Stephen. *Renaissance Self-Fashioning: from More to Shakespeare*. Chicago: University of Chicago Press, 1980.

Greenblatt, Stephen. *Will in the World: How Shakespeare Became Shakespeare*. New York: Norton, 2004.

Griswold, Wendy. *Renaissance Revivals: City Comedy and Revenge Tragedy in the London Theater, 1576–1980*. Chicago: University of Chicago Press, 1986.

Gurr, Andrew. *The Shakespearean Stage 1574–1642*. Cambridge: Cambridge University Press, 1980.

Halliday, F. E. *Shakespeare: A Pictorial Biography*. London: Clarke and Sherwell, 1956.

Harrison, G. B. *Introducing Shakespeare*. London: Penguin Books, 1991.

Hattaway, Michael. *Elizabethan Popular Theatre: Plays in Performance*. London: Routledge and Kegan Paul, 1982.

Holden, Anthony. *William Shakespeare: The Man Behind the Genius.* Boston: Little, Brown, 1999.

Honan, Park. *Shakespeare: A Life.* Oxford and New York: Oxford University Press, 1998.

Honigmann, E.A.J. *Shakespeare: The "Lost Years."* Manchester: Manchester University Press, 1985.

Hotson, Leslie. *Mr. W.H.* London: Rupert Hart-Davis, 1964.

Hudson, Katherine. *The Story of the Elizabethan Boy-Actors.* Oxford: Oxford University Press, 1971.

Hyland, Peter. *An Introduction to Shakespeare: The Dramatist in His Context.* Basingstoke, Hampshire: Macmillan, 1996.

Jones, Emrys Maldwyn. *The Origins of Shakespeare.* Oxford: Clarendon Press, 1977.

Kastan, David Scott, ed. *A Companion to Shakespeare.* Oxford: Blackwell, 1999.

Knight, William Nicholas. *Shakespeare's Hidden Life: Shakespeare at the Law, 1585–1595.* New York: Mason & Lipscomb, 1973.

Kott, Jan. *Shakespeare our Contemporary.* London: Methuen, 1964.

Levi, Peter. *The Life and Times of William Shakespeare.* London: Macmillan, 1988.

Maguire, Laurie, ed. *How to Do Things with Shakespeare.* Oxford: Wiley-Blackwell, 2008.

Marshburn, Joseph H., and Alan R. Velie, eds. *Blood and Knavery: A Collection of English Renaissance Pamphlets and Ballads of Crime and Sin.* Rutherford, NJ: Fairleigh Dickinson University Press, 1973.

Matus, Irvin Leigh. *Shakespeare: The Living Record.* New York: St. Martin's Press, 1991.

McMullan, John L. *The Canting Crew: London's Criminal Underworld, 1550–1700.* New Brunswick, NJ: Rutgers University Press, 1984.

Mullaney, Steven. *The Place of the Stage: License, Play, and Power in Renaissance England.* Chicago: University of Chicago Press, 1997.

Orgel, Stephen. *Impersonations: The Performance of Gender in Shakespeare's England.* Cambridge: Cambridge University Press, 1996.

Paster, Gail Kern. *The Idea of the City in the Age of Shakespeare.* Athens, GA: University of Georgia Press, 1985.

Poel, William. *Shakespeare in the Theatre.* London: Sidgwick and Jackson, 1913.

Potter, Lois. *The Life of William Shakespeare: A Critical Biography.* Hoboken, NJ: Wiley-Blackwell, 2012.

Quennell, Peter. *Shakespeare, the Poet and His Background*. London: Weidenfeld and Nicolson, 1963.

Raleigh, Walter Alexander, Sidney Lee, and C. T. Onions. *Shakespeare's England: An Account of the Life & Manners of His Age*. Oxford: Clarendon Press, 1916.

Rappaport, Steve. *Worlds within Worlds: Structures of Life in Sixteenth-Century London*. Cambridge: Cambridge University Press, 1989.

Schmidgall, Gary. *Shakespeare and the Poet's Life*. Lexington: University Press of Kentucky, 1990.

Schoenbaum, Samuel. *Shakespeare's Lives*. New York: Oxford University Press, 1970.

Schoenbaum, Samuel. *William Shakespeare: A Compact Documentary Life*. New York: Oxford University Press, 1977.

Schoenbaum, Samuel. *William Shakespeare: A Documentary Life*. New York: Oxford University Press, 1975.

Shapiro, James. *1599: A Year in the Life of William Shakespeare*. London: Faber & Faber, 2005.

Shapiro, James. *The Year of Lear: Shakespeare in 1606*. New York: Simon & Schuster, 2015.

Shapiro, Michael. *Children of the Revels: The Boy Companies of Shakespeare's Time and Their Plays*. New York: Columbia University Press, 1977.

Sheavyn, Phoebe Anne. *The Literature Profession in the Elizabethan Age*. Manchester: Manchester University Press, 1967.

Slack, Paul. *The English Poor Law, 1531–1782*. Basingstoke: Macmillan Education, 1990.

Snyder, Susan. *Shakespeare: A Wayward Journey*. Newark: University of Delaware Press, 2002.

Southworth, John. *Shakespeare, the Player: A Life in the Theatre*. Stroud, Gloucestershire: Sutton, 2000.

Speaight, Robert. *Shakespeare, the Man and His Achievement*. London: J. M. Dent, 1977.

Styan, J. L. *Shakespeare's Stagecraft*. Cambridge: Cambridge University Press, 1971.

Thompson, Marvin, and Ruth Thompson, eds. *Shakespeare and the Sense of Performance*. Newark: University of Delaware Press, 1989.

Thompson, Peter. *Shakespeare's Professional Career*. Cambridge: Cambridge University Press, 1992.

Thompson, Peter. *Shakespeare's Theatre*. London: Routledge, 1992.

Thorne, Allison. *Vision and Rhetoric in Shakespeare: Looking Through Language*. Basingstoke: Macmillan, 2000.

Wells, Stanley. *Shakespeare: A Life in Drama*. New York: Norton, 1997.

Wells, Stanley. *Shakespeare and Co.* London: Penguin, 2007.

Wells, Stanley, and Lena Cowen Orlin, eds. *Shakespeare: An Oxford Guide.* Oxford: Oxford University Press, 2003.

Wickham, Glynne, ed. *English Professional Theatre, 1530–1660.* Cambridge: Cambridge University Press, 2009.

Willbern, David. *Poetic Will: Shakespeare and the Play of Language.* Philadelphia: University of Pennsylvania Press, 2016.

Wilson, Ian. *Shakespeare: The Evidence.* New York: St. Martin's/Griffin, 1999.

Zimmerman, Susan, and Ronald F. E. Weissman, eds. *Urban Life in the Renaissance.* Newark: University of Delaware Press, 1989.

Index

About the Author

Douglas J. King is associate professor of English at Gannon University, teaching courses in Shakespeare, film, and drama. He received an MA in Education and Human Development from the George Washington University and a PhD in English from Duquesne University. Dr. King has taught Shakespeare to students from kindergarten to graduate school. His dissertation focused on adaptations of Shakespeare for children.

In 2018, Dr. King published his first book for ABC-CLIO, *Shakespeare's World: The Tragedies*. Other areas of interest for teaching and research include film and Native American literature. Dr. King also enjoys directing and performing in plays as well as the occasional film production.

Dr. King has led twelve trips with students to international destinations including Greece, Italy, France, Spain, England, and Wales, and continues to develop courses and trips to facilitate student experiences of globalization.

Dr. King enjoys playing and writing songs, singing in the church choir, mountain biking, kayaking, and studying to become a deacon in the Byzantine Catholic Church.